"The value of Jason's experience is inestimable, and I have no doubt it is precisely what many families facing this crisis need to hear. His practical advice for family members is sound and sage. This is why *Unhooked* is not only critical, but valuable to people and families who stand on the threshold of recovery. Jason's narrative gives voice to what others have not previously had the terms to describe. It leads addicted people and families out of stigma and shame and into a world they could have scarcely believed was possible because it is so good! Recovery is good, and I have no doubt that Jason's story and hard-won wisdom will lead many people and families to that good.   – **Dr. Kevin McCauley**, Co-Founder, The Institute for Addiction Study

"Jason Coombs has a brilliant way to reach the hearts and minds of the second-degree sufferers of addiction—the forgotten loved ones. I have never read a book that shows the inside of addiction so clearly, yet gives the strength of practical advice that Jason does. This book belongs on the shelf of every loved one caught in the web of co-dependency—and better yet, open on their lap. His personal story, which reads like gritty fiction, is filled with necessary, eye-opening truth. This truth mixed with interlocking, valuable advice will save lives and sanity."

   – **Bridget Cook-Burch**, *New York Times* and *Wall Street Journal* Bestselling Author, Transformational Speaker, Passionate Activist

"I love everything about *Unhooked*. It is a must read for anyone that is dealing with addiction in their own life or with someone they love. This has now become my go-to guide!"

   – **Randy Garn**, *New York Times* Best Selling Author and Entrepreneur

"In *Unhooked*, Jason provides a raw, heart-rending look into the depths of addiction and recovery. More importantly, he helps family members facing addiction learn how to 'be okay, even when they are not okay' by utilizing God's enabling, healing, and strengthening power as they surrender to Him. This book beautifully guides readers through the process of spiritual surrender, which is key to having peace, success, and creating lasting change. I highly recommend this book to anyone facing the devastating difficulties of loved ones dealing with addiction."

– LAURA M. BROTHERSON, LMFT, CST, Author

"Who better to walk you through the heart-wrenching experience of helping an addicted loved one than Jason and his family? They have personally felt what you are going through, and they have transcended it. This book is a must read!"

– KIMBERLY GLYN ZWEIGER, Mrs. of America 2019,
Award Winning Author and Opioid Awareness Advocate

"As an author, consultant, international speaker, and performance coach, I guide hundreds of high-level individuals along their path to purpose and abundance. Frequently, the barrier of a family member with an addiction arises, holding them back from reaching their highest potential. Jason Coombs and his outstanding work, *Unhooked,* are my go-to resource."

– KEVIN HALL, International best-selling author of *Aspire*

"Jason Coombs is the real deal. He's lived it, breathed it, and overcame addiction. His story is riveting and walks you through the path of addiction, and more importantly, recovery. This is what you've been waiting for. This is the hope, the new life, and the steps you need to survive and climb out of addiction. Thank you, Jason Coombs, for breathing life and courage into the world. We need you." – RONDA CONGER, Award Winning Author
of *Better Human: It's a Full Time Job*

"As a mother of an addict, I don't have enough words to praise Jason's helpful and practical guide/personal memoir as a road-map to help parents know what to do when they love an addict. These lessons are wrapped up in a compelling personal story to help you understand *why* certain approaches work better than others. It is unique among self-help books for those who love and want to help the addict in their lives because it is researched-based, practical, and helpful; at the same time, it is a fascinating read that you will find impossible to put down."

— **BECKY JOHNSON**, co-author of *This is Your Brain on Joy* (with Dr. Earl Henslin); *Nourished: The Search for Health, Happiness and a Full Night's Sleep* (endorsed by Dr. Daniel Amen) and *Understanding and Loving a Person with PTSD* (with Steve Arterburn).

"*Unhooked* is so inspiring. Watching a loved one struggle with addiction is painful, but knowing that I can be a part of that addiction in such a negative way is even more painful to realize. I loved reading Jason's mother's perspective and her wisdom in setting healthy boundaries. This is a book I can refer back to when I slip up to remind myself to "get off the beach.""

— **SARA S,** a mother of an addicted loved one

"With the backdrop of his own story of entry, maintenance, and recovery from addiction, Jason provides his readers with an understanding and education that specifically defines how to get *Unhooked*. In an easy to read and personal style, Jason beautifully explores the internal process of drug use and recovery, as well as the challenges that are experienced by their loved ones. His personal narrative combined with the research that supports interventions that create sustainable recovery, Jason identifies solutions that work. This is a great read for anyone associated with addiction and recovery." — **CORY A. REICH**, PH.D., L.M.F.T., Co-Founder, The Institute for Addiction Study

"I remember like yesterday the first time I met Jason Coombs. He showed up at our home to serve an addicted family member of ours. We sat in our living room as he shared his wisdom and insights. 'This has to be in a book,' we all exclaimed! 'In time,' he responded. I have watched him prepare and I always knew that one day he would finally share his personal and very poignant wisdom and story with the world. I wept as I read *Unhooked*. This book is a gift to all who are addicted and their family members. I am deeply grateful that he served our family and now, the world."

— **DAVE BLANCHARD**, CEO
The Og Mandino Leadership Institute and Author

"Jason's authentic and vulnerable description of his journey to the bottom and back helps the reader separate the person from the addiction. I could see myself more clearly in the loved one's shoes, and I also saw into the mind of the addict. I saw some behaviors inside myself that helped me see things from a different perspective. My life has been changed for the better!"

— **BARBARA D**, mother of an addicted loved one.

"Jason's insights are powerful! *Unhooked* is loaded with wisdom born from experience, including the family's perspectives. This book is absolutely a must read for any family dealing with addiction."

— **STEVE CARLSTON**, Television Executive

UNHOOKED:

HOW TO HELP
AN ADDICTED LOVED ONE RECOVER

JASON COOMBS

BRICK HOUSE
PRESS

Brick House Press

3663 N. Lakeharbor Lane

Boise, Idaho 83703

info@brickhouserecovery.com

Editors: Becky Johnson, Deidre Paulsen, Barbara Wilson, Hannah Lyon, Archie Swensen

Cover Design: Ryan Biore

Book Layout: Francine Eden Platt • Eden Graphics, Inc.

Ordering Information:

Quantity sales. Special discounts are available on quantity purchases by corporations, associations, and others. For details, contact the "Special Sales Department" at the address above.

Unhooked by Jason Coombs, Feb 8, 1978

First Edition

Third Printing

ISBN: 978-0-578630-07-6

DEDICATION

To my birth son, Nathan. You gave my life purpose
when I needed a miracle. You are that miracle.

TABLE OF CONTENTS

FOREWORD

BY DR. KEVIN MCCAULEY

Co-Founder of the Institute for Addiction Study

In 2006, I arrived in Utah in the middle of an epidemic.

You would not have known it to look at the place. I observed low unemployment and crime rates, affordable housing filled with cheerful and industrious folks in the heart of a strong, and a local economy that was still glowing in the aftermath of the 2002 Olympics.

But there was a deep, shame-filled threat growing in the very heart of this thriving society: youth and young adults were silently suffering from a hidden plague. Though Utah enjoyed the lowest rate of youth drinking, smoking, and cannabis use due to extraordinary religious and moral cultural resilience against early exposure to these intoxicants—that resilience did not extend to prescription drug abuse.

This growing threat was an addiction to and fatal poisonings from prescription opioid medications. In fact, it was fast becoming an epidemic. This was made all the more horrific because the medical community—trusted physicians—abetted it. While opioid abuse was primarily hidden in Utah, it was happening more openly nationwide.

When I graduated from medical school in 1992, all young doctors were taught that our profession was failing patients: we were leaving them in unnecessary pain because of our own unfounded and foolish fears of addiction. If a doctor did not inquire about and then aggressively treat pain, then s/he was not doing her/his job.

Though it sounds naïve and dangerous now, this was the standard teaching in the early 1990s.

It was the kind of admonition that a young, sincere physician like myself took to heart. We each vowed to be the change our instructors demanded. This ethical shift occurred just as a host of new formulations of common opioids came to market. Novel brands with advertising campaigns were designed by their manufacturers to lower physician's fears of addiction and increase the likelihood they would prescribe these formulations—pills that were far more powerful than previously available. Patients also began to ask for these medications by name. Vicodin and OxyContin, among others, became part of common public vocabulary.

I was not immune to this epidemic, either. After completing medical school, I became a naval flight surgeon. During this time, I was prescribed Demerol to help me cope with pain from a minor injury. I was not worried about addiction, thanks to my medical teaching, but to my surprise I immediately became a fierce slave to the drug. Eventually I was court-martialed and imprisoned for my addiction. This life-altering experience lit a fire within me to study addiction and medicine. Eventually I became the co-founder of the Institute for Addiction Study, along with Dr. Cory Reich and Jim Clegg. We collaborated on methods to provide the most current data in addiction medicine to effectively help people understand that addiction is a serious illness, not a moral issue.

This research was important for Utah in the early stages of the opioid crisis, and it was heartening for me, as an outsider coming in, to see the state as well as local clergy mobilizing to teach, warn, prevent, and treat addiction without attaching it to shame. Addicted persons were not only warmly encouraged, but generously given the tools necessary to reclaim and rebuild their lives with dignity. I have seen no other state in the U.S. react in such an enthusiastic manner. While still under siege like the rest of the nation, Utah remains a shining example to the rest of the nation on how to respond to this still-growing dilemma.

I have been deeply moved by the example of this community rallying around its most vulnerable and misunderstood citizens and creating a path to recovery for them. I felt most fortunate to live in Utah during this tragic and yet inspiring point in time, and especially to have met wonderful people who will always hold a place in my heart. I am a better person for having known them and seeing what they did to serve others.

Most certainly, one of these people is my good friend, Jason Coombs.

Jason and I met in 2009 when he came to work at our sober living house in Sandy. Jason had more than solid sobriety; he had a bearing. It was the bearing of a man who had not only recovered from tragedy, but used it to deepen his character, clarify his values, and begin helping others climb from the depths of their own despair.

Jason was more than tall (he is 6'2") by nature; he had emotional stature. His attitude was invariably positive, and he was unfailingly kind—even to our most difficult residents. Not only were his recovery habits razor-sharp from good practice, it was clear that he had risen far above the indignities of his previous addiction to find his truest, highest self. Where others might emerge from that crucible as hard and cynical, Jason let the experience of addiction and recovery open his heart.

He had what we call in recovery, "Something that you want." You could see it in the way he carried himself. It was visible from one hundred feet away: that paradoxical, deep sense of character coupled with humility, strength balanced by serenity, and wisdom combined with teachability.

Jason was, quite simply, a fine example of a man in recovery. In fact, he was precisely the kind of man I wanted our newly-sober (but still quite impaired) men to meet. Our residents, to a man, liked him instantly. We all—residents and staff alike—respected and loved Jason. The fact that he was willing to work in our recovery home was a blessing.

This book is his story. The value of his experience is inestimable, and I have no doubt it is precisely what many families facing this crisis need to hear. His practical advice for family members is sound and sage. I have loved reading it as I have loved knowing Jason.

Out of my own experiences and in watching Jason, I know this to be true: a critical point in getting sober is for people to grasp their own story—to construct a narrative of what they have been through so they can make sense of it and then change it. An over-arching story, a sense that your life is an unfolding book, makes past experiences meaningful and gives one a sense of purpose as you look at the blank pages ahead—and make choices to create a healthy and happy future. This is, I believe, the foundation of our agency, and it is a spiritual undertaking. It is also one of the reasons people in 12-step recovery meetings tell their stories. In other words, seeing your life as an ongoing narrative is highly effective.

But to construct one's narrative, we must have words—the vocabulary, turns of phrase, frames of reference, and context that become our building blocks. It helps to listen to the stories of others who have walked a similar path. Language structures the mind, and it is only because I have listened to others, borrowed their words and turns of phrase, and followed their advice when I didn't really want to, that I began to make sense of my own addiction and started the sometimes inspiring, sometimes painful journey into recovery.

This is why Jason's book is not only critical but valuable to people and families who stand on the threshold of recovery. Jason's narrative gives voice to what others have not previously had the terms to describe. It leads addicted people and families out of stigma and shame, and into a world they could have scarcely believed was possible because it is so good! Recovery is good, and

I have no doubt that Jason's story and hard-won wisdom will lead many people and families to that good.

I think about the folks who will find this book in their hands. First, this book will reach parents who have found themselves in a predicament with a teen or adult who is addicted to drugs. They tried to do everything right, but still found themselves plunged into a thoroughly unfamiliar and terrifying chaos. Second will be spouses, friends, and co-workers who, despite the shocking and repulsive behavior they've witnessed, nevertheless suspect the person they know and love is still "in there." The final group will be those who have found themselves addicted through years of self-medicating their physical pain or emotional pain. For those who love someone caught in addiction, this book will be a comfort and guide to staying sane and centered in the middle of the roll-ercoaster-like insanity that so often goes with such a relationship. My hope is you will use this book as a manual to wholeness and become a shining example to your beloved addicts as well.

I'm in favor of anything that makes these addicted persons feel less alone, that makes them better understood, and that gives them and their families hope for the future. That's why I'm delighted that books such as this exist, but especially this one because it is Jason's. He is a man with whom I've had the pleasure of work-ing with to help improve nation-wide crisis. He is also one whose recovery I admire and try to emulate. Jason is living a life of love and service that has already helped hundreds, maybe thousands. And one thing is for certain: Jason will leave a legacy far beyond himself.

My hope is that you find the read as powerful as I did.

PLEASE START HERE

I CAN'T THINK of anything more frustrating than watching an addicted loved one tear their life to shreds.

I mean, *seriously*.

It seems like one minute they mean business and are willing to do anything it takes to change their lives, but the very next minute they are back to the same old "bad behaviors" and "poor decision making" patterns. Not only that, but they will often place the blame on those who love them, yet we are the ones who have moved heaven and earth to try to help them. For many parents, spouses, and children, their greatest fear about their addicted loved one becomes their reality.

On the other hand, addicted individuals can be incredibly gifted, sometimes tender hearted, creative, compassionate, and wonderful people when the addiction is not present. We see their magnificent potential if only they would stop using.

I assume if you've picked up this book, you know the pain I'm talking about. Sometimes it feels like chronic torment. Sometimes grappling with an addicted family member causes anxiety, depression, and hopelessness. It's maddening when you try over and over to help, but nothing seems to work.

When my mother discovered that I, her precious son, was addicted to drugs and alcohol, she searched everywhere for resources and guidance for a spark of hope. She researched websites on the topic, only to find a mixed bag of mediocre suggestions and an array of conflicting opinions. My sweet and tender mother was desperate for tools that could drive measurable *results*. However, her seemingly endless search for helpful guidance led her down a rabbit hole with no end in sight.

Gratefully, after years and years, my mother learned exactly what to do in order to transcend and overcome this issue once and for all. This book contains everything you need to transcend this struggle. No parent, spouse, sibling, or friend should have to go through the agony my mother went through in search of real, practical help. I'm convinced that if she had the insights, wisdom, and practical advice found in this easy-to-read book at the time, she would have transcended the dark hopelessness of my addiction much sooner, and she would have more effectively influenced me through the recovery process faster. As she would tell you, my mother suffered longer than necessary simply because she didn't have the proper resources available at her fingertips out of the starting gate of my addiction. (And at the end of this book, my mom will describe her journey in her own words.) If only I could go back in time and give my mother this book to ease her pain.

We can all agree that Substance Use Disorder is a growing public health issue. Every minute of every day, someone's child, spouse, or best friend dies from an overdose that might have been prevented. The loss is devastating, creating a black hole of grief that may never go away. I know how it feels. I've personally lost dozens of friends, including my best friend, who died needlessly from drugs and alcohol. They are part of the 72,000 U.S. residents who died from substances in 2017 alone, according to the National Institute on Drug Abuse (www.drugabuse.gov).

However, as painful as losing someone to death may be, it can feel even more agonizing at times when you have to witness a loved one suffer with an addiction for years, maybe even decades, leaving a tsunami wave of devastation in their wake. The addiction laughs at us as it leaves our children abandoned and hurt, our spouses broken-hearted, and our parents devastated. Inch by inch, it rips the fabric of the entire family system apart.

Now for some good news. (Let's face it, we all need some!) I invite you to join us in The Recovery Movement and together we will rise above this. Although addiction is on the rise at alarming rates, The Recovery Movement is gaining momentum every single day. Celebrities and public figures are passionately using their platforms to raise awareness of the issue and offering hope to millions about all the recovery successes out there. I'm seriously excited about this!

You will find the answers you seek here in this book. There are solutions to this epidemic—scientifically-reliable and evidence-based—that are changing the gloomy outcomes we all see and read about. It is easy to feel isolated when you have an addiction in the family—as if your reality is far removed from anyone else's. It's a relief on many levels to discover that most family experiences with addiction share much in common. There are so many similar feelings and struggles among families in the same boat. You are not alone.

In the beginning, all my mother desired was a life full of peace, hope, and true happiness without the emotional rollercoaster ride. She wanted to feel emotionally strong and stable without stress and constant worry. She wanted to courageously face me with confidence and strong boundaries without fear or resentment. She desperately wanted to know that her approach was productive without being held hostage by the toxic emotions of fear, worry, and the desire to rescue me. She longed for the day when she would feel proud of her inner change, enabling her to pursue her dreams and aspirations, whether or not I got sober. She imagined the day when she could feel protected from the soul-sucking addiction in her family. More than anything, she desired the feeling of transcendence from this problem in order to live an abundant life of helping others achieve joy and freedom, too. Transcendence is a word I will use often throughout this book. In the context of addiction, transcendence means to surpass and exceed your current state of normal. In other words, it means to become emotionally happy, joyous, and free, regardless of whether he gets sober or not.

Today, my mother's dreams have become her reality—she has transcended. This is my goal for you, too. Together, I promise we will arrive there. It will take work on your part, but you will love the outcome. Let's be honest: there is a long road ahead. My experience tells me that you can conquer this beast and transcend, as well.

For starters, in order to move an addicted person into recovery, you will have to adopt a new mindset right off the bat: YOU ARE NOT RESPONSIBLE FOR YOUR LOVED ONE'S ADDICTION. It's true. Let me say it again, kindly, sincerely, and with all the compassion in my heart: you are not responsible for your loved one's addiction. Just sit with that truth for a moment. Breathe it in.

Hundreds of thousands of family members have internalized this basic and vital truth through The Four C's:

- You did _not_ Cause the addiction.

- You cannot Control the addiction.

- You cannot Cure the addiction.

- You _can_, however, Contribute to the addiction, or to recovery. It's up to you which camp you want to be in.

You have more affect than you realize, and I'm here to show you how to influence the right way. This fresh new approach will bring you more peace and balance in your life while helping you and your loved one ultimately transcend addiction.

Sorting Out What Really Works

Have you ever Googled "addiction help"? The search results are crazy-confusing, right? Which direction should you take? Treatment? Therapy? Self-help? Medications? Detox? Ultimatums?

Big megaplex treatment centers even market "addiction cures" and other incredible promises that are designed to drive profit. Some programs bank off the continual repeat business after their customer relapses again and again. Much like with fad diets and get-rich-quick schemes, there are sharks in the water making money off the sick and addicted population without any concern for their client's wellbeing. And their strategies and philosophies are as varied as the addicted population themselves. How do you sort through it all?

To make matters more confusing, many books, podcasts, and websites present recommendations based on the writer's personal experience, strength, and hope. That's not a bad thing, but it can also create confusion. Why? Because everyone seems to know the best answer to the addiction problem, but usually it's only based on their world views molded by what *they* personally experienced. And let's face it, we are all unique. What worked for one person beautifully may not work for another.

So let's simplify the process, shall we? If you're looking for real solutions, my advice is to rely on proven research and measurable outcomes. The best path is to trust some simple, evidence-based methods and practices, reinforced with authentic experiences that drive actual results. This will cut through the muddy waters of confusing information, bringing you safely to dry land. Does that sound good to you? Go ahead, take another deep breath and let it out slowly.

Before you start reading this book, I'd like to ask you a personal question. What are *you* willing to do in order to help your addicted loved one recover? Are you willing to go to any lengths? Because if you are truly interested in genuine, authentic, and sustainable results, you must first look within. It involves self-discovery about your possible *contribution* to the problem and your willingness to tweak your approach a bit (or a lot). It may sound painful, but I promise you will love the results of freedom and peace.

My promise is that if you take these suggestions in this book to heart, and try your best to make them habits, you'll learn what it takes to feel empowered and no longer be driven by anger and fear. You'll learn how to effectively interact with your addicted loved one by dancing rather than wrestling. This is a key concept, and we will dive into it more in coming pages. Just know that the dance approach will undoubtedly influence your loved one toward recovery. Ultimately, this approach will be easier on you than the constant wrestle every time his frustrating addictive behaviors flare up.

As you begin to apply some of these practical tools, you will inevitably run into stumbling blocks, setbacks, and heartache; however, you'll learn how to adapt while finding great treasures of wisdom when things get tough. Furthermore, you will better understand the mindset of the addicted person and why he behaves the way he does. You'll see there are common patterns to what may have seemed bizarre and crazy to you. With this knowledge, your empathy will increase and your desire for collaboration, while seeking understanding, will deepen. I will empower you to set clear and reasonable boundaries, manage your expectations, react appropriately to misbehavior, and do so in a non-judgmental, healthy way. I will teach you how to offer the right kind of help, finding peace in the storm.

To best explain the recovery process, I'd like to begin by doing my best to give you the context in which these principles and tools came to the rescue in my life and that of my family. There is an old saying: "Nobody cares what you know until they know that you care." I want those of you reading this book to know that I care because I'm not speaking from a far-away place. I have been there. I was the "drug addict" in my family. Now, as a person in long-term recovery, I work with the addicted population and their families. I have the unique blessing of seeing this issue from many viewpoints and therefore can be a catalyst to help the sick and addicted sincerely understand what their families have suffered while they have been living in an alternate universe of drugs and alcohol. And on the flip-side, I help the family members better understand the disease of Substance Use Disorder, its symptoms, and the realities of the suffering.

In the next chapter we'll talk about what I call "The Hook," that moment when a normal person took the bait of drugs and found themselves caught in a lifestyle they never dreamed would happen to them. It is important to understand how this happens. It helps to answer the questions everyone who doesn't understand addiction asks: "Why do people continue to turn to drugs and alcohol, even when the risk is so great? Why don't they just stop when it starts getting out of control?"

Addiction is one of the greatest and most misunderstood phenomena known to man. So, I'll begin to try to explain it by telling you exactly what happened to me.

Author's Note:

For the purposes of this book, my primary focus is on chemical dependency. However, these principles and tools apply to any form of compulsive behavior or process addiction: gambling, pornography, gaming, compulsive overeating, and the like. These principles will also help someone with anxiety and depression.

Another important note: I understand that many other factors may contribute to addiction, such as severe and chronic mental disorders, environmental circumstances, mental or physical disabilities, PTSD, depression, or deficiencies in support systems.

I strongly suggest professional help and medication when necessary to treat co-occurring disorders and the like. Many programs, like Brick House Recovery, treat both at the same time, which is a powerful solution. Also, you may find yourself with questions along the way. I am happy to guide you further with these resources. To join us, go to www.brickhouserecovery.com/unhooked.

One more note: I will be using the terms "he, him, and his" to help the flow for reading purposes. However, this book is not gender specific and these principles apply to all.

That said, let's get to the point—influencing, motivating, changing, and getting results!

Chapter 1

THE HOOK

THE SKY WAS BLACK, and the roads were warm and slick from an unexpected August rainstorm. We were driving to visit my parents to enjoy one of Mom's luscious chocolate malts—an end-of-the-week treat I looked forward to each Sunday. I couldn't wait for a soak in their hot tub perched on the valley bench with a view of the breathtaking mountains spreading out behind, and the city lights below. Even if the clouds didn't part, relaxing in my folk's hot tub was my favorite end to a busy week.

My young wife and I were busy creating a prosperous lifestyle for ourselves. We'd been married for three years and were trying to attain everything that professional couples want to achieve and own "keep up with the Joneses", especially with all the high achievers in my family.

Racing down the wet freeway, we were running late, as usual. Actually, to be fair, my entitlement and selfishness always caused me to be late. I carefully pumped the brakes as we approached the freeway exit near Woods Cross, Utah. With all the rain, I couldn't see out my windshield clearly. The sun had already set. Dark clouds and the downpour obscured normal landmarks. The freeway lights reflected sharply off the wet asphalt, making it difficult to see. I squinted hard as my hands gripped the wheel.

Suddenly, the green exit sign appeared in my peripheral vision, but it was too late. Determined to make the exit anyway, I impulsively cranked my wheel at the last second, swerved off the freeway, and barely missed the cement barricades. Fortunately, the fresh tires on my brand new, granite-colored SUV held the grip needed to keep the car from flipping.

Holy crap!

We barely avoided skidding off the road as my body pumped adrenaline and regained control. I brought the vehicle safely to a stop at the end of the off-ramp. My hands shook uncontrollably.

I took a breath and turned my head to see if my silent wife was okay. She was clutching the panic handle above the passenger's seat, aiming a glare of displeasure my way. Her face, now drained of all color, stood at stark contrast to her light brown hair and deep green eyes. For a split second, I contemplated whether I should apologize for nearly causing an accident or blame it on the rain.

Just as I opened my mouth to apologize, WHAM! The sound of crunching metal rang out as my body throttled forward. Instantly, my neck ripped backward into the seat's headrest.

The hit was so hard my vehicle was pushed along the wet asphalt partly into the intersection, where it luckily came to a halt.

Concerned, I turned to check with my wife again to make sure she was not injured. There was no blood. Kelli had only experienced some whiplash, like me. As soon as she said she was okay, my face hardened, and my fear turned instantly to anger.

Who is responsible for this?

I launched out of my vehicle onto the road to see the damage to my beloved SUV, only a few months old. I had worked hard for this car! In my anger, I glared through the night rain, only to see a skinny teenage boy at the wheel of the car behind us. He was maybe seventeen years old, and I noticed he was visibly shaking, the way I had been a few seconds before.

When the boy stepped out from behind the wheel of his smashed navy-blue car, he had a look of terror on his face, made worse by the angry expression he saw on mine. He was clearly afraid of what I was going to say or do to him.

My heart softened, and the anger left me.

"Are you okay, kid?" I asked, clearing my throat.

"Yeah. I'm . . . I'm so sorry, sir!" he stammered, still trembling. "I didn't mean to hit your car, but these wet roads . . . uh . . . really, I'm so sorry."

"It's okay, bud. We are all okay," I said, trying to console him.

The boy's inexperience driving in a storm with bald tires caused him to misread the distance on the wet roads. He had been unable to stop the accident from happening.

We surveyed the damage to both vehicles. My bumper was knocked in a bit, but glancing at the tow package, I could tell the heavy, reinforced metal kept my SUV from further damage. His car—a much smaller model sedan—was a mess, though. He told me the vehicle wasn't his; it belonged to his father.

"Look, buddy," I said, wanting to comfort him, as his trembling hadn't stopped. "I'm safe. My wife is safe. You're safe. Everybody is safe. That's what matters."

He looked a little relieved at my words, until another thought hit him. "My dad is going to kill me," he muttered under his breath.

I looked at the boy, huddled in a gigantic hoodie, making him appear even more childlike. I wasn't a father yet, but hoped I would be some day. Wouldn't every dad just be grateful his son wasn't harmed? Then I thought about my own dad, and the times I crashed his car. My father was a kind and patient man in times like these, and I desperately sought his approval all my life. As I glanced over at this kid, I had more compassion than ever.

My thoughts were interrupted by blinking police lights and frantic sirens echoing from a distance. Help was on its way.

"At least nobody is hurt, man," I reassured him. "I mean it. It's okay."

A police car arrived on the scene about the same time as the boy's father pulled up. The man's face was a mixture of strong emotion: anger at his son, frustration at the wrecked state of his car, but all quickly masked by embarrassment that his kid had caused the accident. As the boy's father walked up to his son and gave him a hug, I instantly appreciated my own loving father.

This was going to take a while, and I was shivering from cold and rain. I really wanted that hot tub now. I climbed back in the SUV with Kelli after the officer saw there were no severe injuries and gave me the okay to do so.

Mom! She and Dad were expecting us. They'd be worried. I quickly texted.

> In an accident.
> Will be a while.

Her response was swift.

> Oh, no! Are you okay?

I replied, getting a little annoyed.

> Yes, Mom.
> We'll be fine.
> Will let you know when we are on our way.

After the officer investigated the scene, he called a tow truck and wrote the boy his first ticket. Then the officer walked to my driver's side window and gave us all the updates.

"You are excused to go," he said. "However, I suggest you go to the hospital to get x-rays of your necks. You may want to have them looked at for whiplash injury."

I glanced gravely at Kelli, and then thanked the officer. In a bit of a panic, I fired up the engine and drove us straight to the local hospital for x-rays. I had only been in a couple car accidents before. I'd never been injured, but I'd heard about whiplash injuries and the horrible symptoms that could develop over time: chronic neck pain, limited movement, headaches, fatigue, dizziness, maybe even blurred vision. This could be serious. It seemed at that very moment, my neck pain started to flare up.

For three long hours, Kelli and I waited in the lobby of the emergency room, the dull atmosphere punctuated only by our quiet, nervous conversation and texts with Mom.

For myself, I was just disappointed to miss dessert and the hot tub. I was starting to think about visiting the vending machine for a candy bar when, finally, we were called and brought back to a small room with a curtain separating us from the hustle of medical staff and afflicted patients.

Waiting again for what seemed like an eternity, the doctor slid the curtain aside. Without eye contact, he asked a couple questions and then left the room. He returned with some suggestions to see another doctor for x-rays in the coming days after the swelling went down, then quickly handed us both a prescription of Hydrocodone for 30 pills each and cleared us to go home.

I looked at the typed and signed prescriptions. The quantity was small; sufficient for my wife, but not for me. A slight tolerance for pain pills originated after a surgery I had in high school.

Kelli went to work the next day. I, on the other hand, milked the injury and requested a few days off from work. During that time, I lay in front of the television watching movies as I took twice the prescribed amount of pain medication. The bottle said to take two pills every four hours. I took four. Within a day and a half, I had gobbled up my entire prescription. I noticed Kelli wasn't taking hers and the bottle sat like an open invitation on her nightstand. So I helped myself to her prescription, telling myself she probably wouldn't notice anyway.

A few days later, I reluctantly returned to work, answering questions about my absence and the accident from my coworkers. By now, my story was embellished and as exciting as possible. I glowed in the attention.

Each time I told the story the roads became slicker and wetter, and the kid became younger—barely able to see above the steering wheel—and the crunch of the car had pushed us to the opposite end of the intersection, nearly getting smashed by oncoming traffic. Embellishments were my way of people-pleasing. I basked in all the attention my coworkers gave me.

Working as an ad salesman for the most-watched local television station in one of the upscale skyscrapers in Salt Lake City fueled my ego. Our sales office was a bull pen of cubicles with all the competitive action happening in the center of the room. Everyone knew everyone else's business, and rookies had to prove themselves constantly to make a decent living.

As a young and ambitious guy, I discovered fairly quickly that a decent living could, indeed, be had. Some of the more seasoned sales executives earned the coveted outer offices, drove BMWs, and managed lucrative high-level accounts, easily bringing home six-figure incomes.

As a motivated self-starter, I was beginning to make great money and a corner office seemed inevitable in a few years.

In addition to my growing income as a media salesman, I enjoyed incredible perks. I had VIP access to nearly every major entertainment venue, including tickets to all professional sports, concerts, and special events in the state of Utah. I enjoyed skiing competitions at Park City Mountain Resort, monster truck rallies at the Salt Palace, and I had tickets for Disney-themed ice shows at my fingertips where I could schmooze my nieces and nephews.

Even better were the media trips to Los Angeles Dodgers' games, house-boating excursions on pristine Lake Powell, along with fishing and snowmobile expeditions in the majestic mountains of Utah. I was convinced I had landed the best job in the world.

For the longest time, I was the youngest salesmen on my floor. In my new SUV and prime access to the whole city with my press pass, I felt like I had it made.

Unlike my siblings, I didn't have to spend eight grueling years in medical school or get stuck with massive student loans to repay. It felt to me like I was on the fast track to success and was already living the dream.

The Oxy Ring

"Hey, Jason," Paul said as I passed by the water cooler. "So sorry to hear about your accident, buddy." Paul's eyes had a friendly twinkle, even if they didn't exactly exude compassion. "Can I take you to lunch?"

I looked at Paul shrewdly. He was just a coworker, but he was a guy I watched carefully. He'd only been with our team about six months. Athletically built and fit with a bigger-than-life personality, I couldn't help but notice that when he walked into a room, almost everyone liked him instantly. That's why I *didn't* like him much—he was too likeable.

My boss had taken him under his wing, and in an instant Paul had stolen my rock-star sales status in my supervisor's eyes. Blond and good-looking, at six feet tall he was nearly as tall as me, and I couldn't help but to compare myself to him. As the young "golden boy" on our team, he became my competition.

I hesitated.

Keep your friends close and your enemies closer.

"Why not?" I said coolly. I felt the tension in my body rising, which didn't help the stiffness I still felt from the accident.

"I'll drive," he offered amicably.

During lunch I became more relaxed around Paul as we discussed the business, swapped hobbies, and did a fair amount of office gossip—the usual topics for young, new coworkers.

After lunch as I sat down in his gray Mazda 3, I relaxed a little. His car was nice, but small, and nothing compared to my new SUV. That helped me feel a little better about myself.

"So, that must've been some accident, almost dying after getting pushed into the intersection by that kid," Paul said. "I noticed you were out for a few days, man. How's the pain? Are you seeing anyone for pain management?"

"Nah, not really," I shrugged. "I saw a doctor and he prescribed me some weak pain pills, but that's about it." I still felt tense in Paul's presence, and a little uncomfortable at his questions. He smirked and then began to tell me about an injury he suffered and how he was being treated for it by a really good doctor. To my surprise, he softly offered a tiny pain pill to ease my stiffness, saying that it really helped him.

His thoughtfulness was touching.

I willingly took the offer, and then he proceeded to open the bottle and pour a bunch into his hand, enough for me to see them in all their glory, like a true salesman. He then pinched one pill and put it into my hand.

"What is it?" I asked.

"Oxy," Paul assured. Then he pulled out an old plastic CD case he stored in his side door while explaining that he liked to crush up the pill because it worked faster that way. He put the pill in his mouth to dissolve the outer coating, then folded the Oxy inside a dollar bill and used two pennies to crush it up. Then he poured the powder out onto the CD case's flat surface and gently chopped it up until the consistency became a fine white powder, which he divided into two lines.

I watched with amazement.

"It also works better this way. Snorting them protects your stomach lining," Paul instructed.

He snorted the first line with the rolled-up bill, then handed me the rolled-up dollar bill, offering me the second line. A little awkwardly, I took it and followed his example.

Like a coke-head, I snorted the white line as my nostrils burned and my throat caked with chalky powder, causing me to cough. Within seconds, I felt my brain release an intense feeling of joy, sending it to every part of my body.

Ahhhhhhhhh!

Wow! Paul was right.

The power of the pill hit me instantly. I began to feel tingly all over my head, face, and neck. That glorious feeling spread down into my chest, arms, and legs. I sighed, feeling all of my pent-up anxiety fade away.

Quite literally, Paul suddenly felt like my new best friend—an angel who had given me a gift, and we would be best friends forever. He was not the competition; he was my buddy, my bro! In fact, in that moment I felt like taking him under my wing and sharing all my secrets to sales that I had learned through the years. Yes, everything seemed right with the world.

At the peak of my high, Paul smiled widely at my dreamy look. Then he made me a proposition I couldn't refuse.

"Look, you should look into some legitimate pain management."

He held up his large, prescription pill bottle, closely watching my reaction as he handed it to me. The label read:

OxyContin

Quantity 120

I looked at him blankly. The competitiveness inside of me was wide awake. *If he can have these, I'm getting some, too. Besides, I have a legitimate injury.*

"I can refer you to my doctor if you want," Paul continued, still smirking. "Seriously. He will hook you up with the good stuff."

In one instant, I felt adrenalin rush through my body. The pills mesmerized me. I had never seen so many in my life! I had only a little history with pain pills after a knee surgery back in high school, but this was different. The power of what Paul seemed to hold in that little bottle enticed me significantly.

"He will hook me up, huh?" I contemplated.

"Do you want a few pills to try it out?" Paul proposed.

"Yes!"

"Seriously, Jason, let me know if you want to go see my doctor. He's great at assessing pain and prescribing what you need. He only sees new patients on Wednesdays from 10 a.m. to 2 p.m. You can come in with me this week if you want."

"Sounds good, man," I agreed, my head spinning pleasantly. Anything to feel like this. "Sure, I'll go check it out."

I was defenseless. I had been high before, but never experienced the high of OxyContin, a pharmacy-grade heroin. I didn't expect to love the feeling as much as I did. The world could have come crashing down in that moment, and I would have been just fine. I felt like I had found the answer to all of my life's complexities. Most important, I wanted to keep on feeling this feeling and never let it go away.

Two days later, I drove twenty minutes from my office in downtown Salt Lake City to the Pain and Weight Management clinic located at the other end of the valley. I was anxious and uptight. I'd rapidly burned through the two pills Paul had shared with me. I couldn't wait to get my own and not be at Paul's mercy to experience that amazing feeling.

Paul had given me the address, set up my appointment, and even insisted on meeting me in the parking lot at the clinic to give me some final instructions. I couldn't understand why he was so adamant about us going together.

Then suddenly he changed his mind.

"Look, buddy, I can't go inside with you today because I need to run some errands in the area. Call me as soon as your appointment is over, and we'll go snag lunch. Sound good?"

"Sure," I said, shrugging. I assumed he expected me to repay him a small handful of pills since he'd shared his with me a few days earlier. It was only fair.

As Paul was about to drive away, he stopped and gave me a sardonic smile. "The doctor is a little weird," he said, "but not to worry. He knows what he's doing, and he'll take care of you."

"Ok," I replied, blowing it off.

As I walked in the front door of the small medical clinic, I noticed that the waiting room was packed with people. Interestingly, all of the patients were somewhere between twenty to twenty-five years old, each of them filling out paperwork. I walked up to the counter and gave the young receptionist my first and last name. She asked for my insurance card, co-pay, and gave me a packet of paperwork to fill out. It seemed standard; however, something felt awkward when she gave me a separate sheet of instructions.

"You are to fill this out precisely," she said, eyeing me. Her stern tone of voice took me by surprise. Sure, the ER doctor had been gruff, but I'd never been treated this way before by medical staff at my dad's office or anywhere else. Since my father was an M.D., I knew his staff would never treat a patient this way—even if the patient was an idiot, which I was not.

"Be sure you follow the instructions exactly!" the woman warned. Then she rushed off to help another patient.

Full of curiosity, I took my seat near the door and looked at the instructions. Step by step, I was ordered to list specific symptoms, such as numbness in my right leg; tingling in my right arm; weakness in my muscles; increased pain when I stood or sat for ten minutes; inability to walk long distances; and migraine headaches.

As I proceeded to fill out the paperwork, my gut warned me. Sure, I was stiff and sore from the accident, and I'd experienced some headaches in the previous few days, but I didn't have migraines and I really wasn't experiencing these symptoms. I knew this procedure was not standard protocol.

I contemplated standing up and walking out, then I hesitated. The withdrawals were setting in. No, I didn't have most of those symptoms, but the past few days, I certainly had experienced other symptoms. My level of anxiety had increased exponentially because I didn't have the OxyContin in my system. I started to perspire, my body ached, and my muscles began to cramp.

Once I got a hold of some Oxy, it would be nirvana. I could escape the anxiety and the pain in an instant.

I stretched my neck painfully for a moment, making sure to wince appropriately, in case anyone was watching. *That's why you're here,* I reminded myself. *Besides, you have a legit reason, remember? Whiplash. It's a serious thing. They should have a surgeon general's warning on every car.*

I stayed glued to my seat and continued to pour over my paperwork. So what if it meant having to bend the truth a little on the paperwork? Besides, did anyone ever read paperwork anyway? I was sure most medical records just sat in their files and collected dust.

I proceeded to finish, line by line, every instruction. I wasn't taking any chances: I needed to get the prescription. I would play the game.

After completing the paperwork, I was called back to the doctor's office. Above the door was an engraved plaque that read, "Dr. Alex." Inside the room, Dr. Alex's degree was framed and mounted on the wall. I started to look at it when a tall, though pudgy Mediterranean-looking man entered, clipboard in hand. Right away, I could tell he had no bedside manner. He was as cold and distant as the emergency room doctor had been. In this room I was given a brief, perfunctory physical before we sat down at his desk. The physical was fake. This whole thing was fake. My mind was screaming, but so was my body. Though I didn't realize it at the time, in hindsight I now know the truth: I was already hooked.

At that point, Dr. Alex finally looked at me in the eye, and without a hint of humor gave me specific instructions.

"You are to present this prescription to the pharmacist with the white beard at the pharmacy at this address, and to no one else." As if that wasn't odd enough, he soberly added these disconcerting orders: "Jason, when you are ready for your next refill, please coordinate with the person who referred you and he will schedule your next appointment."

What? As a doctor's son I knew THAT was not normal medical procedure. Alarm bells rang in my head. Somehow Paul had a tie-in to this clinic. Why else would I have to coordinate a doctor's appointment with him?

Just do it, spoke an urgent voice inside of me. *You don't have to rationalize this one iota. You have an injury. Get your pills and get this over with.*

I felt like I had an angel on one shoulder and a devil on the other, and both were screaming at me. But then the doctor handed me a slip of paper. It was a prescription for a full bottle of 120 OxyContin.

Instantly, my doubts and concerns vanished when I held that valuable slip of paper. As I walked out of the clinic, I felt like I was just given a check for $3,000. All I needed to do was cash it.

I raced over to the pharmacy following the doctor's specific instructions. I walked in the door of the mom-and-pop building and went straight to the counter. There I handed the white-bearded pharmacist my prescription and insurance card. He was no rookie; in a matter of minutes, the protocol was complete. I slid my debit card through the machine to complete the transaction, and he handed me a white paper bag.

That's it? It was as easy as buying groceries!

As fast as my legs could carry me without looking suspicious, I hurried to my dented SUV. Once inside, I ripped open the bag to see the merchandise. A rush of adrenaline flooded my veins as I drooled over the largest bottle of pain pills I had ever owned. I couldn't believe I was actually holding a full bottle of what I quickly learned were the strongest, purest, and most valuable pain pills on the market at that time.

Before I even called Paul, I zipped around the corner to the supermarket parking lot in Cottonwood Heights. Right in my vehicle, I crushed up one of the pills on an old CD case. Using a dollar bill and my debit card, I snorted the lines, just as my coworker had shown me how to do a few days before. Of course, I wanted to protect my stomach lining, but what I really wanted was that high to hit me immediately. And it did.

Then I called Paul. We met up in the parking lot for a quick celebration and exchange. However, it did not go the way I expected.

"Okay, you need to kick me back twenty pills for referring you to the doc," he said. I looked at him blankly. He hadn't said anything like that before. I'd expected just to replace the pills he'd given me.

Reality dawned. Paul had me where he wanted me, and he knew it. "In order to keep this going, you need to agree with these terms."

Be careful, Jason, I thought. *Choose your battles carefully.*

Reluctantly, I handed over twenty pills. I was too high to protest. Besides, he *was* the one who referred me, and I still had ninety-nine pills left for myself. Compared to the thirty weak pills from my other doctor, this was an ongoing party in a bottle. I didn't need to make a big deal of it at the moment.

Paul smiled knowingly, then we drove off in separate directions.

I was a happy camper for days. Over the next few weeks, however, I noticed my dependence on the pills strengthened. I had a need and I had to feed it. It was as if I couldn't get enough. My highs were lessening, and my irritability was increasing. Almost immediately, I started to lose weight and my skin color began to change to a pale white. It was especially tough when my pills ran out and I had to wait a few days before refilling.

Once the time came for my refill, I was chomping at the bit. I followed orders and contacted Paul. I walked through the same protocol as before, except this time I was required to bring $1,000 cash in an envelope and pay it to Dr. Alex.

What other choice did I have?

I was hooked.

After kicking back twenty pills to Paul, I snorted through my second prescription faster than the first. I emptied the bottle in two weeks, which meant I had to wait a full two weeks without my fix until my next refill.

How am I going to cover the gap? I couldn't fathom the idea of waiting that long. That, my friends, was the moment I became aware of my addiction. Over time, like dominoes falling, my life began to fall over one piece at a time. It all began with one bottle of pills. Amazing how such tiny things, no bigger than ¼ inch, can suddenly control every move you make and every thought you think.

People who have Substance Use Disorder don't wake up one day and decide to destroy their lives and the lives of those they love. Most are actually sensitive souls who struggle at some level with high anxiety, a nagging feeling of worthlessness, or an inadequacy that followed them all their life. Their inner emotional life is a constant struggle. A drug or a drink takes all of that pain away in an instant. Of course, many get addicted to prescription drugs because of a medical need to help with terrible physical pain and then find themselves unable to get off of them without horrific withdrawals. Some people can often work successfully with their physician to slowly wean off of the opiates and get back to normal.

But I would say that most addicted people who simply can't stop taking drugs, those especially vulnerable to getting hooked, have had a painful inner emotional life and that may be coupled with a genetic vulnerability to addiction.

Some have suffered a life of constant internal torment that others around them may or may not have been aware of. When they find a "miracle" that makes all the pain go away so they feel normal—or super happy and calm—the psychological hook to the drug is just as big as the physical one. It's a double whammy. A high percentage of those who are addicted also have other co-occurring disorders, such as attention deficit/hyperactive disorder (ADHD), anxiety, depression, bipolar disorder, and the like. Some genuinely have the genetic vulnerability for alcoholism and/or addiction. The substance doesn't matter; it is the same noose, just a different rope. They are fighting a much harder battle than someone who doesn't have the genetic predisposition for addiction and who hasn't struggled with anxiety, depression, or a sense of inadequacy all their life.

Understanding this about your addicted loved one may help increase compassion and understanding, and though his addiction is not your fault—it is important to understand that he is fighting a more difficult battle inside his brain—than others.

You know the old saying, "Don't judge a man until you've walked a mile in his shoes?" I might say, "Don't judge a person unless you've lived with his particular set of neurological challenges and brain make-up for a year."

We don't know what we don't know. But this we do know, based on research and brain studies: some of us are fighting harder invisible emotional and mental battles than others. And without the right kind of help, these folks are especially easy prey to the lure of addiction. I was one of those kids with a vulnerability to addiction, though my family did not realize or see it.

A little more of my story might shed more insight.

Chapter 2

SUPER POWERED

I saw her when no one else did.

Every time she tottered down the school hallway on her makeshift, PVC crutches, she swayed to and fro. Each excruciatingly painful step broke my heart. She was afflicted with a permanent disability that caused her great pain, and she always tried to avoid the other rowdy middle-school kids.

Every time the flimsy support gave way, she stumbled and crashed to the floor. Tears welled up in my eyes as I watched her struggle. And every time she went down, through no fault of her own, I tried to help her back up.

She wasn't popular. She came from an impoverished family. People made fun of her poor excuse for crutches. Still, there were times I would glimpse a bright light that shone from inside of her. I wondered why hardly anyone else seemed to see it.

Most of the time, however, this girl kept her head down, masked in shame and in pain as she survived, step by step, day by day.

The bullies made fun of her. I didn't like it, but I was afraid to confront them. I was afraid of them not liking me, or even worse, turning their focus on me. Growing up, I was a sensitive boy and felt every emotion deeply.

I, too, had been mocked and teased for being chubby, for my mullet haircut, for feeling too deeply, for tears that surfaced too readily, for my own pain, and the suffering of others . . . for not being tough enough. I was teased time and again, so I learned to tell myself over and over to "suck it up", "quit being a blithering idiot", "shake it off", and "be a real man."

So, I hid my tears in my locker, behind my books—whatever it took.

And I learned to shake it off. To be that "real" man.

But my soul never forgot. I never dreamed that one day I would have a crutch even flimsier than those PVC pipes, and that like the poor girl at school, I thought my world would crumble with each excruciating step.

Emotional sensitivity was my curse. Fear was my constant companion.

No one becomes addicted on purpose.

I certainly didn't.

Growing up in a strong family where drugs and even alcohol were taboo, I had no intention of falling prey to the horrors of addiction that were preached against from the pulpit at church and in the classrooms in school. I knew I didn't want to be one of "those" poor losers.

But I had a nagging problem that would grow in size and scope as I grew from a kid into a teenager, and eventually this problem became all-encompassing.

Growing up in a "Type-A" household, with my own Type-A personality, everything had to be PERFECT. I followed suit and became the perfect go-getter in school and at home, until I became a teenager. Then I was perfect at going and getting what *I* wanted, not necessarily what my dad, mom, or siblings wanted me to achieve. My father was a doctor who encouraged us to rise to our highest potential. I took that as a charge to go to school, get exceptional grades, and make a perfect appearance in public—be it church, school, or work. Outwardly, I strived to make all that happen, while inwardly, I was still a scared little kid. I continued to have very tender feelings and emotions, which I hid away as often as I could. I was so afraid of not being accepted or included. In my mind, I always felt "less than" and inadequate. I believed I had to prove myself in *every* possible way or I wouldn't be acceptable to friends, family, or even to God.

So despite my family, my culture, and the fact that it was illegal, the first time I was offered alcohol at seventeen, I tried it without hesitation. That brisk autumn night, my friend Sam popped the lid on his grandmother's hidden whiskey, and, wanting to appear cool, I took a shot. The nasty liquid burned down the back of my throat, and I grimaced at the vile smell and taste. *What was so cool about this?*

Then all of a sudden, I *felt* cool. The instant that alcohol reached my bloodstream and brain cells, it seemed all my insecurities, inadequacies, and fears of what people thought of me vanished. With the help of this chemical, I "lost" the shy and awkward part of my personality; I became outgoing, confident, and carefree. I consumed seven shots of that whiskey in mere minutes. I loved the effect: laughter, loud music, pizza, and best of all, the pure unadulterated escape from that ever-present shame of not being enough.

The next morning, I woke up, sick and confused, lying on the floor in Sam's basement. And then I looked down at my naked chest.

What the...? Why is there black ink all over my skin?

At some point during all the fun, someone had taken a permanent marker and written words and drawn pictures all over my chest, arms, and neck. I had no idea how it even happened, or who had done it. I couldn't remember a thing past the second shot.

I didn't have time to resolve the question before I felt a violent urge to vomit. I lurched toward the bathroom and threw up for the next twenty minutes. When I was done, I still tasted the whiskey on my breath, which made me feel nauseous again. I swished water in my mouth and spit it out in the sink, then looked up into the mirror to find marker smeared across my face. I couldn't let my friends see me this way—I had an image to protect! I quickly washed my face, but the ink would not come off.

Oh crap! I'm going to be the laughing stock of the whole party—the whole weekend. Everyone at school will know about it.

In that moment, I felt overwhelmed by insecurity. Afraid of what everyone would think, I swore I would never touch that wicked stuff again. Then I braced myself and slowly started up the stairs toward the kitchen where I heard Sam's voice.

When I got about halfway up, however, still clinging to the railing, I overheard my friends laughing and telling stories about the events of the night before. Apparently, I had been the life of the party. They couldn't stop talking about me! I stood a little taller, then completed the last step. As I walked into the kitchen where my friends were gathered, they greeted me with cheers and high fives. There were no insults or put downs, and none of the shame I had feared.

"Coombsy, you are the man! You were hilarious last night! Do you remember when you let us draw all over you? Hahaha! That was crazy, man!"

I suddenly felt like a celebrity. The problem was, I couldn't remember most of what had happened. On the one hand, it was awesome to hear my friends talk about me as a fun, party guy; on the other hand, it concerned me that I got drunk enough to lose control over my actions and memory. As the compliments in the kitchen and at school kept coming, I put those fears aside. At the age of seventeen, I'd found the solution to all of my social insecurities. I felt completely and totally alive. To me, alcohol was a new-found miracle.

And as far as my need to please my family and God? My friends took priority. I found that I could hide my party guy persona from my conservative friends, and certainly from my family.

Alcohol became the perfect combination of risk and reward for me. There was an adrenaline rush to sneak, hide, and get away with drinking.

I was in heaven.

So, Sam, my other friends, and I began to drink, and drink often. As the weekend parties progressed, our forays into alcohol escalated into marijuana, and finally other forms of experimentation. For example, at school dances, my friends and I would drink cough medicine with dextromethorphan to get us high. It was harmless, we thought. And the best part? We didn't get caught.

With newfound confidence due to my rising social status, I tackled other parts of my world. My parents never knew about my double life. The good, clean-cut kid and soccer player vs. the secret party animal. I had the best of both worlds.

I hit the top of my game as a senior at Woods Cross High School that spring. A major player for my soccer team, I was proud of my athletic prowess. Pre-season soccer was underway, and our team's mission was to defend the championship title. The year before we had battled the best teams in the state of Utah to win the state championship and earn the coveted ring, and we were set to do it again.

My folks supported me through every spring and fall soccer season over the years, then competition teams and special coaching camps. My parents showed up at every game they could attend, especially my father. He took time off from his medical practice to watch my games and coach me from the sidelines. Dad in particular was fully vested in my success on the field. A distinguished and proper man with salt and pepper hair and an expansive grin, he turned into something to behold on the soccer pitch. He screamed at the top of his lungs from the sidelines, most often at the refs and coaches. Sometimes when I missed a kick, or the opposing team scored on me, he yelled advice and pointers at me, mostly not received well by me. Once, I even dared to yell back at him, "Get off my back! I'm trying my hardest!" It hurt his feelings and he walked off the field. Dad was sensitive, too, though he never showed it. He apologized later, recognizing his loss of control sometimes when it came to sports.

In spite of my double life, I sincerely wanted my father to be proud of me. He was, and always will be, my hero.

On one particularly beautiful spring day, the coaches huddled us up at practice for the annual pep talk. Our first regular season game against our rival, Olympus High School, was only a few days away. The coaches poured on the motivation.

"You're going to go out there and you're going to show them your best. Let them know who the BOSS is in this valley! Wild Cats don't let anyone reign on our territory . . . and we are known to tear apart Titans for just stepping onto our field. WILD CATS RULE!" A roar came up from myself and the players around me. Then the coaches stepped forward and announced that they had selected the prestigious Team Captains.

The team went silent as everyone held their breath. I looked at my friends, my fellow seniors, my best buds, and I could see the hopeful looks in all of their eyes.

"Jason Coombs!" the coaches roared in unison, and the clapping began. I stood for a moment, dumbfounded. I had secretly hoped for this, but never in a million years did I think I'd be made captain! As a teenager, this was the peak of all accomplishments for me.

The coaches then sent us out on the field for a friendly scrimmage game to warm up. I got a lot of high-fives and handshakes from the sophomores and juniors, but not as many from the seniors who felt discouraged. Most importantly, I wanted to impress the rookies with my exceptional skills. I also wanted to prove to my peers that I deserved the title. Plus, when Dad and Mom found out, they would know all of their years of investment and support had paid off.

Wow! Can life get any better than this? I felt like I had it made.

With adrenaline rushing in my veins, I sprinted out on the field and ran up the sideline to go after the ball. I pushed much harder than was necessary. In my exuberance, I hyperextended my leg, tearing my ACL, or Anterior Cruciate Ligament. Grabbing my right knee, I fell to the grass, trying to keep tears from streaming down my face. The physical pain was more than I could bear, but to be truthful, the emotional injury was far worse. As I writhed back and forth in agony on the grass, I knew this was the end of my soccer season and captain status. It devastated my dreams of glory.

Dad was as heartbroken as I was. He immediately scheduled surgery with the best orthopedic surgeon in the state. Along with intense physical therapy, I was going to have to lay off my knee for the next several months. That meant no soccer.

I slipped into depression. I grieved the loss of my high school soccer career, my active routine as a senior who was eager and ready to take on the world, and my lifestyle that had just plunged from perfect to pathetic.

On the day of the surgery, the nurses gave me a surgery prep with a Demerol drip into my vein. The drug helped me feel better. Within moments, I didn't feel so pathetic; I just felt hazy. In and out of consciousness, I drifted from dream to dream between visitors. I loved the feeling. I felt amazing. What I didn't realize was that I was having some kind of abnormal reaction to the drug. It made me want more and more. The nurses giggled as I would flirtatiously ask them to give me a little more pain medicine. They said no, kindly but firmly.

As I returned home, I craved the Demerol drip. There I was, laid up post-surgery on Mom's white couch, while my friends were out partying. My friends were my whole world, but my accident brought my social life to a skidding halt while everyone else's continued on. They were having fun without me, and like many teenagers do, I suffered from FoMO, or the "fear of missing out." I quickly slipped back into that low and lonely depression.

My mother watched my mood darken hour by hour. She did everything she could to help me get through that trial.

"Look who's here, Jason!" I heard her say with a smile as visitor after visitor came by. Over the next two weeks, she invited all manner of friends and family over to cheer me up. I put on my game face and roused myself for company. The moment they left, however, I crashed back into deep depression.

In those dark hours, Mom became my best friend. She seemed to know instinctively how to make me feel better. She comforted, counseled, and listened to me, catering to my every need. I felt emotionally safe enough to cry in her presence as she held me in her arms, her dark hair falling into her eyes, which were also filled with tears for me.

Afterward, she said in her soft and tender voice, "I'll make you your favorite meal tonight. What movie would you like to watch while I make you dinner?" She knew exactly how to make me feel better, to temporarily help me escape the feelings of sadness and numb my pain.

Every four hours like clockwork, Mom brought me two Percocet for my knee pain. She was vigilant to the follow doctor's orders. Each time I ingested the pills, I felt better—similar to how Demerol had made me feel in the hospital, although the effects were weaker. I wanted that powerful feeling again, so I stashed the pills in-between the couch cushions until I saved up four of them.

And when I took them? *Ahhhhh*, that seemed to do the trick, if briefly for a couple hours. In a matter of days, I continued saving more and more until I reached up to ten pills. Then I would take them all at once to relieve my pain and escape my deep sadness.

Just like with alcohol, each time I took the pills, I experienced significant benefits for a few hours. Not only did my knee pain disappear, but my emotional depression did, too. I also became a social "chatty" butterfly with everyone who stopped by to visit me. The pills gave me the confidence to be myself and to say things I usually kept inside. My insecurities vanished and so did my inadequacies –once again, like magic.

The pills were the answer.

The only problem was that I never had enough access with Mom in control.

I got past the surgery and physical therapy, and back into the party scene as fast as possible. Drugs and alcohol continued forming a loyal relationship with me on an emotional, mental, and physical level. They offered me comfort. They protected me from the barbs of negative emotions and gave me a sense of security. They provided entertainment, friendship, and adventure. Seeking and obtaining drugs and alcohol became a game. My only goal was to continue to keep it secret from my parents and siblings.

That summer after graduation, my childhood friend, Adam, and I backpacked throughout Europe. *Freedom!* Since all drugs were legal in Amsterdam, we happily made our way there from southern France through Belgium. We experimented with what we thought were harmless drugs, like LSD, psychedelic mushrooms, opium, exotic strands of marijuana, and strong European micro-brews. I convinced myself that because these substances were all legal in that country, they were safe.

It's not like we're messing around with addictive stuff like cocaine.

Or so I thought.

Without consciously noticing what was happening, the constant stream of chemicals in my system carved deep neuro-pathways in my young and vulnerable still-forming brain, like a rushing stream sculpts a canyon in the desert. My brain became chemically dependent long before I ever realized what was happening. Not only that, but with each use, my sensitivity to right vs. wrong dimmed.

Upon my return back to the States, I felt wiped out. My brain felt fried. Not only that, but my anxiety had reached an all-time high from having to cover my tracks. I looked for ways to change this pattern that had finally become wearisome and could only come up with one—to follow in my older brother's footsteps.

Like Jamie, I made the decision to volunteer for my church and move to Brazil for two years.

That will fix me.

After six months of intense preparation, including becoming clean from all substances including alcohol, the leap to move to South America was underway. I quickly learned the Portuguese language and immersed myself in the Brazilian culture. I loved and served the people. Meanwhile, I stayed clean and sober. I was proud of myself!

One afternoon while playing soccer with the local Brazilian kids, I rolled my ankle over the ball, and heard the crunch as I fractured the bones, creating excruciating pain. I was rushed to the doctor, casted up, loaded up with pills, and sent on my way.

Like before, I had no defense against the magic in the bottle. My old mental obsession ignited as I craved more and more pills. The deep-etched carvings in my brain remembered the old chemical stream immediately as I experienced the instant release of dopamine in my system once again. It sent me off on a pain-pill bender. I gobbled up all the pills in two days.

The high only ended because I could not obtain any more pills from the Brazilian pharmacy. The thought even crossed my mind to make up a story and ask my parents to mail me some pills from the United States so that I could have enough to last me a while longer.

My obsession to get more pills was not normal, but thinking this way had become the norm for me. The overpowering justifications and rationalizations were back. This time, fortunately, when I ran out of pain pills in Brazil, my cravings finally faded, and I immersed myself again in missionary work.

When I successfully completed my church mission, I had a feeling of accomplishment and a sense of self-respect. Upon my arrival back in the States, I committed to creating a beautiful life and a successful future *without* drugs and alcohol.

I began my undergraduate studies at the University of Utah, met the woman of my dreams, and we were married within a year. Nearing my completion from college, I was ambivalent about which career I should choose. At the time, I enjoyed working at the university newspaper selling advertising space. Consequently, I researched the advertising industry and became interested in pursuing a career in television.

At my little brother's wedding, I sought counsel from my Uncle Bob. Although I did not fully grasp the scope of my uncle's profession, we shared a beautiful friendship and I deeply respected his advice. He was on the faculty in the Department of Psychiatry and Biobehavioral Sciences at UCLA, and was well-respected for his research regarding drug addiction among "pedestal professionals" in high profile careers.

As I sought Uncle Bob's career advice, I mentioned my interest in advertising or television. He instantly put his arm around me and said, "Jason, I have to introduce you to my friend, Steve Carlston. He is an executive at a television network in Los Angeles. I think he would take you under his wing and help you get started."

Nervously, I built up the courage to call Steve the next day. Within the first minute of our conversation, he made me feel like the most important person on the planet. He was genuinely interested in my dreams to be successful. Surprisingly, he spent over an hour encouraging and motivating me, and helping me envision a new dream for my future.

A few months later, I flew down to Los Angeles and met Steve in person. He is a tall, athletic college basketball player with a reputation for winning. His warm welcome comforted me.

As his new protégé, I wanted to be like Steve. I watched his every move, tried to memorize his every word, and adopt his gift for making people feel important.

It was a dream come true to learn from a pro. I witnessed how he treated people in every business deal, executive leadership meeting, and intense corporate negotiations. In every setting, with every person, Steve was respectful, funny, and made people feel valued. To make my experience even better, Steve brought me with him to his box suite at the Staples Center for a WWF event, and backstage access to the Tonight Show with Jay Leno. Everybody welcomed us like royalty. By Steve's side, I was a VIP. My ego inflated.

As I set my sights upon my future, I had a new confidence. With the support of my new mentor, anything was possible. A few months later, I landed a job at the top station in the market. Starting out, I worked fifty to sixty hours per week to make a name for myself and to gain traction towards my sales goals. On another note, I deeply wanted to make my father and mother proud. After much sacrifice, I quickly earned the prestigious "Top New Business Salesman" award within the first year.

Under the mentorship of a great boss and co-workers who believed in me, I continued to thrive. Commissions from new accounts began to roll in like the waves of the sea—one after the other. The accolades from my boss and increasing commissions became my new drugs, fueling my ego and pride. I needed more and more. Addictions can come from many sources; they don't always pour out of a bottle.

With all the success, my focus was to enhance my material status and appearance. I bought a new house, two new cars, new clothes, and set out on extravagant travel destinations, including Europe and Mexico.

I had it made.

Until that fateful car accident. Until I took a ride to the dark place with Paul. Until he popped open the lid of that bottle of pills and my world spiraled down as fast as it had spiraled up.

Chapter 3

HOW WE CHANGE

THERE IS A FUNDAMENTAL VIEWPOINT we use at Brick House Recovery for understanding how the process of change takes place. But as I share this, you may find insights into your own life and your own patterns of changing as well. Addicted or not, we are all human beings; change doesn't come easy and it doesn't happen overnight. Because patience is required with the process of change, it helps to understand what is happening *within* as we move toward making major shifts in our lives. Understanding always increases insight and compassion and will help you make better decisions as you respond to your addicted loved one. When you know where he is at in his thinking process, you can better know exactly what to do and how to respond.

The two tools that will be the foundation upon which we will build your new, highly-effective approach, are a graphic we call **Life Domains** and a graphic we call **Stages of Change**. The third graphic will combine the two.

The first graphic illustrates the basic areas of a person's life, or Life Domains. Perfect wellness would be absolute balance in each of these domains. The goal is to strive for a healthy, not perfect, balance. In your own life, which domain is healthy? Which domain is neglected? Which domain needs attention right now, in your opinion? In fact, we suggest that our clients use a little mark in each pie-shaped area to indicate how well they are doing in each area of their life. You may want to do this for yourself, and then also for your addicted loved one. The Life Domains we look at include the following: our social life (including relationships with friends and outside activities), our career and education, our financial situation, our health (physical, mental, emotional), our relationship with a spouse or significant other, relationships with immediate and any extended family that is important to you, spiritual meaning (engaging with a Higher Power and feeling loved and accepted) and, service (what we give back to others).

LIFE DOMAINS

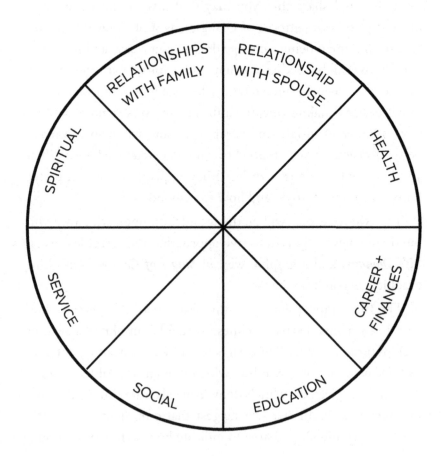

When addiction enters into a family system, over time every Life Domain is affected. Think of your own life and how your loved one's addiction has shifted your relationships, finances, and stress level. It has, in some way, affected every person in your family. Addiction is pervasive and detrimental to one's life balance. It throws everything off kilter and, over time, spreads to every area of our lives like a plague. Before we can stop it from spreading, our lives begin to look something like the next graphic:

LIFE DOMAINS
ADDICTION SPREADS LIKE AN ILLNESS

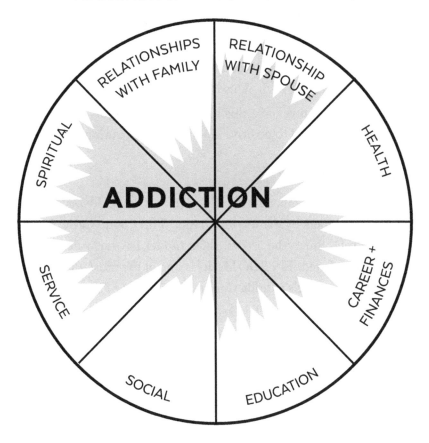

For example, this graph shows how the jagged blot of addiction takes over big portions of your life, reducing them to less and less normal functioning. Imagine someone slowly pouring a pitcher of grape juice in the center of a large, round, white tablecloth. The grape juice spill is like addiction's influence, and as it creeps across the tablecloth of your life, it gradually blots out all the things that formerly gave it meaning and pleasure. Unless we proactively combat its influence, addiction will infect the family system as it takes center stage.

The sickness of addiction causes a person to become myopic; they believe everything revolves around them. Lying and selfishness are like bookends to the disease of addiction. In addition to extreme self-focus and dishonesty, those who are caught in the web of addiction will almost always suffer financial stress; poor performance in work, home, and social settings; risky sexual encounters; declining health, lack of accountability, and insensitivity to anyone's needs but their own. This is what self-bondage looks like.

So how do you reverse this sickness? It all begins with taking small steps that lead to positive changes in the coming chapters.

Stages of Change

The Stages of Change Model (SOC) is an evidenced-based model developed by James Prochaska, Ph.D. and Carlo DiClimente, Ph.D. Since the 1970s, their model has been developed, tested, and refined. The SOC Model is one of the most widely used and accepted models in addiction treatment.

In the book *Changing for Good* (1994), Prochaska and DiClemente describe the six stages of change:

Stage #1: Precontemplation – Not Ready to change

Stage #2: Contemplation – Getting Ready to change

Stage #3: Preparation – Ready to change

Stage #4: Action towards change

Stage #5: Maintenance

Stage #6: Termination [*Transcendence*]

For our purposes, I am going to customize this a little based on my own beliefs and experience. Going forward in this book, Stage #6 will be known as the *Transcendence Stage,* because with Divine help, one can, and will, transcend addiction, *which to me is a more beautiful word picture of redemption and growth than "termination."*

STAGES OF CHANGE
TRANS-THEORETICAL MODEL
(Prochaska and DiClemente)

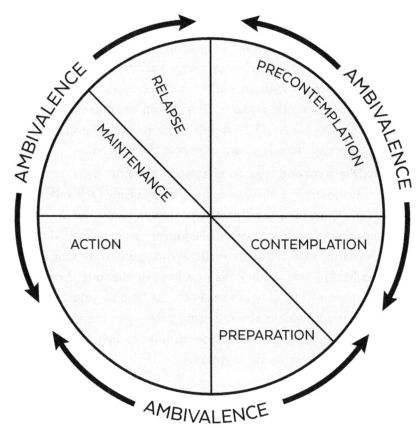

What stage of change is your addicted loved one in today? Is it the same stage as last week? My guess is that you have seen him in various stages over time. This is normal. The old "two steps forward, and one back" (or two back or three back, kind of slow progress). The first five stages are illustrated below, including a relapse stage, which we will get into later in the book.

In the "Stages of Change" diagram, you will notice the word ambivalence is wrapped around all the stages of change.

Have you ever watched your loved one be totally and completely committed to his sobriety, resolved to change for good, but then days or weeks later revert back to the addictive behavior? This generally happens because of his *ambivalence* about lasting change. In other words, a part of him still wants to get high; on the other hand, he genuinely does want lasting change. This "fence-sitting" mentality is common. In fact, you can expect this with your loved one. His ambivalence toward long-term sobriety is why he can't keep promises and continues to revert back to old behavior. In truth, every person with an addiction experiences a great degree of ambivalence; in other words, they are on the fence about getting and *staying* sober. They weigh the costs of using versus the benefits of using. This is a natural part of the process.

Anytime someone tries to change a behavior, there is a tremendous amount of ambivalence happening inside each and every stage. This is normal, and this is why change is so slow. It is best to accept this as a normal part of the journey to recovery. Managing expectations helps you be realistic and respond to your loved one in a healthy way, rather than pushing or shaming them into changing faster than they are ready to. As long as your addicted loved one is ambivalent about getting sober, you can expect setbacks. I will give you more advice on how to help him resolve ambivalence in the coming chapters.

Why are the Stages of Change Important?

Understanding the Stages of Change is vital because people, addicted or not, can't change everything in their lives at once. Think of your own Life Domains wheel. How realistic is it for me to expect you to change all those neglected, out-of-balance domains right now? In fact, you may not even want to change some of those areas in your life, even though you know they are neglected. Am I right?

It is important to grasp that everyone is in a different Stage of Change inside of each Life Domain. For example, the same person may be in *Action Stage of Change (SOC)* regarding her career and her

LIFE DOMAINS

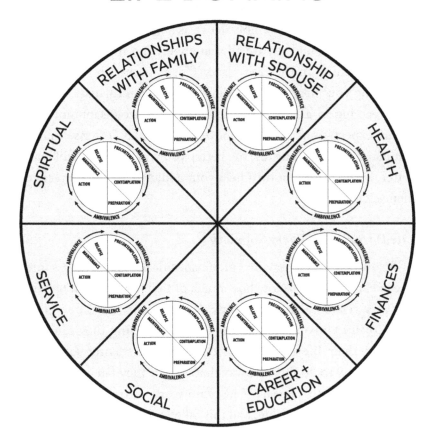

education, yet she is in *Precontemplation* regarding her health and spirituality. See the next graphic, that combines the SOC and the Life Domains together.

In the "Life Domains" graphic, I have placed the SOC wheel inside each Life Domain to help illustrate my point. Can you begin to see why expecting someone to change everything at once sets us up for disappointment? In fact, unrealistic expectations actually prepare the way for resentment. Holding on to resentments is like drinking poison expecting the person you are mad at to die. It sounds crazy, right? But how often do we actually allow the actions of others to make us upset? We are angry because they didn't meet our expectations of how they should treat us or others. What if, by understanding where your addicted loved one is in the change cycle, you could let go of unrealistic expectations and just accept setbacks and ambivalence as a normal part of eventual recovery? You could release all that anger, and in fact, prevent it from happening in the first place. This is going on the offense, protecting your heart and emotions with good information rather than reacting in a defensive way when you are disappointed by unmet expectations. And the more you can play "offense" in this complex relational journey, the better you will feel. You will make better decisions that in turn help your addicted loved one recover themselves.

Life Domains in Early Sobriety

Below is a "Life Domains" graph specifically created for someone in early sobriety. Note how much of their life is taken up with recovery related activities. Think of it as your loved one going to Recovery University—because at the beginning they can't add much to their life beyond concentrating on staying sober and learning how to do this in a way that lasts. If they fall down in the other domains, this is why. The brain works extra hard when we change any area of our life, and this takes energy away from other areas until the new task becomes automatic and routine. Expect this and you will be more patient and at peace.

EARLY RECOVERY LIFE DOMAINS

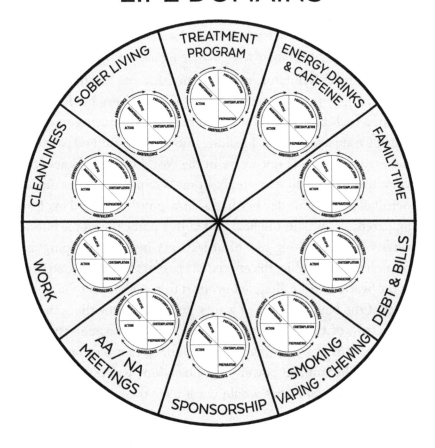

In the next chapter, I will continue my story to show the value of natural consequences. It is no easy thing to walk away and allow your addicted loved one to suffer the consequences of his actions. But you will see why it is the most loving thing you can do if you want to 1) influence lasting change and 2) maintain your own sanity, calm, and joy.

Get Off the Beach!

How do you help someone who doesn't think they have a problem? Let me jump ahead in my story for just a minute. I was court mandated to my first residential treatment program at age twenty-seven. My parents sprang into action and attended the family program. There they were, colossally uncomfortable, sitting in their first rehab facility attending what the therapists called "family group." They felt out of place, overwhelmed, and scared. But it was there they took their first vital step forward in helping me the right way.

The clinical facilitator had them envision me out in the middle of the lake tossing boulders from a boat. Every boulder represented each bad choice I made in my addiction: lying to them, drawing out payday loans, breaking into their house, and pawning their valuables. I had not a care in the world because I knew the worst they would do was simply sit me down for another one of their "talks." (To this day I cringe at how poorly I treated my loving parents.) I was in the boat and at this point the ripple effects weren't really reaching me, or at least my high was keeping me from caring and feeling the effects. My parents lovingly stood firm on the beach shore, calling out in effort to reach me, but the ripple effect of the boulders formed waves, and by the time the accumulated effect of the waves hit the shore, they had gained tsunami strength. (I'm exaggerating the metaphor here a bit, but just go with it.) The tsunami power of all I had done was causing waves of damage and pain that would crash over their heads one after another.

The clinician listened intently and validated my parents' frustrations and confusion. Then she simply instructed the words that would forever change my parents' lives: "You can't stop Jason from tossing boulders because he's not ready to change. So, it's time to get off the beach! You don't have to stand there."

Before that day, my folks had no experience with boundaries, so they lovingly stood firm on the shore for years in effort to help me. With each decision I made, they stood there while the tsunami crashed down upon them over and over, robbing them of their peace, serenity, and financial security.

Finally, and with great relief, my parents took the counselor's advice to "get off the beach!" They became empowered as they learned they were not helping me by standing there trying to rescue someone who had no desire to be saved. In fact, my parents decided to stop allowing me to ruin their lives.

No longer would they allow me to have total access to their home. No longer would they be paying off my debts and bills letting my addiction drain their retirement savings. No longer would they let my addiction keep them from living their dream life. It was time to change all that. They had worked hard to build a good life and they had to protect it from my addiction. They began to love themselves enough to allow me to feel the pain and consequences caused by my behaviors. They "got off the beach."

How do you "get off the beach?" Stay with me and I'll walk you through each step.

Don't Get Caught in the Thickness of Thin Things

Years ago, while working with a client and his family in our outpatient treatment center Brick House Recovery, I had a breakthrough moment. (Outpatient treatment involves intense attendance, but clients go home on evenings and weekends.) This particular client, Chad, lived with his aunt and uncle while in treatment.

Chad's Southern California style endeared me to him right out of the gate. His baggy skater clothing effectively covered his scrawny, emaciated body and his stylish flat-bill cap let his boyish hairstyle slightly cover his eyes, blocking any real eye contact. Chad was twenty-five years old but looked seventeen.

When I began treating Chad, he truly didn't believe he had a problem with drugs. He was in the Precontemplation Stage of

Change, meaning he was not ready to quit using drugs, but was forced to get sober by the Santa Ana Department of Corrections. He was only meeting with me because he got arrested and was required to attend treatment and jump through some additional hoops to please his probation officer and his judge. It's accurate to say that his only motivation was external, and to be honest, that was where most addicted people started.

External motivators help prepare the soil for an internal shift. In this fertile soil, a good seed can be planted and, if cultivated properly, will produce a real harvest of long-term sobriety—a new life.

Days earlier, Chad boarded a plane in Santa Ana, California and arrived in Boise, Idaho to live with his Aunt Julie while attending treatment. In addiction recovery, sometimes it can help to make a geographic change in order to create distance between the addicted person's toxic playmates and playgrounds.

I took Chad under my wing and was encouraged to see him begin to make great internal strides. In a matter of weeks, he attended every treatment appointment and group. He was punctual and began to open up about his deep, internal struggles that caused the compulsion to get loaded on drugs.

One afternoon, my client's aunt called me. She was livid! In her words, Chad was "acting like a junkie" after he came home from treatment every day. She reported that he was staying up all night playing video games, sleeping in late, drinking enormous amounts of caffeine, smoking cigarettes, and continued to dress like a "drug addict." To make things worse, he wouldn't get a job and become a productive member of society. She was at her wit's end because she expected him to be further along in his progress.

She had a lot to learn.

After an ear-full, I validated her concerns.

"You are going through a lot. Can you tell me what your primary expectation was for your nephew Chad before you flew him up to Idaho?"

"Absolutely!" she said forcefully. "We wanted him to get clean and sober."

"Great," I affirmed before she could start her rant again. "You and I share the same goal. Chad has been sober sixty days today! This is a huge success to be celebrated!" I paused, then asked, "Have you celebrated this incredible victory with Chad yet?"

She was silent.

"Starting today," I pleaded, "how do you think it might influence Chad if you make each sobriety milestone the most important date of the century—more important than his birthday and Christmas? What would be his reaction if you made it a family celebration and showed him the entire family recognizes the hundreds of hard battles fought and won? Each and every day clean is a monumental victory, despite your valid concerns."

Then I asked, "How many treatment groups and individual sessions has he attended since he started our program?"

She remained silent.

"His attendance is 100 percent," I proudly reported. "For a twenty-five-year-old who was living on the streets of Costa Mesa with no structure in his life two short months ago, this is a huge victory!"

I further advocated that Chad was making great strides forward in the areas that would build his foundation and character. He was following all the Brick House rules and curriculum expectations. He was on time for assignments and presentations. He was expressing "change talk"—exploring his ambivalence about wanting to stay sober long- term. (We'll get to more of what "change talk" looks and sounds like soon.) And the biggest miracle of all was that Chad expressed his emotions with tears flowing down his cheeks in front of his peers the day prior to her call. Real connections were growing inside him. What a victory!

Aunt Julie wanted the best for Chad, but her unrealistic expectations were hurting both of them. Chad felt her pressure to be more than he could be, so he put up his walls and met her with passive-aggressive resistance. Each time this happened, she felt dismissed, disregarded, and her feelings of frustration and discouragement grew until the point when she called me in a rage.

Clearly Chad, and anyone in early sobriety for that matter, needed a lot of work in many areas of his life. His aunt would only focus on his shortcomings while completely ignoring the fact that Chad was in the *Action* Stage of Change in many areas, especially in his commitment to staying clean and sober one day at a time. Furthermore, he was in the *Action* stage regarding treatment requirements, attendance, assignments, and therapy sessions. There was A LOT to be encouraged about.

During our conversation, Julie reflected on the need to readjust her expectations. She verbally recognized that she was getting stuck in the thickness of thin things. In Chad's case, there were more reasons to celebrate his progress than to be upset.

It is unrealistic to expect that in sixty days all of Chad's unwelcomed behaviors she wanted fixed would suddenly change after he got sober. The truth was that she had set unreasonable expectations, which most family members do. It's okay. The key is that we become aware of them first, then work on changing and adjusting them.

Change is one of the most difficult tasks for any human being. We typically change in small increments in one or maybe two areas at a time.

Parents and spouses often become as addicted to trying to rescue their loved one as their pain and consequences mount from their substance use. The first step for most parents and spouses is to "get sober" from worry and rescuing someone who is clearly not ready to change; and, thereby, show your addicted loved one what sobriety looks like. If you are unhappy and sober, why would your loved one want your kind of life? Get your joy and peace back and show them what emotional sobriety, and a calm, balanced life looks like—come what may!

1. **The best defense is a strong offense.** Let's carefully review our current behavior and become willing to make some hard changes.

2. **Addiction is an illness.** Our addicted loved ones are not losers or morally deficient. They are sick; they are not bad people.

3. **Internal motivation is the key.** External motivators and natural consequences prepare the ground for internal motivation to grow. Real recovery only comes when our addicted loved ones have sufficient motivation to take small and big action steps, one day at a time.

4. **A balanced life is the goal for each of us.** Our loved one's addiction also affects our own Life Domains—creating imbalance, stress, and a discontented life.

5. **Our addicted loved ones will move up and down these stages**, in every Life Domain, as they progress toward recovery. Sometimes two steps forward, one back. Before we change a behavior, we must travel through six Stages of Change:

   Stage #1: Precontemplation – Not Ready to change

   Stage #2: Contemplation – Getting Ready to change

   Stage #3: Preparation – Ready to change

   Stage #4: Action

   Stage #5: Maintenance

   Stage #6: Transcendence

6. **We are all in different Stages of Change inside each Life Domain.** We mustn't expect too much too soon from our addicted loved ones and ourselves. It sets us up for too much disappointment and defeatism. Be kind, patient, and realistic with this process.

7. **We each experience ambivalence at every step.** There are both costs and benefits of making significant changes in our lives. Let's honor our own ambivalence of the changes we need to make within ourselves, while respecting the natural ambivalence of others allowing them their own journey toward internal motivation.

8. **No one becomes addicted on purpose.** Individuals with low self-esteem may be at risk. This includes perfectionists, people pleasers, and sensitive types. They are desperate for others to prop up their wobbly sense of self-worth.

9. **It's time to "Get Off the Beach."** You don't have to stand there. Love yourself enough to allow your addicted loved one to feel the pain of his natural consequences caused by his addiction.

10. **External motivators help prepare the soil where the internal shift will soon harvest.** By doing this, you are *contributing* toward his internal motivation.

11. **Don't get caught in the thickness of thin things.** In other words, become aware of ways you can start contributing toward connection, like celebrating the little victories. Avoid battles over the petty things that drive discord, contention, and arguments. You won't win them anyway because this doesn't evoke internal motivation, but rather drives separation and resistance. What we focus on expands. Focus on the solution, and the solution will expand.

12. **Starting today, make each sobriety milestone the most important day of the year—more important than his birthday and Christmas.** Make it a family celebration and show him the entire family recognizes the hundreds of hard battles fought and won.

13. **Manage your expectations reasonably.** It is unrealistic to expect unwelcomed behaviors to be fixed immediately. It is unrealistic to expect change in every area all at once. You will soon learn which Stage of Change he is at inside each Life Domain, or area of early sobriety. Small steps in any area, particularly abstinence, are HUGE! Change is extremely challenging for any of us. For the addicted, even more so.

*For more help, check out my Addiction Recovery Tips videos for families at www.brickhouserecovery.com/unhooked

Chapter 4

THE ESSENTIAL INGREDIENT: CONSEQUENCES

Now I was in major trouble.

I had purchased my 120 pills from the pharmacy. I gave Paul his "kickback," and I had gone through all 100 of mine in record time.

How am I going to cover the gap between prescription refills?

It is common with opiate dependents to fear withdrawal symptoms enough to continue taking the drug longer than needed for pain. My fear of withdrawals forced me to review my options. The thought of going two whole weeks without medicine made me panic. I called some of my friends and purchased a few pills for $80 each, but that was only a temporary solution. I couldn't justify or afford paying street-market prices for two weeks, let alone two days. After coming to terms that I had no other choice, I made a call to my family practitioner, Dr. Allen.

Without hesitation, I picked up the phone and scheduled an appointment. I made it appear urgent, because it was urgent in my mind. The next day in his office, I delivered my practiced neck-injury speech. I left Dr. Allen's office with a prescription of thirty Hydrocodone, 10 mg. tablets. At least the mediocre strength of these pills would keep me from getting sick from withdrawals. He was now the second physician prescribing me narcotics at the same time.

I tried stretching those new pills out for two weeks, but they were gone in just three days. I was forced back to the black market to buy Oxys for the gouging, painful price of $80 each. In order to hide the missing cash from my wife, I filled up my gas tank with $10 of gas, and asked the teller for $40 cash back, showing a $50 gas station charge on my bank records. Then I went to the local grocery store, bought a few items, and got another $40 cash back from the check-out counter. Both transactions appeared to be for gas and food, which created a solid diversion.

I'm not really being sneaky, I tried to justify. *I'm just taking care of my neck and back pain. I need these pills.*

During those remaining days until my next refill, my "needs" cost me around $1,600 for Oxys out of our household budget.

Two weeks later, I eagerly arrived early to my refill appointment at Dr. Alex's office. By that time, my withdrawals were in full effect, causing intense body aches, sweating, and shaking hands. In his office, I followed the same protocol as I had the last two months.

As I sat there in the waiting room with restless legs that wouldn't stop moving, I couldn't help but notice how sick, skinny, and frail all of the other patients appeared.

Do I look like them? Yes, I did. The drug had them in its ugly clutches, the same as it was grasping me in its vice-like hold.

But I wouldn't admit it. At least, not out loud.

Therefore, I continued to "play the game" with Dr. Alex for a few months as my dependence grew. The benefits I received from the pills were incredibly high. However, a few more natural consequences began to surface. First came my inability to focus at work. My sales plummeted, and my commissions began to vanish. I dropped thirty pounds in three months and was quickly down to 165 pounds because opiates numbed my appetite. My skin color turned pale because I wasn't eating, exercising, or sleeping well. My clothes became baggy, and my smile disappeared. My boss and co-workers began to ask me if I was okay. I sensed they were genuinely concerned, so I tried to avoid them. The accolades in sales meetings stopped, and the questions increased. Every day, co-workers and family members asked me why I was losing so much weight. I brushed them off responding, "I am just training hard for ski season."

That response seemed to satisfy them, if temporarily.

With all the pressure mounting at work, I needed to take a trip to St. George, Utah for a little sunshine and relaxation. I wanted to make up for a little lost time with my wife, too. After all, work wasn't the only place where I was emotionally and physically absent.

That Saturday night after dinner with her, I received a text from Paul:

Call me ASAP!

I stepped outside and called him. His voice was panicked.

"Jason, did you see the news?" he cried. "Dr. Alex's office was raided by the FBI, and they are launching a *huge* investigation! Make sure you don't share *anything* about what happened!"

My heart skipped a beat, and then began to pound in my ears.

I'm going to jail!

Another thought suddenly loomed large in my mind, and it seemed much more important: *Where am I going to get more Oxys?* Luckily, I still had most of this month's bottle left. I hurried into the bathroom to snort another pill in an effort to kill my anxiety.

Over the next couple of weeks, I watched the news closely to learn more about what would be my fate. With growing anxiety, it baffled me to learn that I was involved in Utah's largest OxyContin drug ring in history. Over the course of a few months, Dr. Alex had prescribed over 73,000 pills to his patients. Apparently, compared to other pain clinics during the same time frame, the doctor prescribed up to twenty-four times more than the average doses. Remembering the clinic, the stern directions, and more, I understood why.

The drug ring operated like a business, consisting of just shy of 300 people, a full organizational chart, incentives, and recruiters. I didn't know who was involved until their names were publicly released by the Insurance Fraud Division. The doctor's entire goal was to recruit patients with insurance policies that could cover pain management care and OxyContin prescriptions, get them hooked, and deliver a kick-back of pills to the doctor and the recruiters. What about the $1000 cash? That went directly into the doctor's pocket under the radar from the Internal Revenue Service.

And I had gotten myself right in the middle of the scheme. Purdue Pharma, the company that makes OxyContin, had called Utah's FBI headquarters.

"We have a problem," they conveyed. "We have reports of one of the top prescribers of our drug in Utah, only we can't find his office as being registered with the state." That raised one big, red flag. Another was raised by a technician at the pharmacy who overheard some young people in line bragging about how much money they were going to make selling prescriptions. That's when the FBI set up a healthcare fraud task force.

On May 4, 2006, Dr. Alex was indicted on eighty-three Federal Counts. A warrant was issued for his arrest, and he was arraigned before a U.S. Magistrate the next day. He faced massive counts for Continuing Criminal Enterprise, Conspiracy to Distribute a Controlled Substance, twenty-two counts of OxyContin Distribution, Falsification of Information in Health Care matters, Fraud against the United States, and Aggravated Identity Theft.

For me, I was more worried about immediate consequences. After the raid, I quickly ran out of pills. I then turned to Dr. Allen for relief. His receptionist notified me that Dr. Allen would no longer take me as his patient. Apparently, the Drug Enforcement Agency (DEA) got to him before I could. I was embarrassed and chagrined. I had to find something. I searched high and low for another hook up. I even tried to get my dad's prescription pads from his office, but I was unsuccessful.

My last option was to hit the black market again. Since the raid, the supply could not meet the demand on the streets. The cost of pills sky-rocketed to $100 per pill. That meant my habit would now cost me $10,000 or more every two weeks! That was $20,000 a month, and there was no way that my dwindling income could afford that outrageous price. I had heard that some of my acquaintances found a cheaper solution. Still, I savagely promised myself I would never do the "hard stuff," like heroin.

The decision to abstain from heroin forced me into acute withdrawal symptoms. For the next two weeks, I called in sick from work, stating that I had the flu. I lay in bed for what seemed like an eternity. The violent shakes, tremors, chills, sweats, nightmares, goosebumps, nausea, stomach cramps, fever, vomiting, diarrhea, runny nose, and intense migraine headaches tormented me to the point where I literally considered suicide. I switched from my bed to a hot bath, trying to ease the withdrawals, but nothing helped. A couple of times I tried to beg Paul to bring some pills to my house, but he wouldn't answer my calls. He was hurting as badly as I was.

At the end of the second week of detox, I knew I was not out of the woods. I looked deathly ill and there was no way I could perform my basic work duties. In order to save my job, I just had to get back to work. This was the job that Steve, my wonderful and good-hearted mentor, had helped me secure and if I got fired, I could never face him!

What am I going to do?

I had no choice but to break my promise to myself.

The boundary I committed to never cross.

I could not see any other way out.

Without the leisure of a prescription or any more time off of work, it was time to consider the "hard stuff" just for a day or two until I made it through the withdrawals. Or so I thought.

I called up an old coworker friend. He had connections to get a little cocaine. That would at least give me enough energy to go back to work. The justification made it an easy choice.

Use cocaine vs. lose my job.

I chose cocaine.

Cocaine became my new Oxy overnight. The drug helped me work my way back into good standing with my boss, become productive again, and drive sales results. I began working around the clock in effort to make up for the months I had been lazy and unproductive. I promised myself I would never use opiates again because of how addictive they were. On cocaine, life was getting good again. I was in the *Action SOC* regarding abstinence from opiates, yet I was in the *Precontemplation SOC* regarding cocaine. Do you see how that applies?

The benefits of cocaine increased, especially with the help of alcohol. I began making good money again, started taking care of myself by going to the gym, and I became more social at concerts, parties, and networking events. My work associates and my family were no longer concerned about me. Before long, I hunted for and was offered a better job with another company making even more money, including a base salary. Once again, my relationship with Steve Carlston helped me get an offer. Things got better.

Another benefit was that it seemed the DEA, and the whole Dr. Alex scandal, was going away. There was no contact with Federal Agents, and the whole thing seemed to be resolved.

Ignorance was bliss.

What I didn't know was that the DEA, the state's FBI unit, and local law enforcement were following every string of individuals in that drug ring to get to the other sources of Oxy on the street, and the drug's counterparts, too. Men and women from every walk of life, in every neighborhood, were caught in this insidious ring. In-laws, neighbors, church members, coworkers, and best friends had gotten hooked, and they were all about to pay the price.

One sunny Saturday morning, I was out mowing my lawn when a brown, unmarked car pulled up alongside the curb. Curious, I turned off the lawnmower and my headphones and watched a DEA agent step out of his car. He and I made eye contact through my sunglasses. His shiny badge attached to his belt caught my eye as he approached me.

"Jason Coombs," he said. It was a statement, not a question, and it went with the look in his eye that said he fully knew who I was. With cold determination, he handed me a manila envelope.

"I recommend you get an attorney," he said simply. "Have a nice day." Then he turned and got back into his vehicle.

In speechless shock, I went inside after he drove away, careful to make sure my wife wasn't around. When I ripped into the envelope, inside was a long list of criminal charges against me: Doctor Shopping, Obtaining False Prescriptions, Insurance Fraud, and Distribution. And the combined length of prison time, if I was convicted? Over thirty years in the Utah State Penitentiary. My blood went cold. I had to sit down. Then I had to stand back up again.

The game was over. My life as I knew it was over. What was I going to tell my wife? My parents?

How will I ever get out of this one?

STAGE ONE:
PRECONTEMPLATION (NOT READY)

In high school, drugs and alcohol provided me with adventure, excitement, and a host of new friends. They were also the answer to my insecurities and social anxieties, so . . . I never wanted to stop taking them. All I wanted was *more* to make the feelings last longer. These benefits are important to note. During those early years of using, I formed an emotional and mental bond with pills, alcohol, and marijuana. Because this wasn't accepted in my family, my primary goal was to keep my addictions secret and avoid any consequences that could potentially arise. Though my mother asked me a few times if everything was going alright at school and with friends, I always quickly dismissed her concerns. I was clearly not ready to change my behavior.

There are six Stages of Change (which I will sometimes abbreviate as SOC) that we will talk about in depth in chapters to come, but for our purposes here, let's talk about the first stage of change: the Precontemplation Stage, or rather, the "not ready" stage, because this is the stage I was in at this point of my journey.

Most Precontemplators don't want to change themselves; they really just want the people around them to stop nagging and disrupting their behavior. This group often shows up in treatment centers motivated by pressure from others—spouses who warn of a separation, parents who threaten to kick them out of the house, judges who hang prison time over their heads, and employers who are on their last leg.

One of the most common pressures comes from spouses or parents who give an ultimatum. This may help someone get sober initially, but as soon as the pressure is lifted, more often than not, Precontemplators will resume their old using behaviors. Note here that they are externally motivated. They have no deep and real desire for lasting change. They just want to avoid the consequences of their addiction, like staying out of jail or avoiding relationship conflict with their family and/or spouse.

On the bright side, if external pressure is used the right way, it can help jump start internal motivation, which is critical for them to move into the next stage—the Contemplation Stage. (More on that in a moment.)

TRUTH Nuggets

1. Precontemplators may often be at least somewhat aware of the solutions to addictions, but they are blissfully ignorant to the problem underlying their addictive tendencies. Most Precontemplators don't want to change themselves; they really just want the people around them to stop nagging and disrupting their behavior. They do this through ignoring you or accusing you of some random default or personal defect. There may even be some truth in what they accuse you of, and it's always good to look at and acknowledge our issues—but don't be deceived. Any accusations pointed at you are usually meant to distract you from their addiction and get you off of their backs for a while. Their motivation is for you to stop looking at their addiction.

2. In order to help an addicted loved one the right way, we must face our biggest fear, even if it is allowing him to go to jail. Soft-hearted mamas have the hardest time imagining this, but please believe me: jail is often the place where hope begins. Jail is no picnic, but most moms tell me they eventually sleep better at night when their addicted loved one is in jail, because they know they won't die of an overdose on the streets. Forced sobriety means there will be some time of clear thinking, and it is often in this place that

contemplation can take place, resolving ambivalence, and progressing along their inner journey toward recovery. Even if it is two steps forward and one back, as recovery most often is.

3. People change when the pain of staying stuck is worse than the pain of change. Please do not deny your loved one his pain, because the pain will evoke internal motivation in the weeks to come.

4. Often times we discover our life's purpose in our darkest hour. I call this hour the "Gift of Desperation," because it blossoms out of pain, creating humility inside the person. They become willing to take the suggestions of wiser people.

I don't want to interrupt the flow of my story here, because the consequences are just beginning. I'd like you to read how they led me to the Gift of Desperation. My hope is that my story will sustain you to be strong when your loved one runs into a brick wall of consequences.

Chapter 5

THE SPIRAL

I T TOOK WEEKS before I could muster up the courage to tell my wife and parents what was going on. The secrecy was my way of controlling the situation with hopes that it would all just disappear. In my ignorance, I prayed everything would just resolve itself. However, that was not how it worked. After anxiety levels reached an all-time high, I finally confessed to my family and shared the legal documents with them. I was so scared. We all were.

By the next morning, Dad had already made the call. I was scheduled to meet with the best attorney in the state and he would be paid to solve my problems. Believing that their son was a victim of medical malpractice, my parents even agreed to cover the legal fees. Things were looking up. They even wrote me a check to pay my bills and mortgage. That meant, to me, that my relationship with Kelli would mend quickly, too, and I wouldn't have any more nagging calls from bill collectors or fast loan places.

My attorney succeeded in moving my case up to Davis County. This was good news because apparently the judge in this county was more lenient and understanding. I pegged him to be naïve just like my parents. All I had to do was drop in for a quick "book and release" so they could get my fingerprints. Other than that, I was home free. The judge allowed me to plead guilty but would hold my plea in abeyance for one year until I completed some classes. If I stayed out of trouble, then the charges would be dropped entirely.

What a deal!

I immediately began the charade. Again. As far as my parents, attorney, and wife knew, I cleaned up and was on the straight and narrow path. Sure, at first, several whole days went by and I stayed clean. It wasn't so bad. But, by the end of the week, the voice in my head figured that I could have just a little cocaine as long as it was only for one night. I contacted my dealer again and bought $40 worth—just enough to get me high, but I convinced myself I could get it out of my system by the time I had to give a drug test. The mental hold returned, and I was off on another bender.

In order to pay for my daily habit again, I had to get creative. I knew a handful of people who wanted some occasional "blow" (cocaine). I became the middle man in order to get my cut. One afternoon I called my buddy Scott, who threw the best college parties in town. He had long hair, wore tie-die clothing, and listened to music like Jack Johnson, Dave Mathews Band, and my favorite, Pearl Jam. He was a friendly man with an insatiable desire to have fun—just my kind of dude. He answered the phone and after some small talk, I asked him, "Hey man, I'm just about to pick up some 'blow.' You want any?" My hope was that he would buy some so that I could skim off the top.

"I'm all set up man . . . Do you want to come over?" hinting that he would graciously share his with me.

"I'm on my way!" I was out the door before I clicked off the phone.

As I entered his apartment in the avenues near the university, I smelled a funky, burning odor. I brushed it off while Scott and I chatted for a minute, and then Scott pulled out a straight glass pipe with a little Brillo wire stuffed in the end of it.

"Have you ever tried smoking it?" Scott asked, smirking a little.

"Naw, man. I only snort it," I replied proudly. I wasn't one of the hard addicts, anyway. I just needed a little blow.

"Oh, bro!" Scott cried. "You get way higher this way!"

I watched carefully as he placed a tiny white crack rock on the end of the Brillo wire, flicked his cigarette lighter, and then he proceeded to gently bump the flame up to the drug, slowly melting it as he rolled the pipe in his fingers. The drug began to melt, and I heard the sounds of crackling as he inhaled.

About fifteen seconds later, he exhaled a billow of white smoke that filled the room as he closed his eyes and drifted into another realm. Watching him was all it took. "Hey, can I try that?" I asked, already salivating for a high. Besides, I knew that I was going to have to quit soon for the judge. Why not try it before I had to get sober?

I followed Scott's lead and he coached me along. Within seconds, I felt higher than I *ever* had before. My ears began to ring, my body felt numb, and my mind went to that blissful place where all my problems were gone—but even more intense. I felt as though I was having an out-of-body experience, never wanting to come down. I believed in heaven, and I thought I had actually found my way there. There was not one slight physical or emotional discomfort, and all was right with the world. An atomic blast could have gone off next door and I would have been just fine.

Suddenly the high wore off as quickly as it came on.

"Hey, can I have some more?"

"Patience!" barked Scott. His soft demeanor hardened so I tried to sit patiently, but it was excruciatingly difficult to wait for my turn. The second hit gave me the same feeling as the first, although it was slightly less potent. I asked for more, and more, and more. By the time we finished smoking all of Scott's stash, I was determined to go find more. He reluctantly gave me his dealer's phone number after I pushed him hard for it. With every bit of determination, I knew I had to get more crack no matter what! Besides, I still had a few days before I needed to drug test for the courts.

I set out to get some cash, and since I had no money the quickest way was to try and cash an old check from my recently-closed bank account. When one bank denied me, I went to another, then another, and finally I went to a pay-day loan center and was able to get enough to buy a few grams. Once I got the cash, I called Scott's dealer, Sergio, and within fifteen minutes, I had my own stash. The best part was I didn't have to take turns with someone else.

I didn't arrive home until after Kelli was asleep in bed. By this time, she had emotionally separated herself from my constant storytelling, absence, and unpredictable behavior. She started to set up some emotional boundaries, almost like she was wearing an emotional raincoat and letting all the rain of my behavior roll off her back. She did this for her own survival and it worked for her.

I snuck inside carefully and laid in my bed for hours—heart racing—scheming about how to get more money so that I could meet Sergio again in the morning. I finally resolved to write another fake check to the pay-day loan center. If that failed, I could always pawn something, or last case scenario, head down to the homeless shelter near Rio Grande Street and Pioneer Park. Down at "the shelter," crack cocaine was sold on every corner at all hours of the day, making it a feeding ground for the addicted. I was warned how sketchy it was downtown, but in a pinch it would suffice.

I finally leapt out of bed before the sun rose to get a jump start on finding more crack. I skipped showering and brushing my teeth, checked my wife's purse for loose cash, and luckily found a twenty. I immediately hopped in my car and went on a mission to get my fix. Because it was so early, Sergio wasn't answering his phone. I had no other choice but to head downtown to the shelter. I slowly drove down Rio Grande Street. The dealers, knowing I was searching, were watching me, giving signals that they were holding (street slang for "had crack in hand"). I pulled over and handed the dealer the $20 I stole from my wife's purse. Before long, I was free once again for a few seconds.

But almost immediately, I needed more.

I spent all day down at the shelter hustling more crack. The opportunities were endless as long as I stayed around all the action.

The hunt for drugs, getting the cash, dodging the cops, and hiding it all from my wife was an adrenaline rush; an addictive behavior in-and-of itself. Crack, however, hooked me psychologically like no other pill, drink, or drug had ever done before.

As I slid further out of control, my parents became even more suspicious and tried to set some rules. Since they were helping cover my bills, they really tightened up on my spending. A rule was set that I could only spend my allowance money on basic living expenses, such as gas and food. Every other expenditure needed to be approved by them. I was also required to save every receipt and account for each dollar spent. I never could provide proof of receipts. How could I?

Money meant for food went for drugs. And the money meant for gas? I would fill my tank only partially, enough to get me downtown, and maybe back. The rest I used for drugs.

With each missing receipt and lie about where the money went, Dad got more and more angry. He was bending over backwards to help me, and I couldn't even meet our basic agreement. He was the type to stuff his anger deep down inside, masking his irritation more often than expressing it to me. I used that to my advantage and simply avoided him.

But I knew this couldn't last. I had to get a job. After a few weeks of spending all day down at the shelter hustling drugs, I had been called into my boss's office. He told me that it wasn't working out and I left without a job. Meanwhile my wife picked up another job in desperation to financially keep our heads above water. She was nearing the end of her rope, and I couldn't blame her.

I first thought about my old coworker, Paul, then turned away from that thought in disgust. The man who had been so integral in my addiction to OxyContin and so many others had just gotten off on a plea deal. I heard he was even going to work for a pharmaceutical company. Just the thought of it made my skin crawl. I assumed *he* snitched on everyone else and got off without punishment. *The next time I see him there will be hell to pay.* In my addiction, I could not accept any accountability for my own choices and actions because emotionally, I was as mature as an adolescent.

Instead, I called one of my best friends and college roommate, Bronny, because he had no idea of my recent history. He was working at a local ski resort and willingly put his "stamp of approval" on me with the hiring department. I charmed them into hiring me on the spot. The position was for a Public Safety Officer giving oversight to the entire resort. It was also a graveyard shift, allowing me to spend every night away from home. They even gave me a badge, a master key, and 100-percent access to every lodge, hotel, store, and bar on the mountain. And the best part? They gave me a season pass to ski! I could go anywhere and do anything I wanted. I literally felt as though I became king of the mountain.

I proudly called Mom and told her the news that I found a job. She and I celebrated with a brief conversation. She started asking me more questions, so I quickly made an excuse to hang up. I was in a hurry to smoke some more crack. Often times, when we are in our addiction, we keep conversations short and want to get off the phone. This could be a sign that we are actively using. We want you to know we are alive and okay, but we don't want to engage in conversation or get peppered with questions. This is why most of us will hide behind texts.

This job was going to be perfect because it was a graveyard shift. I worked while my wife was asleep, and I was at home while she worked. I quickly developed a system. In the evenings before work, I figured out ways to get cash, then stocked up on enough crack to last me the night until I went to get more in the morning. The drug kept me awake for two to three days at a time, barely needing to catch a few hours of sleep. Every second or third day, my body would shut down and I would need a short nap. Once I woke up, it was off to the races again.

As the weeks passed, the drugs and lack of sleep caused me to slip into a state of paranoia. It was awful, to the point of visual and auditory hallucinations that haunted me throughout the day and especially at night. This level of drug-induced psychosis and paranoia was the result of high stress caused by drug and alcohol use, poor sleep, lack of nourishment, and zero exercise, over a period of time. I was losing my mind. I began to develop a deeper appreciation and dependence on alcohol because it balanced out the anxiety. A few hours into my shift, I would illegally treat myself to a few beers or shots out of the liquor closet to help curb my paranoia. Besides, the resort had an endless supply, so I felt entitled to as much as I wanted.

Isolation kept me safe, so I stayed away from everyone. The only constant companionship I had was the addict voice in my head controlling my every waking moment.

Blackouts became consistent. I started waking up in locker rooms, behind the bar in the resort restaurants, and in custodial closets. Regularly, I passed out for six hours at a time while on the clock.

It became dangerous.

One morning after work while driving down the canyon, I fell asleep and hit a patch of ice, allowing my car to skid off the road. Luckily there was no oncoming traffic and I was unscathed. On another occasion, I fell asleep at the wheel on Interstate 15 and sideswiped an SUV with an entire family of children on board. Nobody was hurt, and the police did not notice I drove under the influence, so we went on our way with only minor car damage. That particular "close call" rattled me after seeing the children's faces in the back seats of the SUV. I could have killed them! Right then and there, that was enough to want to change for good. However, later that night I used drugs and alcohol to cope with my growing paranoia.

The cycle had me in complete and total captivity; I was

powerless against it. At this point in time, my parents broke the news to my siblings about my addiction with worry and concern in their voice. My loving brothers and sister, Jamie, Cory, and Melissa wanted to jump in and help. It became a heavy load to carry alone for Mom and Dad. Just sharing the truth to my siblings brought my parents great relief and emotional support.

The Intervention

A week later after working the graveyard shift at the resort, I received a phone call from my brother Jamie. When I answered, my siblings, all of whom lived out of state—going to various medical and dental schools—were on the phone. Jamie, the oldest sibling, began the call. "Jason, we want to let you know that we talked to Mom and Dad and they told us about what's been going on with you. We want to get you some help." After he said that, I paused for a long minute. Then each of them took some time to personally express their concern for me. The hardest thing to hear was how my addiction was affecting them and my parents. I need to add that the manner in which my siblings addressed me was perfect: it was full of love, non-judgement, and genuine concern for their brother.

It is hard to describe how I felt at that moment. On one hand, I was mad at Mom for telling them my problems behind my back. I was angry that they thought I needed help, and I was angry because I knew they were right. And I was afraid, because I knew if I didn't get help, I would go to prison once the courts caught up with me. On the other hand, I felt relief knowing that my siblings loved me even after they learned the truth about my shameful problems. I felt valued that they loved me enough to call me and express concern. It was a mixed bag of emotions and contemplation, but immediately as a default, my ego took over.

Sure, this intervention was a nice gesture, but I couldn't hear it. I didn't need them to tell me to stop using drugs and ruining my life! I already knew what I needed. I knew everything. While they talked, I discounted, dismissed, discredited, and disregarded their pleas. I mentally threw away every comment they made.

My siblings' intentions were good; they just didn't understand what I was going through. They couldn't comprehend what it was like to crave something so badly that it became more important than family, faith, or even freedom. They couldn't possibly know what I would be sacrificing if I simply stopped using. Drugs and alcohol were my solution to life. After the call, I immediately resumed my addict lifestyle. I was not ready for change—not yet. (Remember the signs of the Precontemplation Stage? All the natural consequences began to move me into the Contemplation Stage.)

A few weeks later, on one cold winter evening before work, Kelli asked me about more missing money. I tried to lie my way out of it again, but it wasn't working this time. She got tougher and pressed me for the truth. In my frustration, I got defensive and blamed her for not trusting me and not supporting me. (Remember the tactic of shifting blame, so common in Precontemplation? I was good at it.) After a winded, manipulated attempt to get her off my back, she looked at me with the love she had for me still in her eyes, and yet a hint of steel I had never seen before.

"I want a divorce, Jason," she said, her voice still gentle.

This stopped me in my tracks.

"What do you mean, you want a divorce?" I cried.

"I can't do this anymore. You've lied to me more times than I can count, and I don't trust you," she said. The truth penetrated my soul, and it hurt. She was right.

To be honest with myself, as rare as honesty was, I knew this was coming. I had seen divorce etched upon her face every time I left the house, with every unaccounted dollar that I spent, and with each mysterious incoming text or call I wouldn't share. Finally, after five years of marriage, it seemed I had crossed over her boundary one too many times. As much as she expressed her genuine love and concern for me, there was the truth that she couldn't do it anymore. She had tried to support me, but my continual lying killed our relationship. That night, my wife finally held to her boundaries. She asked me to leave the house, and I became instantly homeless. Soon I would also be single.

My life was completely unmanageable, yet I still tried to hold it together. During those crazy months I had been asked to come down to the jail for a quick "book and release" protocol so that the judge could have my fingerprints. I followed orders that day, but I had skipped at least eight mandatory drug tests. Knowing that I was on a short rope, it wouldn't be long before the authorities would capture me and force me to stop using in jail. So I absconded to the streets.

PRACTICAL ADVICE

Though I was still in the Precontemplation State of Change, at this time my family had moved into their own Action State of Change—they were taking charge of their own emotional and physical health. In doing so, as painful as it was for them and for me, it gave them the space and freedom they needed and gave me the gift of facing my consequences alone.

Recently, one mother asked me, "Jason, at some point a spouse or parent is going to ask: But what if my loved one overdoses or dies during the stage where I detach from them? What would you say?" Because this does happen, I want to prepare you for any outcome. In the coming chapters I will guide you through the process of surrender, which will bring you great peace and protection from unfair or unnecessary guilt, and help you influence the right way to prevent this from happening.

The Emotional Raincoat

In order to "Get off the Beach," imagine putting on an emotional raincoat as Kelli had to do in order to preserve her peace and sense of emotional safety.

How do you do this? I suggest actually practicing letting all of the words and actions of others roll off of you like drops of water dripping down a rubber raincoat. You might even have someone (a good friend or therapist who "gets it") to role-play with you, offering all the excuses and blaming that your addicted loved one will likely throw your way. Get prepared and get strong. Go on the offensive and be proactive, unless you want to continue playing defense and living in a state of reacting. No thanks. I would highly suggest a good counselor or addiction expert at this stage to help you through the process, as it is so easy to fall back into old patterns when our addicted loved ones act helpless or sad or angry.

I will never forget the day that my ex-wife looked me in the eye and asked for a divorce. She had prepared herself emotionally and mentally for that moment, and when it arrived, she felt confident in her decision and had calming strength in her voice. She had detached emotionally from all of my reactive responses—guilt missiles, tearful manipulations, and silent scorn. She weathered the storm extremely well because she had put on her emotional raincoat. With the help of her support group (therapist, a good spiritual leader, and attending some family group therapy sessions) she learned how to get on the offense.

In other words, set up your emotional boundaries. Research expert and best-selling author Brené Brown teaches, "When we fail to set boundaries and hold people accountable, *we* feel used and mistreated." How true is that statement in your relationships? Well, let me echo Brené and remind you that you deserve to feel respected.

By putting on your emotional raincoat, you begin the transcendent process of becoming empathetic and powerfully influential. This seems counter to the natural thought. How does setting a boundary and detaching help us become more empathetic? Or influential? Because when we are "well-boundried," we emotionally protect ourselves from feeling mistreated, angry, and afraid. We learn where we end, and others begin. This level of self-love allows us to step into their shoes empathetically, without becoming enmeshed in toxic relationship entanglement.

In dealing with a difficult person, a wise mentor once advised, "Bite your tongue, shut your mouth, and don't get defensive. What they have to say is important for them to express. Just listen and validate them even if the words they say are inaccurate." Our addicted loved ones may try to intimidate us, manipulate us, and pepper us with guilt and angry comments, but we can stay *firm* without being mean. We can kindly and firmly say, "I love and care about you. And my answer is NO." Too often we feel we have to get angry back and mirror emotion for emotion, escalating the tension. But that isn't helpful. We can firmly and kindly say, "I love you to the moon and back. I always will. I'm here for you when you are truly ready for change. But you cannot live here anymore. You can't come over when we are not home. I will not give you any more money or pay your bills. You are capable of figuring this out, but I won't be contributing to your addiction from this day forward. Please know I am here for you and I ask that you get help." (Be as specific as possible and offer some suggestions of where they can get help and what your role will be in helping them at that point.) Remember, they may still be stuck in Precontemplation, so your job is to simply plant ideas in their heads and illuminate the path for *them* to walk while protecting your emotions, and your assets.

While he is in this stage, take measures to work on constructing healthy emotional boundaries within yourself. If you don't set these boundaries now, you will ride the emotional rollercoaster into the gates of madness. Don't lock horns with him and escalate the problem. It's not okay for anyone to disrespect you for standing up for yourself.

If he gets violent and abusive, don't hesitate to call the police and seek safety. There are professional counselors and therapists in your area who can walk you through this process. A good professional is worth every cent. If you suspect he may get violent or abusive when you have to deliver bad news, make sure you deliver in a place where you are not alone, and someone is nearby who can come to your aid. In these moments of impact, remember we are dealing with a sick person who is suffering mentally, emotionally, physically, and spiritually. Try to empathize.

These powerful moments of impact are opportunities for us to really make a difference in helping resolve ambivalence. Let's not squander them any longer. Let's start contributing the right way by putting on an emotional raincoat and allowing the negative reactions to roll right off our backs.

Natural Consequences Create Ambivalence

When my parents put in an alarm system with a security code at their house, it was a step in helping them "Get Off the Beach." During the months prior, I had free access to everything inside their home. In my entitlement, I curiously rummaged through their house, and "borrowed" some of their money and valuables. The alarm system was a physical boundary they used to protect themselves from my reckless behavior. At first it hurt my feelings, and then I was angry. In my hurt, I blamed them for not trusting me. It took time for me to understand the truth—I broke trust by stealing from them. Sometimes you just need to lovingly remind your addicted loved one that *their* actions broke your trust, but you still love them. Trust is an earned privilege. It is okay to love someone while not trusting them (Remind them of that.) Being honest with others establishes strong fences, and strong fences make great neighbors. They also make for better and more balanced family dynamics. You might also let them know, "I want to trust you again. In time as I see your actions change for the long haul, I will gradually increase my trust in you. You can earn it back. It is just going to take a long time."

This one act alone caused me to consider how my addiction and behavior affected my most valuable relationships. I noticed a huge difference in my parents as they started working their own recovery program to treat their obsessive worry about me. They appeared to be getting stronger against my addiction. Their actions caused them to become happier. Through their example, recovery became attractive and subtly this increased my desire to change a little bit.

When you begin to set and enforce personal and emotional boundaries, you begin to feel empowered, like my parents did. As you consistently hold to a boundary, your loved one will feel a downshift in his comfort level, especially if he relies heavily on you for money, emotional support, or any form of enabling. This discomfort will help create more ambivalence inside your addicted loved one, which is a sign they may be moving to the next stage of change: Contemplation.

For example, when you set a boundary to keep a curfew while he lives under your roof, and he continually breaks the curfew, he will begin to lose privileges that may ultimately get him excused from your household. In that scenario, he will feel the emotional discomfort as a natural consequence to his actions.

When you enforce a boundary, remember to calmly remind him that you love him, but it was *his* decision to break the agreement with you. Make it crystal clear that you will not enable his behavior any longer. He will most likely react poorly and blame you for being unfair and unreasonable. That's okay. Don't take it personally. Remember, put on your emotional raincoat and let it roll off of you. It is perfectly okay to put the responsibility back on him, but do this without locking horns with him. In other words, don't go into a back-and-forth conversation that will take you under in an alligator roll. Keep the conversation short, kind, and firm. Remind him that when he broke the boundary, he made the choice. You didn't kick him out; he kicked himself out. Tell him you love him and then leave as soon as you can. Don't hang around for verbal abuse.

"Blaming" is a common ego defense mechanism. An ego defense mechanism is like a hand-grenade that is thrown to get us to look away from them; it is a distraction technique used to defend one's fear, vulnerability, and authentic self. People will defend their egos when they feel threatened. This is common among all humans. Understanding these human behavior trends will arm us to be protected from their harmful effects. There are many of these mechanisms, so to see a list, visit www.brickhouserecovery.com/unhooked.

TRUTH Nuggets

1. By putting on your emotional raincoat, you begin the transcendent process of becoming empathetic and powerfully influential.

2. Remember the words of my sponsor: "bite your tongue, shut your mouth, and don't get defensive. What they have to say is important for them to express. Just listen and validate them, even if the words they say are inaccurate."

3. Allow your loved one his natural consequences, because natural consequences create ambivalence.

4. Sometimes you just need to lovingly remind your addicted loved one that their actions broke your trust, but you still love them. Trust is an earned privilege. It is okay to love someone while not trusting them. Being honest with others establishes strong fences, and strong fences make great neighbors.

5. An ego defense mechanism is like a weapon used to defend one's fear, vulnerability, and authentic self. People will defend their egos when they feel threatened. See www.brickhouserecovery.com/unhooked for a list.

Now let's continue with my story as I show how my family's actions contributed in moving me closer to long-term recovery.

Chapter 6

THE GIFT OF DESPERATION

A BLIZZARD'S WHITE FLAKES covered the city's bright decorations just a few blocks away from where I stood, hunched against the cold. The howling wind ripped into the narrow tunnel across the street from the homeless shelter downtown. I left my dented parked car a few blocks away behind an old warehouse so that it wouldn't get stolen. It was all I had. The car and these dirty streets had become my home since Kelli and I split a few weeks before. As long as I stayed loaded, I didn't have to feel the pain.

My body was growing weaker by the time I weighed a slight 165 lbs. My 6'2" slouching frame had once held a healthy 230 lbs., but that was long ago. I knew what my body looked like in the reflection of the austere glass buildings downtown, but I was strangely, eerily proud of the emaciated figure because most of my life I struggled with a poor self-image of feeling chubby. Interestingly, I never looked at the reflection of my face anymore.

Like other addicted people I'd known, I wouldn't look into my own eyes. Not ever. But my body . . . I watched its sure deterioration in fascination. I could see in my reflection how much I had shrunk. My black leather belt earned a new hole each week as I continued to cinch it tightly around my shrinking, malnourished waist. Very little muscle was left on this body now, and certainly nothing to help insulate or keep me warm.

Living on the streets of Salt Lake City was no joke. I was as used to the bitter cold of Utah as I was used to depression, but tonight everything seemed significantly more relentless and dark.

I wasn't sure what night it was on the calendar. All I had was on my person: a ten-year-old goose-down coat so ragged it was unrecognizable; an old skiing beanie, filthy, baggy jeans that had once fit me, and torn Adidas basketball shoes. I hadn't showered in weeks. I had no socks, contributing to absolutely no feeling in my toes, now numb from the cold. I should have been appalled. I had seen the horror of hypothermia; I was repulsed and revolted by frostbitten noses and the loss of toes. But I didn't care in that moment. I was only feeling one thing: fear.

Just an hour before, I'd decided to take a walk to see if the rumored new shipment of crack had arrived. As soon as I turned the corner of the building, I noticed a wiry Honduran man in his late twenties approach me, his cheeks puffed out like a squirrel holding nuts.

Spitters, we called them, advertised their product through enlarged cheeks and slight, hand-eye motions. Using this method, the pushers wrapped the dope in tiny balloons protecting the product while holding it in their mouths. Another benefit was that if the police came by to do a search, they could swallow the product and vomit it up later, salvaging their investment, arrest records, and in some cases, deportation.

This dealer and his chipmunk cheeks seemed to hold the promise I needed. The surge of craving washed through me, stronger than the cold. After his signal, I stepped forward boldly and held out my hand with the cash I had from selling some stolen items a couple hours before. I should have known better. In every drug deal, there is a moment just as the money and the fix are exchanged, where neither dealer nor user can trust one another. Alarm bells went off in my head, but it was too late.

Something sharp pressed against my throat. I had drawn in my breath when he jabbed the metal tip into my skin, nearly piercing through the flesh.

It was a rusted, filed-down screwdriver. I should have seen this coming, but lacking any energy, I was helplessly slow to react. Sure, he was smaller than me, but I was extremely weak and defenseless.

"Give me da' money!" he snarled, his Hispanic accent noticeable. At that moment, I knew it was going to end badly.

Wincing, I tried not to cry out as he snatched the cash from my hand. As he turned to dart down the street, I desperately lunged at him. Immediately he spit some balloons out on the ground to deter me from chasing him. The last I saw, he vanished into the night around a building.

I threw myself to my knees to begin my search in the dark, despite the biting cold. My hand felt something wet and warm compared to the surrounding ice and cement. I found one. With a sense of relief, I ripped open the balloon and plastic sack inside. My heart dropped fast and heavy as an anchor in the ocean. Inside that balloon, inside the tiny plastic sack, was a carefully packaged piece of small gravel. A terrible feeling of impending doom and rage overcame me.

I screamed threats into the snowy night, irate and fierce. Overcome by my hostility, I launched myself in the direction of the Spitter, with every intention of beating him severely. I searched every abandoned lot, street corner, and alley way. He was nowhere to be found. After an hour of searching, I gave up.

I was out of dope. I was out of money. I was out of hope.

It wouldn't help to go to my car. I would not only freeze, but I would be too far away from anyone who might share a little dope with me. Instead, I made my way back to "the tunnel," which was a little hallway between two buildings that would shelter us a bit from the wind and snow.

I hunkered down and leaned back against the grey, cinderblock wall that led to the dangerously dark alley behind a low-income housing project. These two walls gave me only a slight reprieve from the stinging cold. I pulled my threadbare coat up around my frozen ears to block the blowing-sideways snow, little good that it did. I glanced around.

A tattered band of a dozen men and women were lining both walls, shoulder-to-shoulder. We were not friends. Crouched beneath blankets or whatever clothing we could scrounge from the homeless shelter's donation pile, we had banded together to survive another bitterly cold night. Shapeless forms against the darkness, our only light beamed dully from the faraway street lamp and the flickering of cigarette lighters. I was grateful when it was too dark to see again.

Darkness, as always, was our ally.

Despite the blowing wind, a pungent stench reached my nostrils, reminding me I was surrounded by a battered array of humanity. It was an all-too-familiar smell: the stink of soured alcohol and chemicals seeping through pores, salty sweat, and stale cigarette smoke. It permeated the air around us to the point where we hardly noticed it. Every corner of life and every background imaginable scrambled to survive among us. I could vaguely see bloody scabs on their lips and white-blue frostbitten noses. It didn't matter. They were mostly nameless to me, but not faceless. I surveyed and studied each face. It doesn't take long to become acquainted with the personalities in the homeless community. I knew some of them had violent tendencies and others had criminal minds. Clearly, many suffered from a variety of mental illness, just like me. I kept tabs on those faces and kept my distance.

While I never knew their once-vibrant countenances, I recognized the lines so deeply etched in their faces that thirty years looked like fifty, and forty years like seventy. Whether twenty-six or sixty, we all looked like walking death.

At all costs, I avoided their eyes. And they avoided mine.

Hunkered down in that tunnel now, I needed a fix—that hit of crack or heroin, which could grant me relief and escape from the voices in my head and could numb me from the bitter cold—if only for a few, blissful minutes. Every cell in my wasted body obsessed over the thought.

I was angry at being ripped off. I cared more about getting loaded than I did my own life.

What am I going to do now?

A sigh rolled up from somewhere near my soul. I leaned back against the rough cinderblock wall, jealously watching a man shove a dirty, dull needle into a woman's arm. I looked away. I saw this stuff every day, but all I could think was that she was getting a fix and I was not. No one here cared about anyone else. She might be his wife. She might be a hooker accepting payment. She could be dying under the blanket and no one would notice until morning. Then we would all leave so no one would be blamed. Maybe someone would call the police. Probably not.

It didn't matter. All that mattered was my insatiable craving—to feel the hard burn down the back of my throat and into my lungs that brought blissful escape. As I mentioned, this was no longer about pleasure or getting high. It was about avoiding, at all costs, the physical pain, and the familiar state of depression, anxiety, shame, loneliness, restlessness, and irritability. It was about blissful relief when it all went away—for at least a few minutes.

With each hit the vicious voices in my mind quieted for a few minutes and I could think for myself again instead of being a slave to the constant barrage of mental interference. Never had it felt this dark before. It felt like being attacked by countless evil spirits frenzied to possess my emaciated body to gain a sense of pleasure with each and every hit. Each hit seemed to bring these evil spirits great pleasure as the drugs kept me strapped down against my will. People who suffer with Substance Use Disorder and mental illness know about demons. We have felt and seen them breathing their dark and loathsome thoughts down our backs and, to some degree, possess our souls.

This level of addiction wasn't only about avoiding the terrifying withdrawals that soon came after the dope ran out. No. On this level of darkness, my mind was completely controlled by a malicious puppet master. On a very real level, I felt overcome by an outside entity that was full of hatred whose only intention was to destroy me. At this level, it was about pleasing the dark master by feeding the beast of addiction that thundered inside my soul. In other words, it was hell on earth.

That cold, dark alley was a hall of mirrors. They were (I was) dirty, hopeless, selfish, and addicted. We were engulfed with self-loathing in the midst of being consumed with the obsession to get high, or at the very least, be rid of the onset of withdrawal nausea.

A blast of the arctic wind howled through the tunnel and snapped my mind to my humble conditions in the cold, dark alley. I thought of the Spitter, the sour stench, the needles, the broken pipe, the crowds, fights, the robberies, and the murders. My life was at an all-time bottom.

Suddenly my cell phone vibrated in my pocket. I hardly noticed it in the midst of my shivers. A cellular phone was vital in the business of addiction: it was my main connection to relief. I pulled it out with shaking hands to see who it was.

It was a text message from Mom.

> I am cooking a roast for dinner.
> You are invited.
> I love you.

A vision of Mom flashed through my jangled brain, and I could see her petite frame, dressed in one of her classy outfits, pushing back the bangs of her carefully styled short, black hair. She had the biggest smile which ignited her infectious personality and drew people to her. But she had no grip on my reality. Echoes of the family intervention rippled through my thoughts. I then remembered her look right after my confession and her words of denial, "Jason, you're not addicted to drugs. No, Jason, you're not." It was too difficult for her to admit that her little boy was a hard-core slave to substances.

Not only could she not fix me, she couldn't even say the word, "addict," which carries detrimental stigma.

But fix me she continued to *try* to do, over and over. Her inability to see my addiction had made her easy to manipulate. After all, she was the churchwoman that the majority of other women flocked to with their problems. Coming from a family famous for church and civic leadership, she was a leader herself. Her attractive and vibrant personality influenced others for good. Her life had been seemingly picture-perfect until my addiction rolled through our family like a steamroller, wreaking havoc in its wake. That havoc could no longer be hidden from view, so, of course, that made her want to fix me even more.

I grudgingly ignored her text and dropped my phone back into my pocket. I was not allowed at their house unless my parents were home. My folks had finally set some boundaries. They didn't want me scoping their home for something easy to pocket and pawn for my next hit.

As I sat there in the tunnel, I couldn't push away the memories of the countless attempts my family tried to help me. They tried everything. I had let them all down time and time again.

Maybe I can change all this and get sober, said a soft, prodding, kind of voice. For once, I didn't push it away. It made me question some things I hadn't questioned in a while.

How I wished I could get sober and gain my family's trust back. How I longed to be able to start a new life—maybe get a job and earn an honest paycheck. I could pay off all my debts. Life could be good. I could become something. Maybe . . . maybe I should ask for help.

Then another voice, grittier and full of fear, doubt, and dread filled my mind.

"It won't work! Even if you tried, you can't stay sober! You've tried and failed over and over. What makes you think this time is different?" it yelled adamantly. I felt my own self-hate cause my heart to race. "Your family is disgusted with you. You have no friends. You aren't even worth the oxygen you are breathing. You should just end it all."

I contemplated taking my life.

Maybe it would be better for everyone.

Depression laced with ego sunk in while my thoughts swirled around me, often fighting against one another. The thought of going back to rehab was better than prison, but I shuddered as I thought about living through the intense pain and hell of alcohol, heroin, and crack withdrawals. As much as I wanted sobriety, in so many ways sobriety sounded miserable. If misery was my lot in life, I was going to remain loaded until the bitter end, which could be very soon.

I miss Mom, I thought as a tear dripped down my cheek. I hunkered further down into my coat to hide my tears. "You are a failure. You are a junkie—a disgrace to your family. You've tried. And you've tried again and again. Maybe you should just kill yourself. Then everyone doesn't have to worry about you anymore."

The voices in my head reinforced my self-hatred.

The great wafts of icy snow were spiraling down at a faster pace now, matching my thoughts. The wind changed directions again. I pulled the collar of my old ski jacket higher around my neck and face, trying in vain to protect myself against the gusting flakes of dirty ice off the sidewalk. Across the tunnel from me, three men huddled under a stained blanket to smoke a hit of crack from a sharp, broken, glass pipe. Sulkily, I continued to contemplate my life and future.

Somehow, I have to get sober, or I truly might die like this.

Then came the voice of what felt like reason: "You'll quit. Sure, you'll quit . . . tomorrow."

Every single time I began to contemplate getting sober, the voice always convinced me to wait and stop tomorrow, or next week, or next month. So, my procrastination kept me trapped in my addiction, creating intense ambivalence and lack of self-efficacy.

I stared out of the tunnel at the blizzard, and the wind and bizarrely large flakes created patterns and pictures in my mind. I remembered when life was good—before I became a slave to drugs and alcohol.

Then reality hit again. For the first time, I started asking myself some real questions.

Did I really want to stop getting loaded?

I took a long, hard look.

No. Not completely.

My brain spit out a list of the benefits of using—benefits I felt my family would never understand. They had never understood me—not as a kid, and certainly not as an adult. How could they possibly have a clue about the benefits I received in using, or what I faced trying to quit? The rougher, fear-filled voice was winning.

"Better the devil you know," it snarled, "than the devil you don't."

Truth be told, this is a conversation I'd had over and over again with myself every time I hit an emotional or material rock bottom. It was mental torture. As I tried to slump into the cement wall to guard against the insidious snowflakes, I sunk deeper into despair.

I couldn't go home.

Mom was left wondering if I was alive or dead. It didn't matter. I didn't have a single human being who understood me except for the nameless people in the tunnel. Just as the snow was obliterating some of their hands and toes and noses from frostbite, I felt the same sickness eating away at me on the inside. Hanging my head and closing in on myself yet again for the false promise of more warmth, I knew I would spend another night in an unholy place, at least until I'd get caught by the authorities that would put me in the slammer.

STAGE TWO:
CONTEMPLATION (GETTING READY)

It is extremely difficult to understand why we behave the way we do in our addictions. The experience above partly illustrates the crazy-making in my mind, the constant insanity while listening to the voices in my head, and the emotional rollercoaster of shame, anger, hopelessness, self-pity, and self-hatred. For my parents and family members, they rode the crazy train with me for years while I contemplated change. Once they learned about the *Contemplation Stage (SOC)* they were empowered from the simple understanding of why I was constantly on the fence.

People in the Contemplation Stage have become aware of problems associated with their behavior. However, they are ambivalent about whether or not it is worthwhile to change. In other words, they sit on the fence of a decision. They still see and *want* both benefits that come from the current behavior, as well as making a change. As the natural consequences of drinking and using increase, their motivation for change grows. This is the process we call *resolving ambivalence.*

In other words, the addicted person explores the potential to change by weighing the pros and the cons of getting clean—a cost benefit analysis. He also has a strong desire to change but lacks the confidence and commitment to do what it takes to recover—at least at that point in time. He has the intention to change at some point in the future, but the timeframe is unspecified, which I admit, can be exasperating as we wait in the wings for them to finally change.

For this reason, all too often, contemplators are pegged as being lazy about their recovery. The truth is that they are most likely not lazy; they are simply doing the internal work, sifting through the cost and benefits of sobriety, and trust me, this is hard work.

At some point, the negatives of drug and alcohol use will outweigh the positives. This decision point to change represents a shift in the right direction, although he might not stay committed to his decision, and may even back pedal again. This is to be expected. This is where your emotional raincoat, managing realistic expectations, and setting up strong fences come in.

They may be wavering to and fro, but you have to remain steady and calm, no matter their choice of the day or the hour. You can only control you. You can't control them. Truthfully, the best thing you can do for your addicted loved one is stay steady emotionally. Stay calm. Stay at peace. This book is designed to help you achieve that level of serenity. When they are ready for action steps, you will be, too. You won't be worn out or angry and depressed or sick. Excitingly, you'll be healthy and ready to dive in to support them when the time is right while managing your expectations along the way.

In the rooms of recovery, we use the acronym H.O.W. for honesty, open-mindedness, and willingness. In the Contemplation Stage, we slowly become more honest with ourselves and a tiny bit more open-minded about our options, but we can still be unwilling to take other's suggestions that would help us. In fact, to avoid the pressure, we tend to isolate ourselves from the people who seek to help us during this stage. Don't take it personally. It's part of the inward journey toward the gift of desperation and internal motivation.

We are stubborn. But I believe that is because we know that we will only change when we are ready to do so, internally—of our own volition.

Even as the more serious consequences start piling up, we may not completely want to get sober. For example, I was caught up in the aftermath of the OxyContin drug ring and was served felony charges. I lost multiple amazing jobs and became a repeat in rehabs and an inmate in jails, as you will soon learn. My sweetheart divorced me, and I was robbed at screwdriver point, and lived homeless on the cold streets of Salt Lake City. Nothing was significant enough for me to change long term, even if at times I wanted to. Even when I was forced into sobriety by a judge, I wasn't ready for action steps to change when I was released. The point is that during these hard times, I considered my options, but I was still ambivalent about changing because I had no confidence that I could do it. My *self-efficacy,* or the belief in my ability to change, was depleted. More on self-efficacy in the coming chapters.

So how do you help someone in the Contemplation Stage? Read on to see what worked for me and my family.

Strong Fences Make Great Neighbors

Now that you have decided to "Get off the Beach," let me take you one step further and let's set some boundaries. As you think about what areas of the relationship you can change, let "boundary setting" be at the top of the list. Remember that to achieve true empathy, there must be fences. As I've mentioned before, "Strong fences make great neighbors." And they also make for healthy relationships, especially when you are talking about a relationship with someone who is ensnared in the traps of an addiction.

Without strong fences, you are vulnerable to be mistreated and your love, kindness, and concern for them will be taken advantage of. If given an inch, an addicted person will definitely take a mile every time. If your fences are weak, then your addicted loved one will not respect them or take them seriously, causing you to feel frustrated and disrespected. Our fences must be strong going forward. Believe me, he will test them. He will push them. That is to be expected. Regardless, you must hold to them, or you will continue to suffer. This is how you can *contribute* to his eventual recovery . . . the right way.

Boundaries

Personal boundaries are the limits we set for ourselves in any relationship to protect us from being manipulated by or enmeshed with emotionally needy people. In other words, boundaries help us establish where *I* end, and *you* begin.

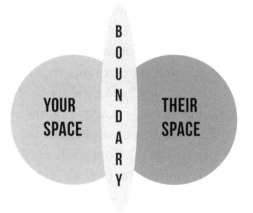

Where does your responsibility begin, and where does it end? The famous Serenity Prayer offered in almost every 12-step meeting across the world reminds us that we cannot control everyone and everything. We will be better off if we focus on changing the things we can about ourselves first. The most powerful venue my parents found freedom in was family support groups, such as Al-anon, and the family programs at the treatment centers. They began to walk through the 12 Steps themselves and discovered complete freedom from their own life-long internal struggles. We all have "stuff" that needs attention, and these resources will help you recover from them. To start, they were taught the powerful and life-changing Serenity Prayer:

God, grant me the Serenity to accept the things I cannot change

Courage to change the things I can, and

Wisdom to know the difference.

In other words, the more time we spend working on our own self-improvement, the easier it is to set up and hold boundaries. Let's think back to the areas in our own lives (Life Domains) that have been neglected. Where do we really need to put our attention? Write them down in a list because you can so easily drift off into Worryland if you aren't very specific and proactive. Get out your own Life Domains graph and decide where you need to put your attention and action in order to focus on your life and balance it. (If you need to think about your "addicted loved one," set aside some small amount of time each day to pray for them. If they come to your mind another time, say to yourself, "I'll pray for my son at 3:00 pm today," and then get back to your tasks at hand.) The idea is that these weaknesses are the areas in our lives that we can work on today, especially because we cannot force our addicted loved one through the Contemplation Stage. So why not take the pressure off him and get to work on ourselves?

We may have serious concerns about our addicted loved ones. However, this does not mean he feels the same way or has concerns or thoughts about you and how his addiction is tearing you apart. My guess is that you tried, and bless your heart, you have done the best that you knew how. I validate your efforts and the painstaking road you have traveled.

One thing I can unequivocally say, without reservation, is that any attempt at forcing, manipulating, or shaming an addicted person to change his thinking or behavior will not do the trick. So what can you do to help the right way?

It's time to clarify. Ask yourself, "What is within my control?" And "What is outside my control?"

For example, you have control over your personal physical, emotional, and financial boundaries. Boundaries are not easy. Period. However, no relationship, and certainly no growth in your relationship is sustainable without boundaries. Boundary setting is a method of protection and an act of self-love.

Boundary expert Brené Brown explains, "Daring to set boundaries is about having the courage to love ourselves, even when we risk disappointing others." She also says, "Empathy minus boundaries is not empathy. Compassion minus boundaries is not genuine. Vulnerability without boundaries is not vulnerability."

Boundaries are healing to your soul. It is difficult to help someone else if you are not well protected yourself. Take the oxygen mask protocol on an airplane: before you help your child put on their mask, you must make sure your mask is on securely first. Then, and only then, will you operate at optimum efficiency. This example may seem trite, but it helps point out the obvious. It saves lives, just like good boundaries do.

Astoundingly, the moment we courageously set a boundary with an emotionally-needy person, it will expand our self-love, self-respect, and purpose. In the world of healthy boundaries, you are free to feel peace, serenity, and happiness again regardless of whether your addicted loved one recovers. You can be happy no matter what! Isn't that extremely liberating to hear?

Anger

You may feel some anger toward your addicted loved one. You actually have every right to feel this anger if it comes up for you. However, if you approach your loved one with anger in your heart, any attempt of building rapport and trust with him will be useless. Why is rapport and trust-building a vital part of helping an addicted loved one? Because genuine influence is channeled through rapport and trust. We will get more into this in the next few chapters.

For now, please understand that anger kills rapport and your ability to influence your loved one the right way. Anger also kills peace—*our* peace. Believe me, if we are upset at him, he will feel our anger, even when unspoken, and this will contribute to and probably help perpetuate his addictive behaviors. When we become free of anger through this process, rapport and trust will flourish and our ability to influence will be magnified.

In the rooms of recovery, we say, "Resentment is the number one offender," robbing us of the connection we seek. This applies to both the addicted and those who love them. To be effective, we must begin to work through our resentments. As we do, we will be more effective in our boundaries and in our relationships. The beautiful Al-anon program is one of our best resources available. For meeting schedules in your area, visit www.alanon.org.

Fear

Fear is also a huge "progress killer" while on this journey. It kills boundaries, which literally takes lives. If we operate in fear, we will not effectively hold to our boundaries in a relationship, and the cycle will continue. Similar to anger, operating in fear can perpetuate our loved one's addiction and contribute to the problem.

A primary example of this is when my mother failed to impose her boundaries because she was afraid that her addicted son would have to suffer discomfort, homelessness, or death. So, she gave in, over and over. This enmeshment between a mother's genuine love for her child and rescuing me from my natural consequences, pain, and discomfort proved a near lethal combination. Bless my mother's heart for what I put her through, until the day the counselor told her to "get off the beach," and she was ready to do so, and did.

Without boundaries, the addicted continue to take that mile, and another mile, and another because they are allowed to. Because they are sick, they will do this again and again until they die.

As we read my mother's experience in this book, we will learn from her mistakes, and ultimate successful triumph over "a mother's fear" for her child's wellbeing. Again, she has a powerful insight and will take you to the top of the learning curve.

To take ourselves off the hamster wheel, we must learn how to work through and channel our fears. Not to worry, because I will hold your hand through my Steps to Surrender in the coming chapters. I have great respect today for the effort my parents made in establishing and holding to their boundaries. It took courage, resilience, and commitment to protect their quality of life, and it worked.

Rescuing

If we are afraid to hold firm to our boundaries and allow our addicted loved one to feel the natural consequences of his actions, we may never witness the miracle of change. There is no gentle way to put it: rescuing is like slowly executing our loved ones. Many parents have contributed to the death of their loved one out of fear of imposing strong boundaries. They rescue him again and again from his consequences. My parents nearly did also—bless their hearts. But every time you rescue your addicted loved one from his pain, you are hammering a nail into his coffin.

At this point, again, you are likely wondering "what if my addicted loved one dies while I'm holding to my boundaries?" This is a valid question indeed. What if I HAD died in that tunnel from frostbite or overdose? What would my mom have told herself? Every parent asks these questions. Sadly, not all stories turn out like mine, even if parents do all the right things. You need a lot of reassurance that even if your addicted loved one dies, you can peacefully know you did the right thing. You can choose the path that will most likely help your loved one get into recovery.

At this time, I want to bring you back to the Four C's.

- We did _not_ Cause the addiction.
- We cannot Control the addiction.
- We cannot Cure the addiction.
- We _can_, however, Contribute to the addiction, or to recovery.

There are no guarantees, but the research shows that the best thing a family can do is keep strong boundaries coupled with affirmations of love. Showing love is entirely possible without rescuing. One mother expressed, "I never hung up the phone with my addict son without both of us saying 'I love you.' Unless he was abusive. If he was, I would say, 'Zach I love you and I'm hanging up now. Call back when you can be respectful and kind.' I also made a very distinct internal shift when I could tell Zach was high or profane or rude. I knew at these times I was talking to the 'drug'—like a demonic force—and not to my real boy. This helped protect my heart. I wore the emotional raincoat every day and it resulted in his ultimate recovery."

We must stop rescuing.

In this process, remember to tell your addicted loved one that you love him, but you are setting boundaries for your own good, and for his good. Please remember that pain is the great motivator for change. Let's not deny him of his natural consequences, whatever they may be. I recognize that this might _feel_ impossible to do, especially if he faces homelessness, jail, divorce, loss of custody, unemployment, and death. Please, I beg you to allow the pain and discomfort caused by his actions to move him to the next stage of change. You must allow him the pain until he becomes willing to try something different.

The beginning of an internal change, and an enhanced spiritual life, is most often through desperation. You may be able look back on your own life and note that the biggest shifts or changes you made for the better often followed times of pain or despair. Pain is an amazing motivator.

How to Help While He is Using, Homeless, or in Jail

What are some things you CAN do for your loved one that won't enable him while he is in active addiction? Take him out for a meal, listen to him, and tell him you love him. But only do this if you can say no when he asks you for a little cash afterward. Because he will. You have to be ready to say, "I can't give you money, but I'm happy to take you to rehab or a shelter." You can give them an old blanket, shoes, and a coat or hat and jacket, but if they are homeless, they can't carry very much and anything that is of real value will likely be pawned or sold. There are many places where the homeless can get food and shelter and warm clothing. You can give your loved one a list of resources with phone numbers. Some moms purchase a cell phone so they can remain in contact with their child. If you do this know that the phone will also be used for drug meet ups and sold at some point. It is astounding how many "phones" he will "lose" and ask you to replace. The truth is, they can borrow someone else's cell phone to call you almost anytime if they really need you. You can give them an inexpensive paperback book if they enjoy reading (the lighter the better for their backpack). If they can behave themselves in your home, having them for an occasional meal is fine. But quite often, at some point, they can't be trusted to be sober and not steal from you. Better to meet them for a restaurant meal. You can give them coupons for fast food. Bus tickets to get around town might be appropriate, but again, many charities offer free bus tickets. If they are very sick, you can offer a ride to the free clinic and take them to get antibiotics. But never, *never* give them cash. Use this litmus test: what would you do for any homeless person that you know is using drugs? Be kind, be humane, but don't be stupid.

Feel free to memorize and repeat these words to him when you get tangled up: "I love you, but you will remain the same until the pain of remaining the same becomes greater than the pain of change. I am done rescuing you from your pain. Again, I love you, but I need to take care of myself right now."

When the law finally caught up with me and I was put in jail and forced to get sober, my parents set a boundary that they would not visit me, but they welcomed a phone call once a day. On the phone, they wouldn't let me whine or complain, but rather we talked about my life and about my desire to change. Selfishly, I made sure the conversations were always about me, me, me. I don't think I ever asked them how they were holding up during that chaos. In jail, I actually wanted to talk to my parents, so they enjoyed getting to know me better without the drugs on board.

I would then always ask them if they could put money in my jail account so that I could buy treats and snacks each week at the commissary. They obliged, putting a small amount each week in the account, but they wouldn't let me talk them into more, and trust me, I tried. They also did not pick me up from jail upon my release. They knew the jail would give me a bus pass. This was hard for Mom, but she was learning how to help me the right way, and she was.

How to Help Without Losing Your Mind

The building of emotional and physical boundaries, or "good fences," will potentially set you free regardless of whether or not he changes. But let's assume your addicted loved one would like to get into recovery and you want to help and encourage this. If he lives with you, uses drugs, and does nothing to stop the use, then I would recommend protecting your home and having him move out. Your home is your safe place. Having someone in active, full-blown addiction living in your space is toxic to you and all who live with you, and it will only encourage their using. At this point if you want to help your addicted loved one with any financial or material support, it is perfectly okay as long as you set up appropriate terms and reasonable expectations, all the while preparing yourself to erect a taller or stronger fence with each broken rule. Make sure you write down the terms of the agreement you make with him to eliminate ambiguity and confusion.

Here are a couple examples of strong boundaries:

AREA OF HELP	BOUNDARY	CONSEQUENCE
Allowing him to live with you	**Agree to:** • Submit to random observed drug/alcohol tests • Must be clean and sober • Must be home by curfew • Must complete daily chores • Required to pay rent (when appropriate) • Must respect house rules • Must be active in recovery plan	• Reduced privileges • Report to police (if using on property) • Move out
Financial Assistance	**Agree to:** • Check into treatment • Submit to random observed drug/alcohol tests • Must be clean and sober • Must be gainfully employed or, • Show proof that he is actively seeking a job • Attend regular financial/accountability meetings for progress evaluation • Must be active in recovery plan	• Reduced privileges • Cut off from financial assistance completely

When he chooses to bend the boundaries you've set, remember that we expect progress, not perfection. You and he then sit down and bring the fences up a little more, allowing him to feel the discomfort of his consequence. He may not take you and your fences seriously at first, especially if he is in the Precontemplation Stage. But remember, the past is the past. You are a new you! It is time to let him know that you are never going back to the old you and he needs to understand you are not rescuing him this time.

For example, say he doesn't respect one of the house rules, which might be cleaning up his own mess. If that happens, the consequence may be to have him clean up the whole house that day. He pays the cost and then you can start again and hopefully he will remember to honor the rules next time.

It may get to the point where your addicted loved one is obviously using again and shows all the signs of it. An occasional slip or short relapse is one thing, but if the fences are being kicked and knocked over and he is obviously using and continuing in this lifestyle again, then he has to go. Period. He doesn't respect your boundaries. Your home is your save haven. You deserve peace within your own walls. You may have to kick him out on the streets if he doesn't have another place to stay. That's what my ex-wife did. That's eventually what my parents did. As hard as it was on them, all three of them saved my life. I love them for it. It was the best thing for me to finally receive that beautiful gift . . . of desperation. The motivating power of desperation is almost always the only thing that will change their lives. My dear friend, Becky, shared her moment of courage: "I dropped my son off at a homeless shelter, gave him a hug goodbye, and pointed him toward the door. At least I knew I left him where help and a hot meal could be found." Today, she has her son back and he is sober.

True love sometimes is tough love. Be strict yet loving. Family members tend to enable as a default. This behavior is predictable, but remember, we are taking a new approach, so let's do this the right way. Begin to make those fences taller and stronger, allowing him to feel more natural consequences from his actions. He's a big boy (although he acts like a two-year-old sometimes). He can handle it.

It is not our job to protect others from consequences. In fact, the longer we protect others from consequences, the longer it will take for the internal change motivation to kick in.

Love yourself enough to start setting up your fences now! For more ideas, check out the Boundary Series videos at www.brick houserecovery.com/video-library/

1. Contemplators want both the benefits that come with their addictive behavior as well as sobriety. As the costs of drinking and using increase, their motivation for change grows. This is the process of *resolving ambivalence.*

2. At some point, the negatives of drug and alcohol use will outweigh the positives. Slips backwards are to be expected while in the Contemplation Stage. This is where the emotional raincoat, managing realistic expectations, and setting up strong fences come in.

3. Practice honesty, open-mindedness, and willingness (H.O.W.).

4. Personal boundaries are the limits we set for ourselves in any relationship to protect us from being manipulated by or enmeshed with emotionally needy people. In other words, boundaries help us establish where *I* end, and *you* begin.

5. The more time we spend working on our own self-improvement, it is easier to set up and hold boundaries.

6. Remember that any attempt at forcing, manipulating, or shaming an addicted person to change will not do the trick.

7. When we become free of anger through this process, rapport and trust will flourish and our ability to influence will be magnified. "Resentment is the number one offender."

8. If we operate in fear, we will not effectively hold to our boundaries in the relationship, and the cycle will continue. Similar to anger, operating in fear can perpetuate addiction and contribute to the problem.

9. Rescuing is like executing our addicted loved ones. There is no gentle way to put it.

10. The beginning of an internal change and an enhanced spiritual life is gifted through desperation.

11. Rather than force him to change, we should start by setting up our fences and reasonably healthy expectations but be prepared to raise the fences after each broken boundary.

12. When he chooses to bend the rules, remember that we expect progress, not perfection.

13. It is not our job to protect him from consequences. In fact, the longer we protect him from consequences, the longer it will take for his internal change motivation to kick in.

In the next chapter I will share how my mom, with her good, kind, and worrying heart, unwittingly enabled my addiction to continue . . . until my dad drew a boundary I could not cross.

Chapter 7

THE VOICES

FTER LIVING ON THE STREETS, the law finally caught up with me again and I had to pay my debt to society. As I mentioned in earlier chapters, the judge sentenced me to Drug Court and locked me up in jail. Upon my release, I still struggled to stay sober, so they locked me up again and again six separate times over the course of that year while I continued in Contemplation.

Mom had always been my best rescuer. Once out of jail, she and Dad got me a little apartment so I wouldn't be homeless. What she didn't think about was this allowed me to get loaded in a safe place on Mom's dime. She often stopped by early in the morning and dropped a little care package on my porch. She made sure I had the basics: clothes, soup, bread, and milk. Inside each care package there was a little note, written in her precise, beautiful handwriting: "I love you, son. Love, Mom."

She always loved me twice in every note.

She loved me so much; she often loved me right out of my pain and my consequences. Yes, I would have gone hungry if she hadn't fed me sometimes. Yes, I would have been homeless without the apartment. And yes, I probably would have hit rock bottom much more quickly. Her way of loving me and comforting me allowed my addiction and helplessness to linger.

Every once in a while, Mom invited me to go to lunch with her. It was her way of keeping tabs on me. It had been a couple of months since we last talked face to face, so one day I agreed to go.

I did miss her. I knew she was worried about me, and that made me sad inside. Just not too sad. I *wanted* to be sober. I just *couldn't.* The voices of addiction that hijacked my brain were in full control.

The day we agreed to go to lunch, I waited on the curb near my apartment for her to pick me up. Conspiring thoughts kept creeping in—two voices in my head arguing like Gollum and Sméagol in J.R.R. Tolkien's famous *The Lord of the Rings.* (If you don't know the reference, you will still get the idea.)

There was an evil voice, which I will call my "addict voice," and it was like a real person inside my head.

"What's the plan?" the ugly but surprisingly charismatic voice questioned. "You need money—at least sixty bucks. Tell her whatever she needs to hear. It worked last time. And quit feeling guilty about it. You know you'll pay her back later."

My own voice thought softly, *Maybe I should just forget the money and try spending quality time with Mom. We never spend time together anymore. We used to be so close. Besides, I shouldn't treat her this way. She doesn't deserve it. All she has ever done is love me.*

"Exactly right!" my other voice answered. "You know you can use that to your advantage."

The addict voice never stopped. It was constant, insistent, and intrusive. It lied. It was nasty. It robbed me of sleep. It stripped me of my agency and human decency. It controlled my actions. The addict voice was king.

No matter how hard I tried, I couldn't silence that voice—until I got the next fix.

Mom drove up in her new luxury car. I couldn't control the first thought at the sight.

"How much money can you score from her this time?"

Not sure.

I got in. As she glanced at my disheveled clothing, she forced a smile and told me how good it was to see me. I leaned over to hug her. The stench of stale cigarettes and beer filled the car. She flinched a little but acted as if she didn't notice.

"How are you, Jas? Is everything going okay?" she cleared a slight tremor from her throat.

"I'm fine, Mom. How are you?"

I wasn't fine at all.

I couldn't bring myself to look her in the eye. If she really knew how sick I was, it would've broken her heart.

She clearly knew I had a real and terrible problem with drugs and alcohol since the Dr. Alex scandal, the winter I spent homeless after my divorce, and the year I spent in jail once my charges caught up with me. However, Mom struggled to admit how bad it really was. She had convinced herself that I had to be doing much better now that I wasn't sleeping on the streets. I had to continue to convince her of that in order to keep my parents paying the rent.

She wanted so badly to believe me—that I was really okay in this situation. The denial kept her safe emotionally. The stone-cold truth would have crushed her.

We arrived at the restaurant, a decent place that Mom knew would have good food that might stick a little to my gaunt frame. I couldn't engage in conversation. My legs were shaking, and I couldn't concentrate.

"Excuse me, Mom. I need to use the restroom and wash my hands before the food comes."

With my head down to avoid anyone I might have known, I excused myself and darted for the men's restroom. I had come prepared for a quick hit of crack cocaine and heroin. My pipe, cigarette lighter, a couple balloons of drugs, and a piece of tin foil were stashed in my sock. I couldn't go anywhere without my stash and keeping it in my socks was the safest place to hide it. Mom would never know.

The flicker of the cigarette lighter was so loud that I masked the sound with a forceful cough. As I lit up, I carefully blew the smoke up into the bathroom fan to cover up, just in case someone entered the public restroom.

Suddenly very high, I sat down on the toilet as the euphoria set in. I heard the blissful, pulsating pinging sound in my ears. I couldn't help it. I remained in the bathroom stall for a good twenty minutes while Mom waited at the table wondering . . . worrying. I wanted to be with her. It's just that I needed a few more "blasts" before I went back out to see her.

Taking great care not to stumble or sway, I finally left the bathroom after finishing the last balloon of dope. I found Mom at the table. She looked at me, confused and irritated. Suddenly I felt more anxious than before, because the drug elevated my heart rate to racehorse status. I quickly buried my face in the menu, avoiding her eyes and acting as if I was reading the line items. I wasn't hungry. In fact, I couldn't eat if I tried. The drugs wouldn't let me hold anything down.

After we ordered some food, the interrogation began. I was prepared for this. Mom peppered me with questions, and I fired back with quick, short, and vague answers. She questioned me about my bills, job search, court hearings, friends, and my plans for the future. I shucked, jived, and dodged them all. These simple topics about life should have been easy to discuss; however, I felt overwhelmed, anxious, and stressed out to the point that I just wanted to get up from the table. Then the irritability and defensiveness rose inside me. I didn't care if I had to walk home, I just wanted her to stop. I couldn't tell her the truth.

Maybe I shouldn't have come. This is not going to end well. She can tell I'm high and this is going to crush her tender heart.

The addict voice quickly shut me down.

"It doesn't matter," it said viciously. "Just get the money and let's get out of here. Just tell her what she wants to hear. It works every time. You'll pay her back later. Be a man!"

Maybe I can just ask for a little bit and pay her tomorrow. If I don't get it from Mom, I might do something that will get me arrested sooner than later. It's probably better if I ask her.

"Yeah, that's a good idea," said the Gollum-type voice. "She wouldn't want you to get arrested."

I instantly turned up the heat into getting money from Mom. Even though I was still high, the stress triggered an insatiable craving inside me and I needed to speed up our meeting. I knew exactly what tactic to use because I was good at it, and she was great at responding. I built a story that triggered her fear response.

Like any mama bear, if she believed I was in danger, she would do anything to rescue me. That's what I counted on. I didn't have to make it complicated. The old tried-and-true addict line was good enough:

"Mom, I need to ask you for another favor," I said. Noticing the untrusting look in her eye, I pressed on. "If I don't pay my phone bill today, my phone will be shut off and you won't be able to reach me if I am at risk of slipping backwards into using again."

At that, my mom's face went pale. She had already spent too many months over the last few years not knowing where I was, and constantly worried and wondered if I was safe. The line I'd given was perfect. And to make me feel better, I added, "I promise, I'm going to pay you back once I start my new job." I didn't have one, but I was sure to deliver my story with enough emotion and sincerity to make it believable.

Mom took the bait—hook, line, and sinker. She couldn't stand the thought of not being able to text or call me to check in and see if I was safe.

As she drove me to the bank, she gave me a windy speech about how much potential I had and all the things I "should do" to fix my life. As we pulled in front, she looked at me hesitantly.

"How much do you need?" she asked. I still couldn't look her in the eye.

"I only need sixty dollars to get me through to next month," I lied. Sixty bucks wouldn't last me the night.

She reluctantly went inside the bank, got the cash, and promptly returned handing me three, crisp twenty-dollar bills.

"You did it! You won!" the addict voice celebrated. "Maybe you should ask her for $100! She will probably give it to you."

I fought that addict voice inside of me all throughout the rest of the time in the car. I felt ashamed.

As she drove me back to my apartment, I commenced to validate Mom with statements about how I planned to go back to church, maintain solid work, and how I planned to change my life. These were all important goals to her. I knew how to say what she wanted to hear to take advantage of her kind nature. At one point, before the drugs, these goals had been important to me, too.

We pulled up to my apartment and I quickly opened the door to jump out. As much as the addict voice was celebrating, I felt a deep knot in the pit of my stomach. I had just manipulated Mom again. I decided not to ask for more money—at least not that day. I hugged her and said goodbye. Even at the end of the hug I still battled, considering asking for more. The addict voice kept hammering at me until it was interrupted. Mom smiled at me, concern in her voice.

"I love you, Jason."

Now I hesitantly wondered if I should apologize for lying to her. Instead, I stepped outside her car and said, "I love you too, Mom. Thank you." I watched as she backed out of my apartment driveway and drove down the street.

"She fell for it," the addict voice purred.

SHUT UP! I responded, hating myself, hating my addiction, and feeling utterly pathetic.

Mom thought she was helping me.

She was.

She was helping me buy drugs.

She just didn't know it.

Before I even reached my apartment, I checked to see if Mom was out of sight. She was. I pulled my phone out of my pocket and made the call. No guilt, no shame could compete with my intense need for relief.

"Now go see if we can get some from Dad," the voice tempted.

No. Not today. Maybe tomorrow.

A couple days went by. It was about 12:30 in the afternoon and I was craving. My parent's front door was locked. It was always locked since my parents got a security system to keep me out. That was their physical boundary after I stole some valuables from their house. I rang the doorbell over and over, but nobody answered. I wondered if they were really gone, or if they were hiding from me hoping I would leave. I walked around the side of their house to peer through the window into their garage. Dad was home. I wished it was Mom, but I'd see what I could do with him. I was angry that he didn't answer the front door.

I pulled my phone out of my pocked and tried to call him. The call went to voicemail. He wasn't answering my calls those days. Either way, I'd find a way in to talk to him. I walked around to the backyard and the snow crunched loudly under my feet. I peeked through the kitchen doors and didn't see him in there. There was no sign of anyone. Maybe he was in the bedroom or bathroom.

I knocked insistently, repeatedly on their bedroom window. Finally. The shutters spread open just enough for Dad to see me, but I couldn't see him. He slammed them shut. Moments later the back door opened to the kitchen. Dad stood uninvitingly in the doorway, silently glaring at me. Memories of the past where I stole, lied, and manipulated my parents, especially Mom, flooded across his face.

He had so many reasons to be angry, but this was worse than it had ever been. Just a few months prior, I conned my parents into paying one more month of rent. After making them a sincere promise that I would straighten out my life, they gave me the check.

It worked every time.

Only this time I had taken the rent check made out to my landlord and forged a higher dollar amount. Then I carefully altered the name on the check, after which I had signed it over to myself. Smugly, I took it down to the wrong side of town to a 24-hour payday-loan center . . . and cashed it.

As he stood there, Dad had every reason to be fed up with me—my lying, my cheating—in fact, all of my behavior. Every time I was in desperate need for money, they were targeted. Multiple times I had broken into my father's medical office where I stole cash and syringes. While staying in their home, I took cash, pills, valuables—including Dad's rare and prized coin collection. I didn't stop there. The list of stolen items expanded to luggage and my mother's jewelry. I pawned them or traded them all for drugs. The sentimental value didn't matter to me or the people I pawned them off to. I needed what I needed. Lying and selfishness are the bookends of addiction. They are a package deal.

Dad stood there in the backyard doorway with a disgusted scowl on his face. To say Dad was disappointed in me was a huge understatement. He had watched my mother cry thousands of tears. He had woken up countless nights to find her wide-awake, worrying about me. He was done with it—he was done with me.

I launched into my well-rehearsed story. With a shaky voice and Visine-induced tears in my eyes, I said, "Dad, I owe my dealer a hundred bucks. If I don't get him the money immediately, he's gonna kill me."

Dad's response shocked me.

"I don't believe you, Jason. You will never see another dime out of your mother—or me."

"But Dad," I pleaded, "they are going to kill me!"

"I hope they don't hurt you too bad." Then he closed the door in my face.

His expression was direct, flat, cold, and final.

I was offended. *Doesn't he care that I could die?* I forgot that it was all a lie. Sometimes I got so caught up in my stories I started to believe them myself.

I stormed off his property and made my way down the street. I felt disregarded, disrespected, and angry that he didn't give me what I wanted. I acted like an adult baby.

As I passed by the neighbor's yard, I noticed some lawn equipment sitting outside.

"You can always pawn those for cash," the addict voice ordered. "Take them." So I did. I took them down to a pawn shop and scored enough to cover the afternoon drug fix.

Dad finally practiced setting a boundary—a wall strong enough that I could not break through it. He was willing to say no and make it stick. He was becoming powerful at sticking to his boundaries. This one act alone got me thinking about making a change, but I was still a long way away from taking action to change. Because my parents began setting and holding to their boundaries, my life became more unmanageable. I began considering change, and actually contemplated ways to do something about it. Their tough love was helping me move through the Stages of Change.

Maybe I could stop using once and for all. A few days later, however, I was court ordered to complete a drug test and I failed again. It appeared the judge knew I wasn't obeying the terms of my probation and locking me up was the only way he could keep me sober. Once and for all, I promised him that I was going to obey and stay sober. I truly didn't want to continue my life this way.

Upon release, I stayed committed and gained some positive traction towards change. After all, I was motivated by the fear of prison and homelessness. The days of sobriety turned into weeks, and then months. Life was becoming manageable again. The external consequences forced me to change certain behaviors; however, I still fanaticized about drinking after I completed Drug Court.

1. The erratic behaviors while in addiction are in large part because of this hijacking addict voice in our heads. It links to our broken brain chemistry, and in sobriety, over time, it will heal.

2. You can see how both my mother and father reacted in these circumstances. They did the best they knew how. Once they knew better, they did better. When boundaries are set, and the emotional raincoat is on, you can expect and allow the escalation of natural consequences to help the addicted surrender. You may need support to stay strong—to not give the money, not pay the rent, and not put up the bail.

3. Again, it is vital that we hold our strong fences up and allow them their pain.

4. Become willing to say no.

Chapter 8

THE SHIFT

*O*N A BEAUTIFUL, warm late-summer afternoon on the lake, turquoise reflections danced off the limestone particles in the water, giving me the feeling of being at the ocean. Instead, I was seated next to a gorgeous mountain lake. I wasn't hallucinating; this effect gives Bear Lake the nickname the "Caribbean of the Rockies." The lake straddles the Utah-Idaho state line and is one of the most popular summer vacation spots in the region. I had the entire weekend to spend with my sister Melissa, her husband Jamison, and her three children. It was an invitation of a lifetime to join her on their annual family trip to the lake. The pleasant weather and the soothing, dazzling, blue-green water should have been a balm to my soul, but I was in a real mess.

It amazed me that Melissa allowed me around her kids with all the trouble I was in. I was only a couple of months sober, and barely hanging on for dear life. During that year alone, I had been court-ordered to a residential drug rehab, had been homeless, incarcerated multiple times for failing drug tests, and was still required to drug test up to four times per week in a rigid drug court program. If I didn't show up for the random tests, I would go straight to prison; the judge had made that very clear.

If I successfully completed the drug court program, my felony charges would be reduced to misdemeanors. If I did not success-fully complete the program, the judge would send me directly to prison to serve my sentence of up to thirty years. Before taking the trip up the glorious canyons to the lake, I was obligated to contact and obtain permission from my probation officer to leave the area. Only because of my recent good behavior did he grant me a hard-earned break for the weekend, and I was very grateful.

Melissa was sensitive to my pain. She always had been. The soft voice of tender compassion during my intervention, she was the closest to me of all my siblings. After my parents shared with her that I was addicted to pain pills, her mission was to love me better. Her letters to me in jail were tender and sympathetic. They motivated me to want to change because she never showed any judgment. She sincerely tried to rally around me while I was down and out. She showed consistent support through unconditional love, and it worked. Because of this, I didn't want to let her down.

In preparation for my visit a few days prior, I had made a promise to myself that I would try to make up for lost time and spend some quality time with family. In this stage of addiction, I meant every promise I made, and I intended to keep them all. Long gone were the days of breaking my commitments to those who loved me most. I had a laundry list of relatives to make amends to, and I wanted to start right away. This weekend with Melissa was going to be different, I promised myself. I had the perfect plan, and this was the perfect place to reconnect with her and her kids, especially in one of my favorite settings.

Everything was in place for an amazing trip and I was going to capitalize on it.

Or so I thought. My addict brain had other ideas. Like a thief in the night, the addict voice seductively whispered into my ear.

"You should call Sergio before the trip. A couple pills would make the trip better. Besides, you can get away with it. For one thing, you won't be using the hard stuff. Just flush your system in time for Monday's drug test. No one will ever know." The voice was mesmerizing with its implications.

I shouldn't risk it, my more rational brain said. *I don't want to blow this opportunity with my sister. I really don't want to go back to jail.*

"Just make the call!" the addict voice began demanding loudly. "You don't have to use the pills! Just have them in case you decide you want one later. You have plenty of time to flush them out of your system. Call Sergio!"

Like a slave to the voice, I made the call. Fifteen minutes later, I was getting loaded in my car—a silver Hyundai Elantra—the car my parents bought me to help me get a new start in life.

That was all it took. One insane thought. Like a puppet, it was as if I was being controlled by someone else. I had no defense against it.

Over the next few hours in secret, I experienced that temporary, blissful escape once more. I ignored the fact that my nephews were given special permission to stay up past their bedtime eagerly awaiting my arrival. Many hours later, long after the kids went to bed, I pulled into the driveway at the lake house. All of the lights were out. It appeared everyone was asleep.

Good.

"Stay quiet," the voice instructed as I took the last pill in her driveway. Then I grabbed my suitcase and walked up to the front door. Melissa had left it unlocked for me when she realized I was not going to be arriving at the scheduled time.

The next morning, I woke up late with a clouded head and a knot in my stomach. Fear of getting caught combined with the shame of relapse was nearly too much for me to bear. Paranoia set in.

How did this happen again? What about all the promises I made to myself, to my family, to the probation officer, and the judge?

My addiction saw a window of opportunity and took advantage. The addict voice inside my head convinced me this time would be different—that I could control it and it would just be one time. But it was too late now. The phenomenon of craving had already kicked in. The mental obsession was back in full force.

I heard my nephew's laughter in the kitchen as I lay in bed isolating.

"Mommy, can we go wake up Uncle Jason?" Dallin begged.

"No, son. Let him sleep a little longer," Melissa replied.

I had to figure something out, a story to tell my sister that would explain my late arrival. "Car trouble," the addict voice hinted inside my head. Perfect.

"You should make up a story and drive back to Salt Lake for some more dope. You could be back by this afternoon and still have time to play with the kids at the lake," the addict voice tempted.

No, I argued back. *I won't blow this opportunity with my sister and the judge. I won't have enough days to flush my system and my drug test will come up positive on Monday. It's not worth it.*

I crawled out of bed feeling sick to my stomach because of the anxiety. I put on some basketball shorts and a hooded sweatshirt and made my way out to the kitchen area where my sister and her kids were making some of her "world famous pancakes." The moment the kids saw me walk into the room, they ran up to me, armed with hugs and kisses. For a brief moment, I felt significant; at least I was important to them.

As soon as breakfast was over, we packed up our beach chairs, towels, and a snack to take out to the sandy lake front. All morning, I forced a smile and played with my niece and nephews in the water, built sand castles in the pristine sand, and threw the Frisbee around in the sun. Although I struggled for energy and felt intense anxiety, I was able to put on the façade.

Later that afternoon, my depression dropped to an inevitable, miserable low. As withdrawal symptoms started to set in, I excused myself from the fun to take a nap on the blanket and attempted to isolate from reality. All I knew was that somehow, I had to combat the nausea, shaking, and anxiety that were beginning to set in, soon to be followed by terribly aching joints, muscles, and bones.

However, something was about to happen that would alter my life forever.

I slept for a few hours. I awoke to the vibration of my phone alerting me of a text message. The text came from the friend of a woman I dated in my drug court program. It read:

> Lisa is pregnant.
> The baby is yours.
> Call me ASAP!

My heart sunk like an anchor dropping to the ocean floor. My first reaction was complete and utter denial. Disbelief hit hard.

Surely this isn't happening.

As I mentally traversed back in time, I felt afraid and confused. I had met Lisa in my Drug Court program and she, too, was trying to live sober. The relationship had not lasted long. Like a toxic mixture, we drank together a couple times. The details of our dates were blurry, but somehow, I knew in my heart that I was the father. I wanted to pretend at first that the baby wasn't mine. Mixed in with all the fear, I felt intense shame and self-loathing. *If this is my child, he has no chance at a good life. I'm just a junkie. Look at me! I'm pathetic.*

On top of my heartache, my withdrawal symptoms intensified, leaving me feeling like I had the flu—achy body, hot and cold sweats, and a deep and dark depression. *What am I going to do now? How in the world will I raise a child?*

My stress induced a craving for more drugs.

"I'm sure there is something in the medicine cabinet back at the house, or the neighbor's house," the addict voice tempted.

Stop it! I can't ignore this! I fought back. *This is a big deal! This is my child's life! I'm going to be a father!*

I might have been a degenerate and delusional about myself in that rancid state of addiction, but something deep within me knew that a young, innocent life was nothing to take lightly.

For the rest of the trip at Bear Lake, I was self-absorbed and completely disconnected from my goal of spending quality time with my sister and her family. I tried to play it off and act the part that everything was okay. Melissa could tell something was wrong, but she did not know what it was. She asked me a couple of times to open up and confide in her, but I couldn't talk about it. In fact, I tried with all my might to block it out of my mind.

On Sunday morning, in the midst of my shame and guilt, I packed my bag, said a sincere goodbye, and drove home to my little apartment three hours away. I was a wreck, and to top it off, I had once again completely blown my sobriety. For two days I flushed my system by drinking gallons of water. The next day I passed my drug test because most tests are easy to cheat.

"I told you everything would be alright," the addict voice sneered.

Over the next nine months, I tried everything I could to become a better man because I was about to be a father. I felt so scared and alone. The stress fueled more drug and alcohol use, but I resorted to non-detectable drugs in order to pass the tests.

I wanted to change. The thought of my baby boy gave me added motivation to quit, but I still wasn't strong enough to stay sober. What was I going to do?

One afternoon that winter, I received a phone call from Lisa. She mentioned that she had met a loving little family who couldn't have children. They had been praying diligently to adopt a baby. Lisa really liked them and proposed we consider placing our baby up for adoption, given the circumstances. I respected the fact that she asked about my feelings regarding the matter.

That was the most difficult decision of my life—to give up my first-born child for hopes of him having a much better life. The thought of it was heart-wrenching. I wanted to be able to raise that child. I wanted to be a good dad and provide for him, yet for once in my life I had to put my selfishness aside and consider the baby's needs over my own.

The decision was made to allow the adoption. His mother and I both felt it was the right thing to do. We loved him so much and wanted to make an attempt to raise him but we both felt inside that in order to give our baby a good life, placing him for adoption was the right thing to do. The child deserved more than what we could provide.

Months later in early May of 2007, the night of my baby's birth finally arrived. I was having dinner with a friend at a Mexican restaurant when I received the call.

"Jason," she said quietly, "I thought you might like to know that your baby son, Nathan was born this afternoon." There was a pause, and my heart was already in my throat. "He looks like you. Do you want to meet him?" Lisa asked with softness in her voice.

The world stood still for just a few moments as I internalized the news. Tears filled my eyes. *A son! My son!* I couldn't believe the day had finally arrived.

I immediately got up from the table and excused myself. I raced to the hospital to meet my baby . . . before he was gone forever.

On my drive up, my excitement and joy were mixed with pain and heartache. I was so excited to meet him and hold him in my arms, yet I was terrified that I would bond with him and the adoption would only be more painful.

Upon arrival at the hospital, I discovered a group of Lisa's family was there. I felt like everyone in the crowd was glaring at me with disapproving eyes. As I glanced around, everything in the room sharpened like a razor, painful and cutting, each movement playing like a slow-motion video. My eyes were suddenly drawn to the center of the crowd, where my baby boy lay swaddled in a little green and white striped blanket. His eyes were swollen shut, and his lips latched around his tiny finger.

Lisa looked up and hesitantly smiled.

"Come in, Jason," she said gently, with a sweet and welcoming nature. "Do you want to hold him?"

Everyone watched for my reaction. "Will you let me hold him?" I asked humbly. I was trembling with fear and hesitation, but I was still eager just to wrap my arms around him. She nodded.

With great care, I gingerly took my son in my arms and pulled him near my chest. Emotions flooded my soul as I tried to keep up my tough-guy appearance. His tiny hands grasped my finger and held tight. I came undone. He was perfect: a perfect little miracle.

Everything and everyone in the room seemed to disappear and it was just him and me. In that moment, my perspective changed forever. In that moment, his innocence inspired me to consider my role in his life. Could I make him proud of me? Could I become someone he would want to look up to? I had wanted to change before, but I felt for the first time that I had a real purpose to change my life and attempt to overcome the chains of my addiction.

Up to that point, my life seemed meaningless. I was twenty-nine years old and had been struggling with intense addiction for four years. I felt I wasn't worthy of anything, but just embracing the exquisite miracle of that little baby boy changed me. Everything around me, all of my emotions of shame and guilt over my past, faded to the back. I believed I was not just an irresponsible drug addict anymore. I was a loving birthfather.

I committed that I would never touch another drug or drink of alcohol again in my life. It would be different going forward. I stared down at his little face, eyes closed tight. I felt unconditional love for my son. Nothing he could say or do would ever take that away. At that moment, I was gifted with a real reason to change. I wanted more than anything to one day be a good example to him.

I committed that night in the hospital that I would be the best birthfather in the world. I would leave my old life behind me, for my son, and finally for myself.

That night, I devoted to change for good, not for the judge, or for my family, but on my own volition. Finally, I experienced a true form of internal motivation.

I now had an internal reason to try.

In the hospital parking lot, I sat in my car wondering if I would ever have a chance to explain to Nathan why we placed him for adoption. My mind started spinning as I thought about all the questions he would have growing up.

Why didn't my birthparents want me?

Why would they give me up for someone else to raise?

Did they not love me?

I couldn't live with myself if these questions were left unanswered. Would I ever get a chance to tell him? The thought then popped into my head to write him a letter so that he could hear it from me. I pulled a legal pad of paper and a pen out from my backseat and I began to pour out my heart.

Date: May 8th, 2007

My Boy,

My heart is full tonight since I saw you come into this world and I am so proud to be your birthfather. I pray that you will always know that I love you very, very much. It is out of great love that your mother and I placed you into a home where you will be taught, loved, and raised with a mother and a father. I wish that I was in a place in my life where I could raise you correctly and be a good example to you. I have gone through many hardships that one day will be explained to you, but at this point you deserve so much better than what I can provide. I know that the Martins will give you the wonderful life you deserve. This decision was . . . not an easy decision to make. It tears me apart inside to know that you will not be with me as you grow up. I will always be here for you if you decide later in life that you want to meet and get to know your birth father. I would love that. Right now, I am trying to put my life back in order. I love you with all of my heart and it is out of love that we have placed you with the Martins. I will look forward to the day that you make contact with me and ask me to go to lunch to better get to know one another. By then I promise you I will be a different man and will be excited to share my life with you . . . I don't want you to ever doubt if your birth parents love you. We do more than words can express! Your birth mother is making a huge sacrifice for your better life. She has carried you and loved you during these last nine months in her belly, so the thought of losing you is crushing her, too. But the next few days we will spend with you in the hospital will help us get through this difficult time. Again, I love you son and I will always be proud that I am your birth father.

– Your father, Jason Coombs

Because this experience is so humbly sacred and precious to me, I cannot share even a fraction of what transpired inside me during this event. Needless to say, a few days later, with tears dripping down my cheeks, and extreme grief, sadness, and the fire of commitment in my heart, Nathan was placed in the arms of his new wonderful parents, Dave and Tanya Martin. Would I get to see him again? No matter what, I was going to get myself ready in case that day arrived. It was this sacred experience that caused my internal shift.

STAGE THREE:
PREPARATION (READY)

Looking back through the darkest times of my addiction, I entered premature preparation multiple times—the times I promised myself I would stop using sitting in jail, living in rehab, and when I was roaming the cold streets as a homeless man. I made goals and plans to change; however, the lasting commitment was missing.

In certain moments, addicted people will spring into Action while shortcutting Preparation. Preparation is a vital stage and must not be skipped. It is the bridge between the *decision* to change and the specific daily *actions* taken to solve the problem. In other words, it is the bridge from the Contemplation Stage to the Action Stage.

My period of preparation came after Nathan was born. There were no benefits to using drugs and alcohol any longer. I became "sick and tired of being sick and tired." I finally wanted to get sober, I just didn't know how.

In the Stage of Preparation, an individual will finally accept responsibility to change his behavior. He evaluates and selects techniques to change. Instead of just gathering information and slowly working through ambivalence, the Preparation Stage will focus on finding the best actions to take to overcome the problem, like narrowing down a treatment program online and making the calls to set up a drug and alcohol evaluation.

If he is to be accountable, he will draft a plan of action and begin to make those needed changes. He will also work on building his confidence and strengthening his commitment to change. He sets a clear timeline for change rather than the previous ambivalence.

In Preparation, usually he will have the intention to change within one month; however, recycling and vacillating through stages and longer timelines should be expected. We can describe this person in Preparation Stage as "willing to change." At this stage, he is also anticipating the many benefits of changing behavior. There is also the acknowledgement that the continuing journey will present challenges and obstacles. He begins to plan and prepare accountably for his future.

When they don't see the results they want, they become resentful when they are received with resistance. Impatience and any attempt to control will contribute to the addicted person's complacency.

This forceful approach creates a motivational setback. If you have done this in the past, try to commit to never doing it again. I understand that this is a real struggle, especially for those who stay in the preparation stage for a long time; however, it is vital to recognize the importance of the Preparation Stage of Change. We can use the following skills and strategies to help him the right way.

Now that your fences are set up, you're wearing your emotional raincoat, and boundaries are established, you are ready to begin learning about the most effective, evidence-based approach to help your loved one gain traction through the Stages of Change and see results.

I will begin this section by introducing you to the most effective, results-driven approach in the treatment industry. This approach is called Motivational Interviewing (MI) and was first developed by two clinical Psychologists named William Miller Ph.D. & Stephen Rollnick Ph.D. in the work with problem drinkers.

Today, it is used across the globe to help people change all types of behavior. Motivational Interviewing is a client centered, empirically based intervention that enhances intrinsic motivation to change by exploring and resolving ambivalence to change. In other words, it works! Notice it isn't called Motivational "Lecturing." The word "interview" is used because when you chat with a person in recovery, it is more helpful to ask them questions that help them discover their own internal motivation and draw them out into self-discovery. Lectures or sermonizing almost never work with the addicted population, not if you want them to find the inner resources for lasting change.

In his book, *Changing for Good*, Dr. Prochaska states, "The value of being prepared—as any Scout can tell you—is that it readies you both to take action and to handle unexpected challenges. It is unquestionably worthwhile to gain the skills and have the resources you need to manage the problems of life effectively. The success of most long-term projects is in large measure due to patient preparation; most successful self-change projects similarly rely on a sometimes brief but always thoughtful period of preparation." (p. 145) Your job is to exercise great patience with your loved one during this stage. Let me tell you why.

Most family members begin to get frustrated with their addicted loved one when they don't see any action, yet they hear the words, "I really want to get sober and I am going to stop." Typically, family members get impatient, try to force an outcome, and make shameful comments.

Trust

Before you can influence someone, you must develop a genuine level of trust. Trust is a firm belief in the reliability, truth, ability, and strength in someone.

Let me give you an example. Many of the successes happening in the rooms of recovery are the result of a person in "long-term recovery" helping a newly sober person free of charge.

Honestly, words can't describe the profound respect and *trust* that exists between two recovering individuals who serve and confide in one another. I have experienced this transcending connection myself.

That said, I have heard some naysayers smugly remark, "Talk about the blind leading the blind." Although they have a point to some degree, they are ignorant to the powerful reasons why this peer to peer relationship is so effective.

Another person in recovery is incredibly effective in building rapid trust because of their empathetic, non-judgmental understanding of the suffering addiction causes. They know intimately what the addicted person has gone through, what he is experiencing now, and knows exactly how to help. Why does this work to help motivate someone to *want* to change? Because of empathy. And empathy is an amazing miracle worker.

Empathy is the ability to understand and share the feelings of another. This respectful rapport facilitates wonders and success in recovery 12-step fellowships throughout the world. The mantra,

"What we can't do alone, we can do together," is repeated often in 12-step meetings. This sense of unity and affiliation with others sharing the same problem and same solution is transcending. There is no judgment or punishment. Whether you subscribe to the 12-step approach or not, the research evidence shows that this modality in treating addiction drives real results.

Therapists and family members can replicate a respectful trust with their addicted loved-one in overcoming their struggle if they know how to connect with them empathetically. This is true, even if you have not suffered your own addiction. You can earn "street credibility" by simply following a few basic fundamentals. Let's start with deepening your understanding about the importance of trust combined with rapport.

Rapport

Rapport is a little different than trust. Rapport is a close and harmonious relationship in which you understand each other's feelings and ideas. After a period of time, I experienced this with my parents as they, and I, grew emotionally healthier. Our communication became open and receptive to the point where I felt like I could share my innermost feelings with them and they shared theirs with me. You can begin to develop this rapport today.

The most effective way to build rapport quickly is when two people feel that there is safety, trust, and love between them. Begin by focusing on your addicted loved one's needs, feelings, and thoughts. In other words, don't make it about what you need, want, or expect from them. Turn it around and focus on his needs, wants, and what suffering he might be going through. You may need to bite your tongue and restrain yourself from correcting him or reacting to his sick thinking and behaviors. Just try it and do the best you can. This is a practice that takes time to develop.

The goal of this approach is not to prove who is right and who is wrong, but rather to foster a loving, respectful, and collaborative dialogue about change over time. It honors your loved one's struggle, timeline, resistance, and confusion—his ambivalence. It promotes independence and self-determination. It also can be used to improve your relationships with your other children, spouse, friends, and co-workers. Yes, it is that powerful and applies to all of your relationships.

To be crystal clear, Motivational Interviewing is not just a technique, nor is it about tricking people to do what you want them to do. This approach is not psychotherapy or ill-persuasion. Instead of manipulation, we *must* come from an authentic and vulnerable place in our heart for it to be effective, which means that we can't fake it. It must be genuine.

If this is done well, we can help call forth a person's own motivation and commitment for lasting change. Remember, internal motivation is the key to lasting change. We must create a spirit of love, tolerance, and non-judgment before we will achieve our desired result. How can we create this level of relationship while he is still sick?

We Must Make It About Them, Not Us

We are about to embark on a new approach that is a collaborative, goal-oriented method of communication. The plan is that once trust and rapport are built up, we begin to inspire your addicted loved one's motivation by eliciting and exploring his own arguments for change.

Again, let me make myself clear: it's about *his* own argument to change, not ours. If we can set aside our own agenda, it will help us patiently listen without correction. Pay particularly close attention to the language of change, or "change talk." These are key indicators about making a change, even if ninety-percent of his argument is against change. Remember that even ten-percent is progress. Let's honor it.

Let me give you an example of what *not* to do. Well intentioned, when I first got sober, I began seeking out others to help them find sobriety. I was told that if I carried the message of recovery to another addicted person then it would ensure my own sobriety. I forced myself to do it because I was so desperate.

I went out like an evangelist on a reform mission spreading the good news about recovery to everyone I came in contact with. I pushed my agenda on other people and when I was ignored or received with resistance, I became frustrated, resentful, and opinionated. So what does an adult, childlike man in early sobriety do with that? I decided to push my agenda even harder. I became ever more frustrated and resolved to push until the relationships were nearly severed. I couldn't accept other people's timelines, resistance, and lack of motivation.

I learned a lesson through my mistakes. The more we push and force our will upon others, although it is based in good intentions, the more resistance we receive and our good efforts backfire.

In order to be effective, we must first learn to make it about them. We must learn to be patient and become free of selfish agendas, outcomes, and resentments when it doesn't go our way. Easier said than done, I know.

You may be thinking, "Sure, that's great, Jason, but how do I help my addicted loved one to even open up to me?" Again, stay with me and let's go straight to the best, most efficient approach that you can use every day in your interactions with your loved one and it will drive results.

Tapping into the "Spirit" of Motivational Interviewing

Motivational Interviewing (MI) is much more than a set of techniques and intervention skills. There is a "spirit" or clinical "way of being" that is sincere, authentic, and genuine. This is the "spirit" by which others feel understood, heard, and loved no matter what. In this context, you can inspire and motivate.

We'll go through all of these in a way that's easy to understand, so you can apply them to your situation immediately. There are valuable insights into each of these elements.

Collaboration vs. Confrontation

My first taste of recovery was through my court-ordered treatment experience. None of us—the residents—wanted to be there, but we had to stay or we would go to jail. The culture of that program was founded in confrontational communication and fear-based motivation. There was no love felt or understanding from a client-centered approach. It was all "program forced" and insincere.

Immediately, I became resistant to *everything* they taught me about recovery strategies and sobriety, even though the tools were sound and would work if I applied them in my life. The staff created an environment of confrontation, misused power, control, fear, and resistance. It was no wonder that all thirteen of us relapsed within days of leaving treatment. Some of us even used drugs smuggled into treatment in order to cope with the environment. Let me be crystal clear on this point: confrontation does not work, unless it is backed with sincerity, empathy, and a genuine approach of unconditional, positive regard for the other person.

Collaboration, on the other hand, is a partnership between you and the addicted person that is grounded in respect for the experiences and perspectives of one another. This is a stark contrast to the toxic approach of a parent, sibling, or a spouse when they assume an "expert" role by confronting the addicted person and imposing their perspectives, mandating the appropriate course, and ultimately expecting a certain outcome. This toxic approach is often instinctual but is not effective for multiple reasons. Consider instead the collaboration model.

Collaboration strengthens rapport and facilitates trust, which is the foundation of healthy relationships. Collaboration means working together. It does not mean that we automatically agree with the addicted person about the nature of the problem, or the changes that may be most appropriate. Although we may see things differently, the therapeutic process is focused on *mutual understanding,* not on us being "right" and convincing the addicted person of how "right" we think we are. Collaboration is the opposite of the "my way or the highway" approach. In fact, it is more like taking a relational road trip together but letting our addicted loved one take the wheel for the most part, while you offer practice developing a deeper relationship of trust through encouragement, conversation, compassionate feedback, and fun.

Now, a collaborative approach will also include some honest confrontation, handled appropriately. Confrontation can be framed in a collaborative spirit. It is packaged with empathy, understanding, and accurate feedback. It works when the person being confronted feels a genuine positive regard from the confronter.

Briefly, skipping ahead in my story for a minute to my last treatment center, I was confronted multiple times and I did not like it. However, I could not deny that what my peers and counselors were saying was important to consider because I felt their love and concern for me. They constantly made it known and I became open minded enough to their brutally honest feedback, which inspired me to conduct a much-needed self-overhaul. Collaboration mixed with appropriate and loving confrontation will crush the walls of the ego.

"Drawing Out" vs. Imposing Ideas

As addicted people, we get tired of hearing what we "should" do and what we "must" do. As a result, our resistance strengthens instead of our recovery. Damagingly, this occurs even though the suggestions are probably constructive, just like what happened at my first court-ordered rehab.

The best way to help influence another person is by cultivating *their* own ideas for change. People support what they help create, not what they are told to do. Unless your addicted loved one is clearly in Precontemplation about his destructive behavior, the truth is he has his own reasons to want to change. Furthermore, he has the ability, although he may not believe he does, to co-create a plan for lasting change.

In the rooms of recovery, we are taught that "no human power can relieve us of our alcoholism," and that we must rely on a higher power. Try to accept that *you* are not your loved one's higher power, but that you can be an instrument in "drawing out" sufficient motivation and inspiration from within him to discover his greatness. What you are doing is moving from instructing and lecturing your loved one to drawing out his own ideas as his guide. As you do this, it will illuminate a path to a brighter future in recovery. This brighter path will be attractive to him because it is *his* idea, not someone else's path for him.

Each time I faced a big problem in my early weeks of sobriety, I was given a wonderful therapeutic suggestion. Instead of getting a bunch of advice, I was invited to sit quietly, ponder the problem, and seek solutions through thoughtful prayer and inspiration. If the answer doesn't come immediately, I practice patience, which is also an attribute I need consistent work on. To this day, it amazes me how often and quickly the answers come when I simply sit and ask for help and clarity in prayer.

This process can work for you and for your addicted loved one because it honors our own abilities, gifts, and talents, increasing our motivation for continued growth, even through life's toughest challenges.

The word *inspire* means to breathe life into something. If someone is inspired, they experience an increase of motivation to act. To encourage means to give someone courage. When we inspire and encourage others, we breathe life and courage into their spirit. It is a wonderful gift to share and we can do this by simply shifting from telling someone what to do, to drawing upon their God-given gifts, good hearts, and their intrinsic abilities to transcend.

Rather than imposing your opinion on your addicted loved one, try understanding his thoughts and feelings about change. This process is amazingly powerful if both parties are willing to engage in the exploration of solutions. In all my experiences with an addiction, a person in long-term recovery, and as a treatment provider, commitment to change is most powerful and durable when it comes from *within* the addicted person, not through a series of "should" and "must" statements.

Ultimately, lasting change is more likely to occur when he discovers his own reasons and determination to change. Our job is to "draw out" or evoke his own motivations and skills for change. This creates the foundation for powerful change within *you* and, in the near future, for your addicted loved one.

Individuality vs. Authority

One of the reasons why it took me so long to change was because of my struggle against authority figures. I resisted every person in my life who told me to get sober while demonstrating authority over me. Because I was an ego maniac with an inferiority complex, it felt emasculating and demeaning. The harder they pushed me to behave the way they wanted me to behave, the harder I stiffened up and pushed back on the inside.

The courts, the judge, the probation officer, my ex-wife, my parents, and my bosses all fit into the "perceived authority" category. Because I was so caught up in resisting authority figures, I missed the opportunity to seek my own individuality while expanding my purpose in life. On one hand, these authority figures helped me with external motivation because their boundaries and laws brought about much-needed natural consequences.

On the other hand, I resisted their advice because it came from an authority figure, not an empathetic equal.

Rather than positioning yourself as an authority figure, try to come along side your addicted loved one and be his guide. Try to illuminate his path toward an abundant life in recovery without forcing or controlling him. Forcing your will upon him only creates resistance. Ultimately, it is up to him to follow through with making changes happen; however, you can *contribute* the right way. Recognize that the true solution and power for change rests *within* his divinely created soul. Allow the natural consequences of his actions to apply the external pressure, while you simply support his individuality and patiently support his internal work, which can take time, toward a better life.

This approach is empowering to the individual, but also gives him responsibility for his actions. Try to reinforce that there is no single "right way" to change and that there are many ways that change can occur. Let him decide whether he wants to make a change or not. Honor his individuality by allowing him to exercise his own volition, whether you agree with it or not. What happens if he never changes no matter what you try? There is a solution for this too, and in the coming chapters I will show you how to truly let go and surrender the outcomes in order to receive the much-deserved peace and serenity you seek, even in the midst of the storm. It really works, so stay with me.

The Principles Behind the Results

Every family has their own set of unique circumstances and factors that contribute to the chaos caused by addiction. Because it is so easy to get caught in the weeds and stuck in the mud, I always coach family members to take a step back from the problem and begin to "operate on principles." These principles will help remind us to do this every time we slip into controlling, rescuing, or any form of unhealthy behaviors.

During the process of change, we will most likely experience some let downs, unexpected turns, and recycling through the stages. There are four powerful, guiding principles to live by in each situation to help us and our addicted loved ones move through the Stages of Change.

Empathy

I mentioned empathy earlier in this chapter and want to mention it once more because it is so vital. I strongly believe that empathy is the most important principle to apply if we want to experience real and lasting results in our relationships with anyone, but particularly in our relationship with those along the path to recovery.

Let's start by taking a look at the word itself. Derived from ancient Greek roots, empathy: em- means "in", and pathos- means "feeling". Empathy means "in feeling." Empathy involves seeing the world through another person's eyes, thinking about things as they think about them, and feeling things as they feel them.

Stop for a moment and think about this. Can you see how powerful this is? If we have empathy and we share in our addicted loved one's experiences, then we begin to understand the depth of his struggle. It doesn't mean we let down our boundaries. Instead we establish *rapport*, or a true connection to the individual by hearing and understanding him. In turn and over time, our loved one will be more likely to share his experiences and feelings in depth—a huge step in being able to explore his lingering ambivalence. Instead of having to justify and defend, he will feel that he is in an honest space without judgment as we practice the attributes of listening and understanding. If we want to be understood, make sure that first we seek to understand. This is an ancient principle that cultivates authentic relationships.

Support Self-Efficacy

Another vital principle to anchor our approach is to support self-efficacy. Self-efficacy is a person's belief and confidence in themselves that they actually do have the ability to change. Efficacy instills sufficient hope and motivation in the leap from *preparation* into taking difficult *action*.

As addicted people, we experience a deep core belief that says, "I am a failure," or "I am inadequate." This and other beliefs of self-hatred and shame are common with people who suffer from addiction. As an addicted population, we often feel deep in our core that we are unlovable, inadequate monsters who are not good enough. You may not see this side of us because we are professionals at masking low self-esteem with ego—false bravado, haughty or perverse pride, and self-importance.

Coming to believe that we have the Divine ability within ourselves to change takes time. In order to do that, we have to discover, or rather, uncover our strengths and abilities. This is a strengths-based approach that supports the truth—that an addicted person has within them the capabilities to recover successfully, with the right help.

Try supporting self-efficacy by focusing on successes and highlighting skills and strengths that the addicted person already has within them. The word *Namaste,* practiced throughout the world, means to honor the God-given gifts *within* your addicted loved one. Even if you have to look hard to find it, there is greatness within him.

Try practicing this principle with him, and with everyone in your life. If you do, you will begin to see the world differently. "When you change the way you look at things, the things you look at change." Dr. Wayne Dyer knew what he was talking about.

Roll with Resistance

If you want to gain traction in helping your addicted loved one, then you must become a master at this principle: roll with resistance. Take it from someone who works with addicted people every single day. The most effective way to influence progress through the Stages of Change is to "dance" rather than "wrestle" with him. Resistance happens when there is a conflict between *his* view and *your* view of the "problem and solution."

The moment an addicted person feels his freedom or autonomy is being threatened, you will experience resistance again. This usually occurs when he is told what he "should" do and how he "must" do it. Pushing someone, or forcing an outcome, creates resistance. So does poor communication.

Try changing the words *should* and *must* to "suggest" or "invite." Semantics are important. Words have power. Every addicted person wants to feel that he has some say in his own life. If we give a suggestion or invitation rather than an order, he will be more inclined to consider them after you have built trust and rapport.

Our addicted loved one's volition, or preference, is a key component to long-term recovery. We can positively influence him by offering suggestions to consider while demonstrating empathy, non-judgment, and unconditional love. We need to be careful not to use words like "should" if we want to avoid unnecessary resistance. Learning to communicate differently will drive real results.

Another important note is to avoid forcing him to act when you sense resistance. Don't lock horns with him. Instead, work to de-escalate and avoid a negative interaction by "rolling with it." You can offer direct and honest reflections and feedback, but remember that in order for your relationship to be effective, there must be rapport.

For example, a client named Luke came into my office and told me that he couldn't do the Brick House Recovery program any more. At this point in time, he had achieved two months of sobriety and he was on a good path. But after receiving some devastating news about his employment, he panicked into fight or flight mode. He wanted to quit.

As my heart sank, I remembered to put on my emotional raincoat and roll with it. Instead of responding with a list of reasons why he should stay in the program and continue working on his recovery, I simply nodded my head.

"Sounds like you are under a lot of pressure, Brother. Will you tell me what happened?"

Sensing my genuine concern for him at this critical time in his life, Luke proceeded to share with me the entire story, his feelings of overwhelm, and limiting beliefs that he could succeed. In that emotional state, he was wavering about his commitment to sobriety as the thoughts of drinking alcohol would take the pain away, if only for a few hours.

I put my hand on his shoulder. "I am so honored you would share this with me, Brother, and I am here to help you sort through this if you would like."

He then shared his fear of relapse and what that would do to his relationship with his daughter and his career. He also expressed concern about the health risks if he drank again. He was, in that sacred space, exploring his ambivalence. My job was to empathize, offer support if he asked for it, and to listen. By the end of the conversation, Luke recommitted to the program, not because I told him he should, but because he wanted the benefits of recovery more than the benefits of another drink.

I was honored to witness him create his own arguments to stay in the program and fight for his recovery. This small example of how I "rolled with resistance" proved to be fruitful. However, sometimes the outcome doesn't go the way I hope it will. When that happens, I can step back and feel comfort knowing that I did my part while relying on sound and proven principles. In those cases, I always leave the door open for future conversations when the other person is ready to explore their ambivalence again.

As a treatment provider, most of my clients naturally dig in their heels at one point or another during my efforts to help them. This is probably because they initially view me as an "authority" to resist. I can relate. But after sufficient trust and rapport are built, I have learned that rolling with resistance disrupts any struggle that may occur. The process of collaboration by honoring his individuality and self-efficacy through authentic empathy is a powerful combination for real results.

This is a good place to mention the role of humor, especially gentle or self-effacing humor with a client or loved one. If we can laugh about our own foibles, mistakes, mishaps, or embarrassing moments, it helps to establish connection quickly. I agree with Victor Borge that, "Laughter is the closest distance between two people."

Develop Discrepancy

Motivation increases when an addicted person becomes aware of the discrepancy between where he is and where he wants to be. When an individual sincerely internalizes the severity of his addiction and how much it is interfering with his true, core values and future goals, he is more likely to experience an increased motivation to prepare for change. Taking an honest inventory of our Life Domains and where we are off balance is a great way to develop discrepancy.

This process will naturally facilitate a deeper admission of his problem, leading him to seek a solution by which he can achieve his goals of becoming a better version of himself. This may sound kind of de-motivating to show them how far they are from where they want to be, but it is an important principle in evoking internal motivation.

This is where I get most excited in helping people recover. Without a vision of recovery and a clear pathway to get there, there is no hope and progress will be dormant. I love the perspective of American inspirational speaker, Iyanla Vanzant, "If you don't have a vision, you're going to be stuck in what you know. And the only thing you know is what you've already seen."

Addicted people genuinely lack the vision of a brighter future free from the chains of alcohol and drugs, and how to obtain it. In fact, the idea of long-term sobriety can actually sound miserable. It is helpful to invite them to experiment with recovery anyway. Developing a discrepancy between where they are and where they want to end up will inspire their desire to take action. Action is the only way people ultimately achieve long-term recovery. Without a vision, there can be no hope, and hope is the fuel for action.

How does hope work?

I like to think of hope as a way of thinking or a cognitive process. Emotions play a supporting role, but hope is really a thought process made up of what C.R. Snyder calls a trilogy of goals, pathways, and agency. C.R. Snyder, a former researcher at the University of Kansas, enlightened the meaning of hope for me. He taught me that in very simple terms, hope happens when:

- We set goals to reach our desired outcome

- We see the path ahead, including the action steps

- We believe in our abilities (self-efficacy) to persevere with tenacity until we reach our goal

Consider helping your addicted loved one create a list of action steps that will help him achieve his goals. Then focus only on those initial actions first. Resume this process throughout the journey.

Although this chapter may seem a bit overwhelming and clinical, let me give you some hope. When my parents started attending regular Al-anon meetings, family therapy groups, and reading "bibliotherapy" (recovery self-help books), they naturally adopted this new approach of rapport and empathy, one day at a time. They didn't memorize techniques and study Motivational Interviewing skills. Their change happened organically as a result of their own recovery work and sincere desire to support me the right way. Dive into your own recovery from over-helping or over-worrying about your addicted loved one. There are many other resources, such as self-help groups like Al-anon, and books to help you experience rapid changes that will naturally lead you to better helping your loved one in their own recovery. For a list of other resources, see www.brickhouserecovery.com/unhooked.

STAGE FOUR
ACTION

At this stage, people engage in self-directed behavioral change efforts while gaining new insights and developing new skills. Although these change efforts are self-directed, outside help may be sought. This might include self-help efforts, recovery meetings, treatment, or therapy. Characteristics of this stage include: consciously choosing new behavior, learning to overcome the tendencies toward unwanted behavior, and engaging in change actions. We might describe this person as enthusiastically embracing change and gaining momentum.

STAGE FIVE
MAINTENANCE

People in the Maintenance Stage have mastered the ability to sustain new behavior with minimal effort. They have established new behavioral patterns and self-control. Characteristics of this stage include: remaining alert to high-risk situations, maintaining a focus on relapse prevention, and behavior has been changed for a period of time. They are integrating change into the way they live their life.

1.   In the Preparation Stage of Change, usually an addicted person will have the intention to change within one month, however, recycling and vacillating through stages and longer timelines can be expected. We can describe this person in Preparation Stage as "willing to change."

2.   Therapists and family members can replicate a respectful trust with their addicted loved one in overcoming their struggle if they know how to connect with them empathetically.

3.   The most effective way to build rapport quickly is when two people feel that there is safety, trust, and love between them. Begin by focusing on the addicted person's needs, feelings, and thoughts. "Seek first to understand before asking to be understood." It is powerful.

4.   The goal of this approach is not to prove who is right and who is wrong, but rather to foster a loving, respectful, and collaborative dialogue about change over time.

5.   We must create a spirit of love, tolerance, and non-judgment before we will achieve our desired result.

6.   The more we push and force our will upon others, although it is based in good intentions, the more resistance we receive. Our good efforts backfire.

7.   In order to be effective, we must first learn to be patient and become free of selfish agendas, outcomes, and resentments when it doesn't go our way.

8.   This is the "spirit" by which others feel understood, heard, and loved no matter what. In this context, we can inspire and motivate.

9. Confrontation does not work unless it is backed with sincerity, empathy, and a genuine approach of unconditional positive regard for the other person.

10. Collaboration, on the other hand, is a partnership between us and the addicted person that is grounded in respect for the experiences and perspectives of one another.

11. Although we may see things differently, this therapeutic process is focused on *mutual understanding,* not us being "right."

12. The best way to help influence another person is by honoring the fact that they have the ability to tap into their solution inside their hearts and minds.

13. Rather than positioning ourselves as the authority figure, let's again recognize that the true change rests within the addicted person. Forcing our will upon him only creates resistance.

14. If we have empathy and we share in our addicted loved one's experiences, then we begin to understand the depth of his struggle. In turn and over time, our loved one will be more likely to share his experiences and feelings in depth—a huge step in being able to explore his lingering ambivalence.

15. Self-efficacy is a person's belief and confidence in themselves that they actually do have what it takes to recover. Efficacy instills sufficient hope and motivation in the leap from *Preparation* into taking difficult *Action.*

16. "When you change the way you look at things, the things you look at change."

17. The most effective way to help an addicted person is to "dance" rather than "wrestle" with him.

18. Attending regular Al-anon meetings, family therapy groups, and reading "bibliotherapy" (recovery self-help books) naturally helps us adopt this new approach one day at a time.

19. Stages four and five are the results you will reap after all the work and effort in stages one through three. These sections deserve more detail, but I'll address them more in future writings and on my website.

Chapter 9

DRINK LIKE A GENTLEMAN

GRADUATION DAY from Drug Court was a wonderful experience. My family and close friends came to the courthouse for the graduation ceremony, and all in attendance felt accomplished and triumphant after two years of hard work and effort. Throughout the process, I had slipped up quite a few times, but finally I overcame the addiction once and for all. I was ready to move on with my life and put this all behind me.

By that time, I had completed three outpatient treatment programs and a residential program, which I had failed miserably at staying sober after completion. But I had survived Drug Court, I had made some progress, and I was committed to keeping my promise to Nathan. At the graduation, I was six months clean and sober. However, I continued to suffer with anxiety, depression, anger, mood swings, and other addictive behaviors. Although I was clean, I was NOT *emotionally* well. In the rooms of recovery, there is a distinct difference between those who only achieved years of "clean time" vs. those who have "emotional sobriety"—or rather, those who are happy, joyous, and free.

I proudly squared my shoulders when it became my turn. I stood up from my chair, walked up to the podium, and I delivered a well-thought-out speech to the entire audience, hoping to impress them all. I even mustered up a few tears for effect. I puffed up with pride as they clapped and applauded me for my successful completion.

After the ceremony, my parents took me to lunch and each of them gave me a graduation gift. I had reached the finish line of my addiction. The past was finally behind us.

Soon after we left the restaurant, a text message from one of my coworkers stopped me in my tracks. He and another coworker had planned a celebration trip to Wendover, Nevada, the party-getaway destination for northern Utah locals. He even offered to pay for our hotel room. Without hesitation, the addict voice in my head convinced me that I could celebrate my accomplishment with a few drinks! Besides, drugs were my problem, not alcohol. I knew I could drink like a gentleman and control my quantities.

This is a classic example of someone who is in Precontemplation about quitting alcohol, but in Action about quitting drugs. The truth is, for someone who has Substance Use Disorder, when it comes to substances, there is no difference. In my experience, they all impact the brain, causing the insanity to return in the mind, and the insatiable cravings to return in the body. In other words, it is the same noose, just a different rope.

The three of us packed an overnight bag and drove across the desert for a weekend of drinking, gambling, and nightlife. I felt the rush and excitement during the entire drive through the Bonneville Salt Flats, knowing that alcohol and I would be reacquainted soon.

Upon arrival at the casino, even before checking into my hotel room, I ordered a long island iced tea with a double shot of tequila. The moment the alcohol touched my lips, I felt the blissful release and re-acquaintance with my ol' best friend. After that moment, all bets were off. Just like an allergy, the alcohol ignited a craving inside me that ravished my commitment to control my drinking. A few drinks hijacked my self-control and the addict voice returned.

"An eight ball of cocaine would make this better. Besides, you have earned this celebration after all the hard work."

I had no defense against it. It was as if the memories of being homeless, divorced, the suffering, the loss, and the pain had vanished. The promises I made to Nathan vanished. I had the crazy belief that I could drink like a normal person, and somehow suddenly have the power to control my drinking. Under the influence of those first few sips, I already began to forget where drugs and alcohol took my life. This quick ability to "forget" after just a few sips of alcohol are in fact symptoms of Substance Use Disorder.

What followed was a 48-hour blackout. I was nearly arrested for fighting, I got kicked out of a nightclub for disorderly conduct, and I forgot which random casino I left my car at. To make things worse, I borrowed and spent over $1000 on alcohol, cocaine, gambling, and nightclubs.

That experience in Wendover sent me on a nine-month "runner"—the worst one yet. A "runner" is a stretch of time immersed in using drugs and alcohol. The truth about relapse is that you rarely go back to using a little bit. It hits harder, faster, and worse than before.

The day came when my desperation to get loaded could have put me in prison for the rest of my life. Once again, I crossed lines I had promised never to cross.

On that cold and wet winter day, the kind that settles into an addicted person's dry bones and stays like a plague until a high can take the raw pain away, I was sitting with my phone in my hand. I was in trouble. I needed a fix so bad I couldn't stand up well. Keeping my voice as calm as possible, I called my dealer.

"Hey, Sergio," I begged, "I'm ready. I need three 'black' and four 'ready.' Can you meet me?"

"Black tar" refers to Mexican black tar heroin, and "ready rock" refers to crack cocaine "ready" to smoke. There was a pause on the other end of the line.

"No, you have no money. You lie to me," Sergio answered with his strong, Hispanic accent.

"I got the money this time, Cabron! I promise!" I argued.

I didn't have it, of course.

The last two times he fronted me the drugs because I didn't have the cash to pay for them—and still hadn't paid for them. I would say or do anything to get him to meet me. Then I could figure out a way to persuade him to front me again.

Sergio reluctantly agreed to meet me, under the impression that this time I was telling the truth. I had, in fact, been a great customer up until lately. I had cashed in my entire 401k and all the money in my savings account, which was about $15,000, to buy Sergio's product. I felt like he owed me.

We met up in a residential neighborhood in the town of Sugar House, about fifteen minutes south of the University of Utah. From my rearview mirror, I watched Sergio and his two cronies pull up beside me in his maroon 1996 Pontiac Grand Am. As Sergio carefully passed by me, I noticed his typical white coat (though dirty from wear) made a strong contrast against his dark skin. I recognized him instantly from his thin mustache.

Sergio never smiled. He was always serious and paranoid, and he had reason to be. He nodded at me, checking for passengers in my vehicle as he slowly passed by, and parked in front of my car.

It was go time. I grabbed my Swiss Army pocketknife out of my center console and put it in my pocket. Then I opened my car door. I pushed all other thoughts aside. My mission was to get the crack and heroin balloons—at any cost.

With overblown confidence, I walked directly up to the rolled down window on the passenger side of the car.

"Three 'black,' and four 'ready'!" I ordered again.

"You have the money?" he asked suspiciously. As if I was going to pull it out of my pocket, I reached into my coat gripping the knife and then looked at him.

"I'll get it to you next time."

Sergio yelled some expletives in Spanish and slammed the car in drive.

"Give me the dope!" I screamed, determined not to lose my fix. "I'm not playin'!" I pulled out the knife, visible enough for him to see.

Sergio's foot revved the engine. He looked at me with hatred in his eyes and slammed on the gas. I was desperate. As the car was moving away, I grabbed onto the door and threw myself in the window at him as the tires screeched on the pavement.

Grasping desperately at his coat, I shouted, "Give me the dope or I will kill you!" The seriousness of my tone and the insanity in my eyes scared him enough to spit a few balloons in his hand and threw them out the window, past my head and onto the street. I pushed myself out of the car window just as he furiously peeled away.

Barely missing the rear tire, I rolled across the pavement into the gutter, scratching my face, back, and arms. I didn't care. I picked myself up quickly and frantically ran back to the area where he had tossed the balloons.

There, in the middle of the street and the gutter—in the midst of passing cars—on my hands and knees I made sure I found every balloon. I checked again for good measure.

In the drug game, intimidation worked to get what I wanted. Before I became addicted, I would never have threatened a life to get what I wanted, but it worked. And in this case, I actually didn't feel bad about it. Even though I had crossed a dangerous, dangerous line, the only thing that mattered was getting my fix. Now that, my friends, is insanity.

The hours after the high wears off and you have no way of getting more are always the darkest, and this was the darkest time in my life. The shame and disgust racked my soul. I felt the pitiful and incomprehensible demoralization understood by every hardcore addicted person. I became bankrupt, spiritually and emotionally. Thoughts of making the "grand sacrifice" were entertained.

As I got closer to making that decision, images of my son Nathan's face and the promises I made to be an example to him gave me strength to fight just one more day—to take one more breath. I had to stop. But how? I looked up at the blue, late February sky and asked God to rescue me. I had little hope He would, but my foxhole prayers were my default reaction in hard times.

God, if you are there, I seriously need to get sober, I just don't know how. I need help. I'm ready.

Despite the frequent thoughts of changing, I pushed the procrastination envelope too far. Procrastination always plagues the person who is addicted. A few weeks went by and my daily use increased to an all-time high. By then, I had built up a resource list of at least five different dealers in case one ran out. I heard Sergio's front door was kicked in and he was arrested by the Drug Enforcement Agency, or DEA. No problem. I had other resources. I rang the doorbell at my second drug dealer's house, Leo.

I stood on the front porch, shivering in the cold, impatiently waiting for Leo to answer. I was anticipating my next high when BAM! A DEA agent opened the door dressed in SWAT gear. I didn't have time to be stunned as he pulled me inside and quickly kick-slammed the door shut. Then he proceeded to smash my face against the wall with his hand still on his gun.

It's over. I'm in serious trouble now.

Inside the house, I smelled the sour scent of drug manufacturing. The windows shades were drawn and all the lights were off, but the sunlight from the cracks gave enough light to see shapes and outlines. As my eyes adjusted to the darkness, I made eye contact with my dealer and his Honduran cartel. They were all lined up on the floor with their legs crossed. Each one was handcuffed behind their backs. Three federal agents stood by them, armed with formidable weapons and ready for any sudden movement or attempt to escape. These guys were in big trouble. But my thoughts were not focused on them. I was in perhaps bigger trouble.

This is it. I'm going to prison for a long time.

My heart sank deeper into despair as I thought of Nathan and my parents. I had let them all down . . . again.

I was interrogated by the DEA for several minutes, his voice and his eyes harsh and menacing. He didn't know I had a secret stash in my sock.

Finally, the agent surprisingly let me walk away. I couldn't believe it. As I drove away, I replayed every word in my head. How did I get so lucky? Holy crap, that was a shot just over the bow! I made the commitment again in that moment; I would never touch another drink or drug again in my life.

Insanity returned. Hours later, I was back out on the streets seeking dope to quiet my mental obsession and to soothe the intense physical withdrawal from heroin. I simply did not have the power to stop, let alone stay stopped.

Over the next few weeks, in a state of increasing paranoia, I noticed something odd. Everywhere I went throughout the Salt Lake Valley, a navy-blue Ford Crown Victoria was following me. Then it hit me. I was only valuable to the DEA if I led them to the "big fish" drug suppliers. Consequently, they followed me to watch my every move and learn who the distributers were.

That knowledge threw me into a tailspin. The fear and anxiety propelled me into a drug-induced, paranoid psychosis.

I raced home and where I locked and dead-bolted the door. I pushed my body against it and listened for any sound that I was being followed. From there, each hour that passed by, my paranoia got worse. Finally, I reached a psychotic break. Hallucinations and audible voices devoured my sanity and reason. For nearly two weeks, I barricaded myself inside that tiny apartment to hide from the DEA, FBI, and armed terrorists I believed were outside my door and out on my roof. I stacked up all the tables and chairs I could find and securely wedged them behind my door.

Scrambling around my cupboards and bed for supplies, I grabbed my one remaining chair for a stepladder, then used duct tape to drape blankets and sheets over my windows to keep anyone from peeking in the cracks of the blinds. I wasn't just worried about an arrest. I was convinced that the FBI was waiting for the perfect moment to capture me and lock me in a cage. In a state of acute paranoia, the intense hallucinations of "shadow people" stalking the apartment premises and faint voices in my head consumed me. I held my head in my hands and rocked back and forth on my bare and cold mattress. The voices nearly drove me to end my life. I became a mad man and it got worse after I ran out of my drug supply and alcohol.

On the seventh day after a week of no sleep, bath, food, or water, I received a text message from my best friend from years ago, Dave Pinegar.

> Are you ready to get sober yet?

Dave had planted the seed to check into the same rehab he went through a while back, but I disregarded his suggestion. Now, I considered it. Dave and I had a long history that started when we met in Brazil and after we became college roommates. We had many fond memories together, and we had some painful memories while using drugs and alcohol. He had entered treatment and recovered three years prior. He knew what I was going through. I felt he was the only person on the planet I could trust. I decided to reply to his text.

> I need help. I don't know what else to do.

Dave knew my history and knew that I needed an extreme miracle if I was ever to change. He knew how deep I was into my addiction, for he, in fact, was there by my side years earlier using with me. After his wife found him in a dark basement, cold and blue from an opiate overdose, followed by a drug-induced coma, Dave checked into treatment and changed his life. Not only that, he was emotionally sober, happy, and lived an attractive life of freedom and purpose. He could tell I was on death's doorstep, knocking to come in.

> Let's get you into detox, and then into treatment tomorrow.
> I will drive down in the morning and take care of everything.

It was time for me to surrender. I was either going to change for good this time, or I would die a miserable death. This hadn't been fun for a long time. Drugs had become like air to me, and I didn't know how to breathe without them. I couldn't do it on my own. I had to change.

Dave drove down from Idaho early the next morning at 5:00 a.m. to liberate me. Upon his arrival, he and I embraced like brothers who separated long ago. Dave felt like family. He was family.

"Jason, please. Please give recovery one more shot and give it all you got. I promise you, brother, this is where you will find freedom from the disease of addiction once and for all."

I searched his face for the truth. Was it possible to be free from the demon of addiction that possessed me? I wanted to believe him. I wanted to believe him so badly, but I had so many doubts and fears.

Over the next twenty-four hours, Dave patiently helped me prepare to enter treatment. I had already lost my apartment for not paying rent and was being evicted. Dave boxed up my belongings, cleaned up my apartment, and threw away my drug paraphernalia. This was it. He even agreed to take care of my cat, Cubby, while I got help. Dave did for me what I couldn't do for myself. He rescued me in the nick of time. He became my angel.

Before checking into the hospital on March 19 of 2009, I made one last request to Dave. I wanted to see my boy, Nathan. I needed something of love to hold on to before I entered the uncomfortable world of treatment again. In the Martin's loving kindness, they allowed me to see him.

We arrived at the Martin's home in Lehi, Utah that evening. I couldn't believe my eyes. He was now two years old and looked exactly like me when I was his age. He was extremely shy and reserved at first as I opened up to the Martin's about my plans to seek treatment again. They showed loving support and offered to send me pictures while I was in treatment for encouragement. I tried not to cry at their benevolence as I watched Nathan start to play—not just walking, but running with ambling steps, and not-so-gracefully swinging his baseball bat at everything.

As I watched my boy, there was something inside of me that kept calling me to better things. After all the times my addiction called me back, I was now prepared to do whatever I needed to do to achieve real recovery. I became willing to try. I wanted it on my own volition once again, but this time, it was sincerer than ever before.

RELAPSE

In my journey, I recycled through the Stages of Change and I experienced multiple relapses. With each failure, my shame and embarrassment compounded. My family was baffled, but nobody was as baffled as I was. What happened to my rock-solid? I had made excellent progress in my sobriety a couple of times, but something would trigger me and that was all it took. I lacked *emotional sobriety*.

We have all asked ourselves why someone would choose to get loaded after it caused so much pain and suffering? Why would he decide to have one more drink? What were they thinking?

For me personally, two major factors that contributed to my continual relapses were my environment and lifestyle. I did not protect my sobriety; therefore, I put myself in risky situations around people who were not supportive of recovery. It's been said that we become the average of the five people we spend time with. Since I hung out with drinkers, I eventually drank.

In the rooms of recovery, we advise each new person to "stick with the winners." For far too long, I hung around people who did not help me protect my efforts in sobriety.

Additionally, because my lifestyle was geared toward a selfish pursuit of wealth, accolades, and counterfeit happiness, I lacked the humility and willingness to surrender my life to the process of change. I did not continue the actions necessary to put my disease into remission on a daily basis, so I was a "dry drunk" for weeks or months at a time. Again, I lacked *emotional sobriety*. Inevitably, my addiction flared up again and again and again.

Fortunately, the majority of relapsers do not give up on recovery for good. We may fall apart for a period of time, then get ourselves together, but we will try again, and again. This cycle is what makes addiction so frustrating. We are a resilient bunch and we will fight, even if we only rely on our own self-will, which is insufficient.

In *Changing for Good,* Dr. Prochaska states, "Although relapse is never desirable, our view is that change is often circular and difficult. The spiral cycle of change shows how contemplation, preparation, and action usually follow relapse. Relapsers most often take one step backward in order to take two steps forward." In other words, we need not panic when our loved one's relapse. This does not mean that he is back to the beginning. This is often a part of the journey: it undoubtedly was a part of mine.

Some recyclers, however, become so demoralized after a relapse that they cease to make the effort to get sober again and they give in to their disease. They look at themselves as total failures. Guilt, shame, and embarrassment take over.

Respectfully, some addicted people have grave emotional and mental illnesses and they are plagued beyond understanding. For those in this category, intense work with psychiatrists and mental health professionals are needed to overcome an addiction.

Silver Linings

There are silver linings when we seek after them. A short relapse will sometimes resolve a person's ambivalence about sobriety, moving them through the stages toward *Action.* For example, last holiday season one of my female clients named Grace came into my office distressed and irritable. She was a thirty-seven-year-old woman with blonde hair and blue eyes. Her husband and children supported her recovery; however, she has been stuck in Contemplation for years.

As she sat down, I smiled and asked, "What's the matter?" She let out a big sigh like she was about to share some sad news to me.

"Jason, I want to pause my treatment until after the Christmas holiday and New Year's Eve. I know I am going to drink, and I do not want to feel guilty about it. There will be a lot of alcohol at my family parties over the holidays, and I can't resist. Please don't be mad because I really do want to be sober, but just not during the holidays."

Instead of a forceful attempt at persuasion and a list of things she "should do," I decided to "dance, not wrestle" with her. While rolling with her reasoning, I reflected back to her what I heard to make sure I understood her correctly. "So, Grace, just to make sure I understand you, the holidays are not an ideal time to attempt sobriety and you would like to resume drinking until after New Year's and then get sober. Am I correct?"

"Yes," she sheepishly replied.

"Got it. Many people feel this internal struggle, especially this time of year. I totally validate your feelings."

She let out a sigh of relief as if she was expecting a different reaction from me. I relaxed back in my chair to help calm her even more.

"Remind me, when we first met, what were your primary reasons for wanting to get sober?"

Grace thought for a few seconds while looking up at my family photos placed on my filing cabinet in my office. "Yes, I do remember. I don't want to be hungover on Christmas morning. I want to be present with my kids and give them the best Christmas ever. Last year I was miserable, and the holidays were a mess because of my drinking. I promised myself and my family that would never happen again."

I let her words marinate for a few moments, then asked, "Why is that important to you?"

I could tell she wasn't sure anymore. She was ambivalent. For the rest of the meeting we explored her ambivalence about the pros and cons of staying sober now as opposed to drinking now, and trying it again after the New Year. For twenty minutes, I simply asked her open-ended questions, validated her feelings, and illuminated her options as best I could. Basically, I gave her a safe space to explore her reasons until she made the decision to focus on her sobriety, stick with her commitment to be present for her kids, and in her words, "power through the holidays." She felt relieved after making that decision to do the right thing. It was a good sign, but I knew it wasn't over.

The next morning, Grace woke up feeling depressed. She instantly changed her mind. Instead of fighting for her sobriety, she grabbed her keys, hopped into her car, and raced down to the liquor store before she changed her mind again. That day, she drank herself into another blackout. The following day she called me in tears and told me what had happened. She expressed the embarrassment, guilt, and shame she felt. She was sick to her stomach about it. I asked her to come meet with me again to continue our conversation about what happened.

Believe it or not, something powerfully positive came out of the relapse. For her, the relapse clarified what she did not want in her life—alcohol. She beautifully articulated that the consequences of drinking again far outweighed the benefits. She was able to identify the lies she told herself leading up to the drink. She also articulated that this painful experience helped her decide to stay sober going forward and do what it took to never drink again. She took one step backwards in order to take two steps forward.

After the relapse, she sprang into the Preparation Stage of Change and became ready to take action. Immediately after the relapse, she cancelled her party with her drinking friends. Then she told everyone in her family that she was working on her recovery and asked for their help at the Christmas Eve party. They all rallied around her and decided the party would be alcohol-free. She set herself up for success and now she is in the Action Stage. Much credit goes to her family for their support and understanding.

In many cases, relapses happen to individuals who are still ambivalent about the costs and the benefits of change. A good example of this is the person who commits to diet and exercise. Commonly, they set a start date for January 1st after the holidays. They work hard and stay committed for about two weeks, and suddenly one morning, they decide to sleep in and miss their workout. "I'll make it up tomorrow," they'll justify. Then the recycling begins back into old behaviors. The motivation wears off, and the comfort of eating sugar and flour draws them back in.

Similarly, drug and alcohol relapsers will test the waters because they desperately want to feel the old benefits again. They are trying to find ways to experience the blissful benefits of using, but not reap any of the consequences.

If our loved one relapses, it is not the end of the world. A relapse can be used to help him move from one stage to the next. If relapse does happen, it should be channeled and used as a learning experience. Taken in this spirit, it can serve as an incredible springboard to help someone transition from *Contemplation* to *Preparation*, and *Preparation* to *Action* as they consider the costs vs. benefits. The end goal of ultimate recovery comes as he successfully transitions through each stage. Let's be patient and remember the Four C's:

1. We cannot **Control** his addiction

2. We cannot **Cure** his addiction

3. We did not **Cause** his addiction

4. However, we can **Contribute** to his addiction, or his recovery.

Our main goal is to not slip into angry, controlling behaviors. If our external fences are up, and our emotional raincoat is on, we can react in a healthy, understanding, and loving way, free from anger and judgment. Remember the powerful principles mentioned before:

- **Empathy:** he is a sick man, not a "bad man." Sick people have symptoms, and relapse is a symptom. This mental and physical battle is extremely painful for a person with Substance Use Disorder. Try to step into his shoes.

- **Non-judgment:** he is experiencing more suffering than we realize. Everybody experiences trials and weaknesses in life, including you. Let's not kick him while he's down. Rather, let's check our resentments at the door. Anger won't help get us the results we desire.

- **Unconditional love:** his relapse should not cause us to pull our love away. In fact, the more love we show at this time, the better. Tough love can be useful here, but make sure it is not driven by anger or fear, rather empathetic boundary setting and allow him to experience the natural consequences.

- **Redefine boundaries:** it is perfectly okay to sit down again and redefine our boundaries (financial, physical, emotional, and material) with him after a relapse. This will help motivate the transition into the next Stage of Change faster. Remember, "strong fences make great neighbors." Boundaries create a healthier relationship and resolve ambivalence.

- **Don't rescue or enable.**

Do you remember how many times I was rescued from my gift of desperation? The times my parents softened the blow and denied me my natural consequences? They will tell you, please do not rescue in the midst of a relapse!

During a relapse, remember the fundamentals in this book. All too often, family members deny their addicted loved one the gift of desperation. Family members often "relapse", or recycle through their own negative behaviors, codependency, and shaming comments which always perpetuate the problem. Let's not succumb by falling into this trap.

The most important thing for us to recognize is that we are contributing to the problem if we rescue him. In order to contribute to his sobriety and ultimate recovery, we can become more mindful of our behaviors.

One of the questions I get asked the most by family members is, "What can I do? I have tried all of your suggestions and nothing, I mean nothing, is working. What else can I do?" There is a solution for you even if your addicted loved one is dancing with death and never plans to change. How do you accept the things you cannot change?

Seven Steps to Surrender

What do we do if all of our attempts to influence the right way just don't work? The truth is, some addicted people are simply not going to respond to our efforts, and that is okay. In these situations, we practice the liberating art of *surrender*. Detachment from the outcome is not an easy process; however, we must learn how to surrender in order for us to "Get off the Beach" and enjoy our lives while allowing our loved one's their own journey—for good and bad.

At Brick House Recovery, we work to inspire addicted individuals and motivate them to move through the Stages of Change, but some people down-right won't budge. If I'm being honest, this can be maddening at times. Why won't they accept the help? Why can't they just buy into the solution? What is their deal? Clearly, sometimes I lack empathy and forget what it was like to walk in their shoes.

The frustrating part about trying to influence another human being is that we know their potential, but they don't. We can often see the path to their happiness and abundance, and we desperately want them to achieve greatness. If only they would take our lead. Am I right? Yet, the reality is that we cannot treat people like puppets and expect them to do what we want. We are powerless. Our efforts feel seemingly futile. We cannot control their behaviors or their timelines for sobriety, just like we cannot stop a natural disaster from happening.

When we place certain expectations on the outcome and attach emotionally to the expectation, we set ourselves up to be disturbed. Their success or failure is *not* a reflection on our effectiveness as parents, spouses, or family members. When we are more invested in another person's change than they are, this is a sign that we need to turn our efforts inward to tending our own needs. Melody Beattie, best-selling author of *Codependent No More: How to Stop Controlling Others and Start Caring for Yourself*, said, "Furthermore, worrying about people and problems doesn't help. It doesn't solve problems, it doesn't help other people, and it doesn't help us. It is wasted energy." So, how in the heck are we supposed to stop worrying when it's our child or spouse who is suffering?

Over the years, I have learned an incredibly important truth: when I get disturbed by my client's lack of progress through the Stages of Change, my client is not responsible; I am.

My gifted therapist, Laura M. Brotherson, helped me recognize the detriment of setting unreasonable expectations on other people, especially when they continuously fail to meet them. When we carefully craft a certain set of expectations on other people, which they don't live up to, we remain unsettled, frustrated, and resentful. Unreasonable expectations placed on other people can easily become pre-meditated resentments. So why not give up the expectations, turn to caring for yourself, and skip the resentment?

Surrender put into practice liberates us from fear and emotional battle fields. With Laura's permission, I share her approach and my insights to surrender. I use them in my life and it really works.

1. Figure out where we have control and where we don't.

Recognize that most of the stuff we worry about and seek to control is really outside of our control. Do we have control over his using? Can we control an overdose? Can we control his choices? Can we control his behaviors? Do we have control over death? These are all outside of our control: we are powerless over people, places, and things. Recognize where you end, and others begin.

Make a list of what you do and don't have control over.

_____

_____

_____

_____

_____

_____

_____

_____

2. Make friends with our worst fear and the worst-case scenario. Know that we'll be okay no matter what.

What's our scariest fear that keeps us up at night? What happens if he doesn't change his life and get sober? Are we afraid of divorce, jail, overdose, or death? Or worse, are we afraid that he will needlessly suffer with this disease for twenty more years? Are we afraid his credit score will drop? Are we afraid he will lose his job and can't provide for the kids and spouse? What is our worst fearful scenario? Write it down. Now that we have clarified it, if that were to actually happen, we must honestly ask ourselves if we can still carry on. Can we survive, even though it will be extremely painful and sad? Would we let this destroy us, or would we choose to do the work to transcend and heal from this? Can we be okay no matter what? I'm here to tell you YES!

One friend of mine, a mother of an addicted adult son, told me that her worst fear was that her son would die from an overdose. "I spent a full day imagining everything that would happen if I got the call that my son had died. Where his funeral would be held. What our family would say and even songs that would be sung. I wept and wept as if I had lost him. And then I wiped away my tears at the end of the day of surrender and I was surprisingly . . . okay. I would live through the Worst Thing. I had done all I could do to let my son know I loved him and was here when he was ready to get into treatment. Beyond that, I was at peace. If he died, I would be okay. Love was eternal. My love would go with him, and his with me, no matter what happened to his physical body. He'd either find peace in heaven or peace in sobriety. The end of his addiction story was up to God, not me. Amazingly, God saved my son from addiction. He went into a drug induced paranoid psychosis and, in a standoff involving a SWAT team, he was saved from himself and jailed. Eventually he was sent to a mental hospital where he is getting the exact help he needs."

Write out your worst fear and worst-case scenario.

_____

_____

_____

_____

_____

_____

_____

_____

3. Let go of your attachment to a specific outcome.

Our desired outcome for anyone chained by addiction is to witness them become happy, joyous, and free, right? But what if they never get sober? It is time that we let go of our attachment to a specific desired outcome. Can we let go of the outcome? Can we turn it all over to God and accept the things we cannot change? In this step, strive to let go of any and all outcomes.

Write out the outcome you want to let go of.

_____

_____

_____

_____

_____

_____

_____

_____

_____

4. Become willing to grieve the loss in order to let go of needing a certain outcome.

"Letting go" will undoubtedly bring some emotions to the surface, sooner or later. Maybe we have already started the process of grieving the child, or spouse, or friend you once knew before the addiction took over. Maybe we are still angry, or afraid to let go. I validate the struggle it is to truly grieve the loss of a loved one. One of my favorite therapists told me that we must "feel it, to heal it." Take the time to grieve and honor the sadness, pain, depression, loneliness, and loss in order to really let go of a certain outcome, like my friend did about her son's funeral mentioned earlier in this section.

As you become willing to grieve the loss of that outcome, what feelings are coming up for you?

_____

_____

_____

_____

_____

_____

_____

_____

5. Let go and trust a higher power. There is a better plan for our lives—and our addicted loved one's life!

Now it's time to let go and trust our higher power. This is where we detach from our fears, resentments, and the outcome. Let's experiment with this each morning and see what happens as we trust this process.

What does it mean to you to trust that there is a better plan for you and your addicted loved one's lives?

_____

_____

_____

_____

_____

_____

_____

_____

6. Absolutely BELIEVE in our desired outcome—just LET GO of attachment to it.

Just because we made friends with our worst fear and worst-case scenario does not mean we won't hold onto hope. Now is the time to grab hold of hope and believe that eventually, our addicted loved one will recover. I see miracle after miracle in my work with the addicted population, and I can tell you that people recover all the time. Now that you are contributing toward his recovery, his chances will skyrocket. Try focusing on the positive because what we focus on expands.

What are some positives in your situation that can and will give you hope for a brighter future?

_____

_____

_____

_____

_____

_____

_____

7. Finally, actually surrender the situation with a prayer or expression in writing.

Feel free to use your own words or method. For example:

Dear God,

I humbly acknowledge my utter powerlessness over_____ (name of addicted loved one) and my feelings of _____ (hopelessness, confusion, anger, etc.).

I surrender _____ (name of addicted loved one) to Thee and let them go to you.

I am choosing to forgive myself because I know I'm doing the best I can even with my powerlessness and my human imperfection.

Dear God, please do for me what I do not have the power to do for myself . . . according to Thy will. Amen

This level of surrender will help us begin to interact with our addicted loved ones with empathy, understanding, acceptance, and tolerance. This process really does work. Sometimes I have to do it over and over before I feel peace, freedom, and serenity about a client or a friend who is caught in addiction's grasp. If prayer is not your thing, say these words to yourself and remove any words you want. The whole point is to admit that you can't control the situation or the person, but our loving Creator can and will.

How will this practice of surrender help you contribute the right way going forward?

_____

_____

_____

_____

_____

_____

_____

_____

1. "Although relapse is never desirable, our view is that change is often circular and difficult. The spiral cycle of change shows how contemplation, preparation, and action usually follow relapse. Relapsers most often take one step backward in order to take two steps forward."

2. Most often, recycling will resolve a person's ambivalence about sobriety, moving them through the stages toward Action.

3. Remember to "dance, don't wrestle." Roll with the resistance.

4. Relapsers test the waters because they desperately want to feel the old benefits again.

5. Most often, recycling through the Stages of Change will ultimately resolve a person's ambivalence about sobriety.

6. We cannot **Control** his addiction.

7. We cannot **Cure** his addiction.

8. We did not **Cause** his addiction.

9. Family members often **Contribute** to the problem when we recycle through our own negative behaviors, codependency, and shaming comments, which always perpetuate the problem.

10. If we rescue, we are contributing to the problem.

11. Unreasonable expectations placed on other people are pre-meditated resentments.

12. Detachment from the outcome is not an easy process; however, we must learn how to surrender in order for us

to "Get off the Beach" and enjoy our lives while allowing our loved one's their own journey—for good and bad.

13. When we carefully craft a certain set of expectations on other people which they don't live up to, we remain unsettled, frustrated, and resentful.

14. Surrender put into practice liberates us from fear and emotional battle fields.

15. Remember the Seven Steps to Surrender.

Chapter 10

THE JUMPING OFF POINT

IT WAS A BLUE-BIRD CHIRPING, early spring morning in March. The white caps were beginning to melt off of the Wasatch Mountain peaks into the canyons below. I shivered in the biting spring wind as I waited on the cold stone bench outside the hospital where I had detoxed off of all the drugs and alcohol in my system for four long days. Medical detox was mandatory before entering residential rehab. I closed my eyes and let the sun reflect off my pale cheeks as I took a few deep breaths. For those four days in detox I rested in the hospital bed while they monitored my vitals, managed my detox medications, and fed me three meals a day. For anyone who hasn't experienced withdrawals from alcohol and drugs, try to imagine having the worst flu in the world and then magnify it by ten. Mentally and physically, it feels like torture. Medically detoxing in a hospital setting decreased the discomfort significantly, although withdrawals are agonizing regardless.

Minutes later, a white fifteen-passenger van with rusted rims pulled up to the patient pick-up area. A tall, slender man wearing a gray athletic shirt stepped out of the van. He enthusiastically stuck out his hand to shake mine.

"You must be Jason." He had a big, cheesy smile on his face.

"Yeah," I replied with feigned arrogance.

"My name is 'Shakes.' I'm your ride to The Ranch."

"Okay, let's get out of here!" I barked. "I can't stand hospitals."

I put out my cigarette on the stone bench and flipped the butt across the lawn, expecting someone else to pick it up later.

For the next forty-five minutes in the van, I listened to Shakes tell me about his journey with alcohol, and his experience as a client in treatment eight years prior. He'd earned his nickname from shaking violently when coming down from alcohol withdrawals. We were headed to a residential center affectionately termed "The Ranch." I didn't know much about the place and frankly didn't care. My memory of surrender with Dave Pinegar less than a week prior was short lived. All I knew was that Dave got sober there and it worked for him, although I truthfully believed it wouldn't work for me.

Finally, we pulled into a long driveway lined with white vinyl fencing. Out in the pasture, I saw a beautiful brown horse and two alpacas. All three of the animals stopped and stared at me as if they could read my mind. It kind of freaked me out, like when cops stopped and stared because they knew I was high or doing something else illegal. I quickly looked away and paid attention to the house looming overhead.

Over the last three years, I had been through four rehabs, so I knew what I was walking into—at least that's what I thought. Still, my anxiety rose even as I tried to sling my bag nonchalantly over my shoulder to walk up the steps, approaching the white front door of an older, three-story tan-colored mansion. It boasted six thin white columns from roof to ground; its porticos and porches making it look more like a plantation in Louisiana than a rehab in the west.

Before I even approached the bright white front door, it swung open and a man in his mid-twenties welcomed me with a hug. Stepping back quickly, I thought that was weird. *Really weird.* Then he laughed at my stiff response.

"Here at The Ranch," the man chuckled, "we are all about hugs, not drugs. My name is Justin, and I'm your roommate. Come in and I'll show you around." I left my bag at the door so that Shakes could search it for drugs, weapons, or any other contraband. Over the next few hours, I quickly assessed that this place was *different*.

I was uncomfortable right away. This rehab was not for me. In fact, it felt appalling on several levels. There were solid expectations, a serious structure, a strict schedule, and defined rules. In order to stay, I had no choice. I had to follow the rules.

I hated rules.

According to Justin, rules not only created a safe environment, but they had therapeutic value. *Ugh!* How I hated therapeutic value.

While lost in my negative musings, a woman with a smile that lit up the room walked into the area. Justin made a brief introduction. "Jason, this is Kris and she will be your counselor." Kris was a strongly-built woman with long, brown hair and exceptionally beautiful, candid eyes. I had a hard time looking into those eyes; they were so honest and real.

"Welcome!" she said with a smile. "Dave Pinegar mentioned you were coming. I look forward to working with you." After some small talk, she offered me a hug and then slowly made her way back to her office.

I guess everybody hugs each other around here.

Justin continued the orientation by explaining the program expectations. "Rules create a foundation of honesty, accountability, and punctuality, which will all eventually lead to self-love and self-respect." Sensing my resistance, Justin added, "Rules develop a willingness and open-mindedness, which are required for us to recover."

Self-love and self-respect were just words to me. *Get me through this so I can get out.* Any kind of authority and rules hanging over my head were an added nuisance to my body's lingering symptoms of detoxing, and my mental aversion to authority.

I had an almost allergic response to authority and rules. I ignored structure. The hard life of addiction bore no resemblance to that of a responsible member of society. In the justice "system," I was used to being punished for being late, absent, flakey, unreliable, manipulative, dishonest, entitled, and terminally unique.

I was numb to it all.

In my mind, I was "special." I felt the rules didn't apply to me. "Terminally unique" is a common mindset in addiction, even when we are desperate for help. We can still be wildly narcissistic on many levels.

My addict life only consisted of promises I couldn't keep and excuses I couldn't justify, although I sure tried. Clocks existed for *everyone else*. Time and commitments had become irrelevant to me in the day-to-day scheme of things.

I complained about the smallest irritants, like most other childish adults. Addicted loved ones often get stuck in the emotional age at which they began using. In fact, I am quite sure whining could be heard through rehab hallways in every town, city, and state—at least in the ones I'd attended. I certainly complained about everything, including being asked to do my own laundry, wash my own dishes, and sweep up after myself. It's just the way we cope in the beginning.

From what I had seen of other addicted people and myself, resistance was our knee-jerk reaction to almost anything that was good for us. I made a game of choosing which rules I would and would not follow. I was now thirty-one years old, not a child, but stuck in a childish mindset. Boundaries, in my opinion, were to be breached. Therefore, I immediately had a problem at The Ranch. I put up my walls and my dukes and couldn't wait to prove myself in front of the group.

I became even more resistant as soon as I entered The Ranch's kitchen. Justin was ticking off rules on his fingers and showing the signs posted on the kitchen wall. I wasn't paying attention. I could smell bacon frying; my stomach was suddenly alert with hunger pains; I had not eaten a solid meal and hadn't had much of an appetite for several months in a row now. After detoxing, however, my body was crying out for food.

In the center of the kitchen rose a large island with a laminate countertop. Attached to it were several swinging barstools. I made note of the kitchen's lay out, as I was already planning how I might pilfer in the night like I used to do at my first rehab years before. Off to the left there was another entrance, this one leading into a large dining room. It had two long dining tables. In the opposite direction off to the right was a line of food pantries and cupboards. They were all closed, and my criminal mind noticed there were no locks on them.

Just then my roommate burst my bubble.

"Clients are not allowed in the fridge or cupboards without staff permission," he said bluntly. Had he been watching my eyes and reading my mind, too?

"What? No way! What if I get hungry and I want snacks? I *paid* for them, right?" I growled. He ignored me.

Whatever.

I was so irritated and hungry; I paid very meager attention to Justin while he gave me a rundown of the meal schedule. I would be assigned duties and chores. As the low-man-on-the-totem-pole, I (like every newbie) was assigned to kitchen labor. I was to show up fifteen minutes before and after every meal, staying until all the dishes were done. Washing dishes was the worst chore because it took longer while everyone else got to hangout and chill until the next group therapy session started. I certainly didn't like it.

Here we go again.

I knew the song and dance. All I had to do was to breeze right in and do whatever I wanted, where and how I wanted it. I just had to be sneaky. I looked around, beginning to feel I could make myself at home. This was a men-only facility, which was probably good. But I would have to establish the new pecking order. I would have to make sure people respected me right out of the gate.

Justin sat down in the dining room and read through the stupid "House Rules" which I was to read over and sign:

- Wake up at 6:00 a.m.
- Make your bed by 6:05 a.m.
- Open your bedroom blinds every morning.
- Walk one mile around the track by 6:30 a.m.
- Shower, brush your teeth, put on deodorant, and dress appropriately by 7:00 a.m.
- Be on time to all groups, meals, and scheduled activities.
- Complete all assignments on time.
- Do not leave personal items in common areas.
- Rooms must be tidy and clean at all times.
- Stay in groups of three.
- Naps are not allowed.

Whatever.

Suddenly the men in the other room got out of a group session (or what we simply call "group") and came through the kitchen where the lunch crew was already at work. Each man stopped, introduced himself to me, and gave me a hug. Not one walked by without it. That made me immediately uncomfortable.

I don't fit in or belong here. These guys don't get it. I'm a hardened criminal. I've been in jail. I've lived on the streets in the bitter cold. These guys are soft. They haven't experienced hard-core addiction like I have. My "specialness" was asserting itself.

I didn't speak my thoughts aloud. Addicted people have an egotistical code of respect—if you could call it that—where we try to "one up" each other about how bad it got, levels of intoxication, drug usage, times overdosed, how much time incarcerated, and the number of rehabs we'd chewed up and spit out—almost like a sickening badge of honor.

During my first day I broke over a dozen rules.

The next morning, I decided to sleep in. I felt I deserved it. Then I took my time getting ready, went downstairs, and opened up the cupboards for a bite to eat without permission. I didn't think twice—didn't even blink. Next, I strutted into the meeting room, extremely late, for morning group therapy. All seven pairs of eyes stared at me, but I ignored them as I smugly plopped into the metal chair and relaxed casually, studying the floor. I noticed there was no counselor facilitating the group, but that all the guys had been fully engaged in a productive discussion. They had pens and notebooks in hand—with actual notes written down.

There was a long, long silence as they stared at me.

"What?" I snapped.

"Dude, you're late," one of the guys remarked. Then another guy, Russ, expressed his frustration that I skipped out on the morning walk around the track. For some reason, this apparently bothered him.

I glared back at him. *How dare he speak to me like that?* Everyone was waiting for me to respond. I didn't let them down.

"Why don't you worry about your own 'f'-ing program, okay? I'll worry about mine!" I snarled. I rattled off a bunch more expletives with the expressed intent of intimidating everyone in the room. They needed to know not to mess with me and stay off my back. I had clearly slipped back into Precontemplation in the obedience department.

This tough guy act, using anger and intimidation had worked for years on the streets, jails, and at every rehab I had ever attended. Intimidate first, set boundaries with people next so they knew their place with me, and all would be well, as long as they left me alone.

Only this time, my act backfired.

Well, let's just say that it didn't go the way I expected. For the next hour, the men in the group worked me over and broke me down. They called me on every rule broken, every entitled action, and every manipulative comment I had made since the moment I arrived. They were trying to help me see the blind spots in my character that I was oblivious to.

"What? You guys got nothing better to do but follow me around taking notes on all my mistakes?"

I sat back in my chair and crossed my arms, pretending not to care what they thought.

I was lying to myself. I did care. I had always cared about what other people thought of me. However, I would not show them my weakness. I had to keep up my "don't mess with me!" reputation.

Surprisingly to me, those men and The Ranch staff could see through my façade. They could see beyond my disease and my ego. What I didn't know yet was that underneath they could see the good in me—the hurting boy inside.

The Ranch Brothers, as they affectionately called themselves, were tough men; streetwise and experienced. They had to be tough and wise, or they would have been dead by now. It shocked me to see how motivated and serious they were about their sobriety. I wasn't used to that. I looked up into the faces of these men. Something was so different here. I was used to rehabs where everyone was court-ordered to be there and their only motivation was to get the stamp of approval for their judge or probation officer. These dudes were actually serious about treatment and recovery. These guys were "street smarter" than the men I was used to being around on the streets, and yet these men wanted lasting change. They seemed to be a group of a higher caliber seeking emotional sobriety.

Even so, I knew I was smarter. I just had to up my game. I used every angle, con, and defense.

First, I got hostile. When that didn't work, I went apathetic. Then I minimized. Then I manipulated. Intimidated. Invoked false emotion. I shucked. Jived. Justified. Diverted. Distracted. Dodged.

Addicted people depend on manipulation. But it didn't work. Not here. Not with the Ranch Brothers.

"Why are you here, Jason?" one of the men asked me. Sam was a Native American, with a bright countenance and an easy smile. He was clearly the leader of the group. But he wasn't smiling right then. "Why are you really here?"

"I want to get sober, man," I said, mustering as much sincerity as I could. I'd tell them what they wanted to hear.

"Well, your behavior doesn't show it. You're breaking rules right and left, and that shows us that you don't really care about taking this seriously."

You can't con a con, and this group wasn't buying my schtick. Apparently, I didn't have the right to threaten their chance for sobriety. They stood for something I hadn't experienced in previous treatment programs: Honesty. Integrity. Empathy. Boundaries. Acceptance. They stood for each other. And they stood for recovery. What they wouldn't stand for was my nonsense. They would either get through to me or vote me off the island.

So what? Who cares? They were pushing all my buttons.

With experienced wisdom, they could tell I was full of myself. Their responses shed a light on my ambivalence and lack of commitment to myself and to the program. On one hand, I wasn't sure why I was trying to get sober because it never worked before. On the other hand, I made a commitment to Nathan that I intended to keep. But I wasn't going to share that with a bunch of strangers I didn't trust or know. No way! The streets had taught me to shut down and to shut up and to keep my protection up.

One by one, the men called me out. No matter what ego-defense mechanism I put out there, each fellow "brother" saw right through it and called it out. They knew I was full of myself, and yet, they continued to chip away at my pride. I felt attacked, yet I also felt a sense of empathy. It was weird to me. They brutally told me the honest truth while at the same time expressing genuine, positive regard for my well-being. It was a new approach I had never experienced in other rehabs. In my first rehab, I experimented with expressing my self-worth issues in group. Sadly, it was received with laughter and mocking. Instantly, I believed rehab was not a safe place to share feelings.

Although here, I felt like they were trying to help me. Either way I wasn't about to share my feelings with them. I became more and more frustrated, and my responses became more belligerent, meant to intimidate. This had worked at other programs to get people off my back.

But these guys had on their emotional raincoats and were fully prepared to show me tough love. It was shocking to me how committed they were to helping me on my first day, getting through to the real me.

Russ, a fellow bald man, sat up in his chair. "Dude, I love you brother, but I hate your ego! Get with the program, man," he ordered, "or go pack your bags and leave!" He was speaking directly to my ego, seeking to free the tender little boy inside who desperately needed to break through and breathe some oxygen. But my ego was stronger; it had smothered the "real me" for many years.

The addict voice persisted strongly in my head. "You don't need this! These guys hate you, Jason. You are better off trying to get sober on your own. Let's get high one last time. Then you can get sober tomorrow. Let's get out of here!"

"Fine. I'm outta' here!"

Furious and confused, I stormed out of the group room, climbed the stairs to my room, and started cramming my stuff into my duffel bag. *I don't need these punks telling me what to do! Who do they think they are? I don't have to take this!*

The battle for my soul was in full swing and I was at the jumping off point. I was about a week off of drugs and alcohol, but my disease was fighting relentlessly. A familiar feeling of impending doom gathered like a dark cloud in my head. All I needed was to get high—to make these feelings all go away, even just for a few minutes. This was my parents' greatest fear—that I would leave treatment.

On the other hand, I also wanted, more than anything in the world, to get sober, once and for all. I had fought so hard to get to this point. I'd been given one last opportunity to change for my son Nathan. To change because I wanted to.

I set my duffle bag on the bed and tried to keep a tear from falling down my face. If I left treatment, I would go straight back to the streets within minutes. The realization hit me. I would soon lose my mind again, and I would be dead. I knew if I left, I would not survive one more relapse. It would all be over, and I would have failed Nathan.

My life was at a fork in the proverbial road.

Would I once again get defeated by my addiction—my ultimate enemy? Or would I stay this time? Would I at least try something different? Would I give the program a chance and really surrender for once? Although I didn't have the language for it at the time, I was recycling between stages of change quickly and the ambivalence was escalating.

I was embroiled in an intense inner emotional conflict.

If I left, I had nowhere to go. My family made it clear that they would not bail me out—not even one more time—and not ever again. The truth was, I had burnt every bridge and destroyed every relationship. I had nothing left. I was totally alone. This was due to my family setting up strong fences, letting go of the outcome, and practicing empathy from a distance. Because of my family's own recovery work, I was left with only two options: leave The Ranch and lose everything or stay and see what happened.

I was tired. Exhausted. Too tired to even pack my stuff. Too tired to play the game.

I sat on the bed, my body tense with fury and conflict, adrenaline pumping through my veins, and yet I was completely exhausted: physically, mentally, and emotionally. I felt it in my bones—the penetrating exhaustion from fighting with the addict voice every single day, nearly every single moment. The raging battle was taking its toll. I laid back and when my head hit the pillow, I let out a deep exhale. It was as if I was raising a white flag of surrender from the depths of my soul. In seconds, it felt like a warm blanket covered me and instantly I fell asleep as if I were under a divine spell.

A couple hours later, I was startled to hear the sound of the squeaky door swinging open.

"Hey Jason. You okay?" my roommate Justin asked.

Confused and groggy, I sat up on the edge of the bed and with soft eyes stared at my half-packed bag on the floor.

"I'm okay."

"Are you really leaving The Ranch?" Justin asked.

"I was . . . uhhhh . . . I am . . . I don't know. I got nowhere to go."

"Well, I hope you stay. All the guys hope you stay," he said quietly, then turned and left the room.

They do? Why would they want me to stay?

The addict voice interrupted, "Because they need a whipping boy to pick on. You don't need them!"

What am I going to do? I need to talk to someone. I decided to get up and walk down the back stairs to my counselor's office in order to avoid the guys. I timidly knocked on the door.

"Come in," Kris called out.

I opened the door a few inches, just enough to see Kris sitting behind her desk. It was covered with picture frames, angel statues, and small gifts sent to her from former clients. A calming smell of flowers and candles wafted through the crack in the door.

"Do you have a few minutes to talk?" I asked, feeling my vulnerability.

"Of course, Jason. Come in and have a seat."

Her voice was welcoming, soft, and soothing. Her eyes were kind.

Kris' office felt like a fairytale dream. Her little electric foot heater created a feeling of comfort—warm and inviting. I sat down in a brown leather chair across from her desk. She waited patiently for me to speak. For the longest time there was silence. I couldn't conjure up the words. Tears welled up in my eyes and began rolling down my cheeks. For the first time in a long, long time, the tears were actually real. I felt emotionally raw and helpless.

Finally, I looked into Kris' eyes. She could sense my intense ambivalence and especially the merciless internal conflict between my spirit and my mental illness. She continued to wait with a look of genuine compassion and empathy until, finally, she spoke.

"Sweetie, I can tell that you're struggling." She said it so softly and gently I had to strain to hear. And I actually wanted to hear her. "It's okay to feel what you're feeling," she continued. "In fact, it is essential to your recovery. You have to feel it to heal it."

You have to feel it to heal it?

I'd heard the guys say this a few times already. It sounded saccharine-sweet. It hadn't meant anything. Now, all of a sudden, it meant everything.

"Kris, I don't know what to do!" My voice shook. "I want to leave so badly. I can't stay in this house with these men for two long months. I just want to leave and get high. I want relief." I paused and put my head in my hands. "But I can't go back to the streets. I can't. I can't go back. I WILL DIE."

I suddenly knew, without a doubt, that this was the truth. I had failed for so long at everything. I thought of my little boy, Nathan, and how I had made a commitment to him to be a good role model in his life, even if I would not be the one to raise him. But I didn't know how to become his hero. I was sick and tired of being sick and tired. This program was the last olive branch my folks were giving me. If this program didn't work, I was on my own, and that meant the streets, prison, or death. I knew in my heart this had to work, or it would be over.

"I'm so lost," I pleaded, the tears making my shirt wet. "I don't know what to do. What do I do?"

There was a heavy silence in the room and I realized I had just bared my soul more deeply than I had to another human being in over a decade. Suddenly Kris' face turned to one of determination, as if she knew this was the moment of truth.

"Jason," she said firmly, holding my eyes in the grip of compassion. "What are you *willing* to do for your sobriety?" I didn't even hesitate. Not for a moment.

"Anything!" I cried passionately. "I will do anything!"

As the words came out of my mouth, I felt a rush of adrenaline from head to toe. The hair on the back of my neck stood up and I felt goose bumps. Something was going on here.

"Are you willing to go to any lengths for your recovery?"

"Yes!" I declared. For the first time in my addiction, I actually meant it.

"Okay then," she said firmly. "If you are going to stay here, then you *must* follow the rules. Just stop fighting them and see what happens."

I stared blankly at her. Then I began thinking about the entitled attitude I had brought in with me. She sat quietly watching me "get it." There was another long, uncomfortable silence. I got it.

"Jason," she said, "I'm serious. There are two things you have to do if you are going to stay. One, follow the rules—every last one of them; even the little petty ones. Two, I want you to make amends with your Ranch Brothers. Tell them what you told me—that you are willing to try. Ask them for their help and support, and that you cannot do this alone. Are you willing to do that?"

"Yes," I reluctantly committed, but my heart sunk. I was going to have to face the group. Not them! Not the Ranch Brothers. The addict voice, that enemy inside me, yelled in my head that said that I had to run rather than face those men.

Kris quietly stood up, walked around her desk, and put her arms around me. She gave me a true and loving mama-bear hug. I had not felt something like that in ages, even from my own mother. I hadn't allowed it. But as she held me, I felt safe. This was the boon I needed to fight the real enemy: my addiction.

For the next three hours, however, I hid in my room, thinking of what I would say to the group. Years of not taking accountability had taken its toll. My anxiety rose every time I thought about what I would say and how I would say it. I alternated between tears and more anger.

I was so afraid to face them.

Yet here I was, desperately out of options, and I knew it. I had hit rock bottom. It came down to this one choice. I had to face those men or I would soon be dead out on the streets.

A new feeling permeated every cell in my being. It was surrender. Not hollow surrender, but real surrender. I thought about each man in the group in a different kind of way. They hadn't spoken a word to me that wasn't true. They were just so committed to me that they wouldn't stand for my lies and ego. And I suddenly realized . . . this was unconditional love.

The gift of desperation inspired renewed commitment within me, and a genuine willingness to face my fears. The key to lasting change was about making daily progress, not reaching perfection. Kris and my Ranch Brothers embodied the principles of collaborative confrontation, rolling with my resistance, reinforcing boundaries, and supporting self-efficacy.

This gift, this desperation, combined with my family's healthy contributions beforehand; the inner promises made to Nathan; the honesty of these men, natural consequences if I broke the rules; and Kris' unconditional love, non-judgment, and honoring my ambivalence, were the ingredients to the elixir that could *finally* set me free.

But little did I know, I was about to face my biggest barrier of all.

Making a Spiritual Connection

Who says I have to find a Higher Power to stay sober? What do they know?

People at The Ranch had been telling me that if I didn't find a spiritual path, or a connection with a Higher Power, then I would not succeed in recovery. This presented a serious problem for me. I had grown up in a strong religious family and had some spiritual experiences in Brazil, but I had written off any desire to revisit that life long ago. Period. By the time I arrived at The Ranch, I had conceded to the belief that I was never going to heaven, and even if I did make it through the Pearly Gates after I died, I wouldn't feel comfortable there anyway. Not with *those* people. You know, the perfect ones.

I was cynical and skeptical. How many times had I asked God to make my life better? My life had only gotten worse. How many times had I bargained with God to pull me out of the hell in which I was living? How many times would I allow myself to be let down?

My bargains with God always entailed some kind of barter. "If you do this for me, I'll stop drinking . . . drugging . . . stealing . . ." Well, that never seemed to work, either. I had even tried going back to church. I felt colossally uncomfortable there. Not only did my cigarette smoke-infused clothes, skin, and breath not fit in; I felt like *I* didn't fit in. I had a hard time seeing my part in the larger picture of anything. Therefore, it had been much easier to blame God for my failures.

About three weeks into my sobriety at The Ranch, the thought of connecting to a "Higher Power as I understood Him," was a seemingly impossible order. It presented a series of critical problems and caused me to further doubt the likelihood of staying sober. If my sobriety was contingent upon my relationship with a Higher Power, I just felt I was destined for another failure.

And what if I did find some kind of spiritual connection? The addict voice in my head screamed that there was no way God would forgive me after the things I had done and all the wrongs I had committed. For the first time in a while, all this "spiritual talk" prompted the old loud and menacing addict voice in my head again. It nearly convinced me that I was doomed.

What am I going to do? I paced The Ranch halls restlessly. I went outside to whisper to Mikayla, the gentle-eyed horse. I mopped the floors furiously, swept porch stairs, and took walks with intense vigor.

It was ironic to me that I had landed in a "faith-based" treatment facility, where the topic of a "Higher Power" was not only encouraged and taught, but actually *explored*. State-based and other mental health programs and facilities had encouraged the spiritual connection as supported by the Substance Abuse and Mental Health Services Administration, but they didn't really explore it. I felt a dark cloud settle over me, remembering how I had wrestled with this topic for the last several years as I'd gone in and out of treatment.

So instead of contemplating or trying to reach out to a God who seemed detached and unhelpful, I had tried to stay sober on my own. I'd made hundreds of promises to myself, to my family, to my employers, and to my ex-wife. Over and over, I had failed. I had enthusiastically written plans of attack and lists of goals to help myself accomplish sobriety. I had failed. And, despite the extra support of legal consequences, judges, and a probation officer, I still experienced epic disappointment.

Somewhere deep inside, I realized that the honest truth for me was that without some help from a Higher Power, I could not stay sober. Period. On my own, I knew I would fail again. But how could I trust someone who had let me down again and again?

I was stuck. And I was freakin' ticked off about it.

One Tuesday during afternoon group, it just so happened that the topic was Step Two. It states, "Came to believe that a Power greater than ourselves could restore us to sanity." I went back to an old argument of mine.

I don't trust a Higher Power. And I'm not insane! Am I?

Then someone in the room repeated the quote that "The definition of insanity is doing the same thing over and over again, expecting a different result." Sure, I had heard different versions of that saying before, but this time it inspired a deep question within myself: "Could it be that my spiritual hang up is because I'm holding onto the same old beliefs about God, but expecting the outcome to be different?"

I paused to contemplate that perhaps I *was* insane by that description. So I needed to find a Power to help me with my insanity. Not only did I have a "thinking problem," I was sick in mind, body, and spirit. Unless I treated each of these areas, I would not achieve the lasting recovery and abundance I so desired.

Kris, the counselor, was extremely sensitive to the fact that the topic of God was a barrier for most of us men at The Ranch. Kris knew most of us were not active in spirituality; instead, we had only been active in our addictions. Our god had been our drug of choice, and that god was cruel and relentlessly powerful.

Somehow Kris knew how to guide us through the spiritual weeds. She gently offered a few suggestions on where to begin again with the whole Higher Power dilemma. First, she created an environment of transparency, laying it all out on the table.

"Let's start from scratch," she encouraged, carefully eyeing every man in the room. Some, like me, were squirming a little. "Let's set aside all of our pre-conceived beliefs, experiences, and prejudices—just for a little experiment. Let's just wipe the slate and our brains clean from everything we've ever been taught about a Higher Power . . . just for now."

Kris then instructed us to pull out a sheet of paper and begin to create our own description of our "Ideal" Higher Power.

"Start by writing down a list of personality traits, attributes, and characteristics you would wish for in a Higher Power. Whatever you do, make it personal to each one of you. Don't copy off your neighbor," she said, eyeing me as I leaned over my neighbor's shoulder a little. "I encourage you to really explore this," she said, emphasizing the word, "explore." "And only write down traits that mean something to YOU."

I shrugged. *Personality traits of a God that would mean something to me.* It sounded trite, but I took the suggestion. I put pen to paper, and actually began writing an honest list.

My Ideal Higher Power:
- Likes to snow ski, play the guitar, enjoy the mountains
- Has a sense of humor
- Will still listen if I call him "Bro," "Dude," or "Man" instead of "Thee" and "Thou"
- Understands me and the pain of addiction
- Always listens
- Is forgiving of my past
- Is tolerant and patient with me
- Is accessible
- Loves me unconditionally, with no strings attached

My list was short and sweet. Kris called on me to share it out loud to the group. Reluctantly, I read my list. At the end, Kris asked, "Jason, is this a Power you could begin to believe in? One you can trust?"

"Yes, I can, actually," I said with a grin, "because this guy is more like a cool friend than someone who is disappointed in me and judging me and damning me all the time."

"Good. Why don't you start here," Kris suggested, "and see if you can build a new relationship with *this* Higher Power."

I could try that. It was my last-ditch effort to stay sober. What did I have to lose?

"First, however," Kris continued, "for those of you who have resentments and anger toward God, I want you to know that you can express all of your feelings to Him. He is a Big Boy and can handle it," she said with a smile.

I sat in stunned amazement. I had to think about her challenge for a minute, and then suddenly it made sense. What she was asking me to do was to pray to my Ideal Higher Power and be rigorously honest with Him about my resentments towards Him. It sounded like an oxymoron, but in its own weird way, it made total sense.

Late that afternoon, I found some time before dinner to write out my prayer on paper. Tiptoeing so as not to be heard or interrupted, I snuck down the back stairs to be alone in the basement, behind closed doors, so that I could offer up a real, honest prayer, based on what I had explored that day.

I slowly got down on my knees on the hard floor. Then I let Him have it.

My angry prayer was real and raw, filled with hostile emotions, and laced with colorful expletives. I pointed my finger to Heaven, blaming God for my addiction.

"I don't deserve this addiction!" I whispered fiercely. "I damn well don't deserve this disease! It's your fault! You're the reason I had to get divorced. You tore apart my family because you didn't fix me! And then you robbed me of the opportunity to be a father to my son, Nathan! How could you? How dare you!"

Unexpectedly, in that moment, in that basement room, Nathan's little face came to my mind. A tremor ran through my body as I remembered the tenderness with which I held that miraculous little being. He held onto my finger so tightly, and he had never let go of my heart.

I instantly became aware of my unconditional love for that child. There was absolutely nothing that he could do that would stop me from loving him. Nothing. My love for Nathan was not contingent upon his behavior or any conditions. A father's *true* love was unconditional. Pure. Eternal. Sacred.

All at once, I felt an extraordinary rush of warm energy . . . and Light. Pure light and peace enveloped me. It literally permeated every part of my body, but unlike drugs, it blanketed my soul with a soft and tender essence.

I felt it! I could not deny it. My angry prayer had actually been *heard*.

I was astounded. My New Friend was listening, communicating, understanding . . . and still loving me despite my terrible language and informal prayer. I'd had a taste of this with my Ranch Brothers when they accepted me after seeing my ugly side, but *this!* This Higher Power knew everything—everything about me. He knew my deceits, my lies, and my sins; he knew I had been beyond angry with Him and yet, He still loved me.

Tears began pouring down my cheeks, and like a child, I let them go. I cried violently for several minutes, my body shuddering in ferocious waves. I remembered Kris' words, "you gotta feel it to heal it." As I released the resentment and anger toward Him, the poison in my soul vanished. I felt that unspoken gentle Power of my Creator wrap around me again, like a loving Father hugs his child. Just as tenderly, I realized, as I had held my own son Nathan at his birth.

I finally understood the meaning of unconditional love, and as it washed over me, I was astonished. This, I suddenly realized, was a Power that I could rely on every hour to stay sober! This was a Force I could call on during times of weakness or craving. Most importantly, this was the Friend I *wanted* to surround myself with and be like. My mind and my heart had been opened to a fresh new perspective on spirituality that would sustain long-term recovery and emotional sobriety.

In that sacred moment, on day twenty-eight of my sobriety, the divisive obsession to use drugs and alcohol was taken from me once and for all. Irrevocably, a Power greater than myself had restored my mind to sanity as He released me from the shackles and chains of resentment and fear. It was like I was given a new pair of glasses and I could finally see clearly.

That experience forever changed me. I took that love within my very essence and recognized that it was a knowledge and Light that I could draw upon moving forward. I would not be perfect. I would have my struggles. Yet, I began to realize as I continued my journey in recovery, I could build a life—a life where all things lost could be restored. I began to imagine a life in casual and close communication with a Higher Power who loved me as much as I loved my own son. It was amazing to me to contemplate a life where all wrongs could be forgiven, and all failures could be redeemed.

Although I still struggled with bouts of depression and anxiety with temptations to leave, I at least tried my best to do my chores, follow every rule, make my bed, open my blinds in the morning, and contribute in group. Furthermore, I decided to take some risks with being rigorously honest about some things that I thought I would take to the grave—secrets from my past that were keeping me sick. This set me free on deeper levels, healing wounds buried in my soul.

I was found.

Although I still had my doubts in my ability to change, this was a good start.

It's been said, "For prayer is nothing else than being on terms of friendship with God." I completely agree with Teresa of Avila.

1. *Willingness* to be honest, take suggestions, and become obedient creates humility.

2. *Humility* is a vital attribute for lasting change. We become teachable and open-minded to learn. As we learn, we see new ways to view and approach our relationships and life in a much healthier way.

3. Spirituality can be a major hang up for those with an addiction. Remember not to force your beliefs, but rather, honor where they are at so that they can experience their own personal spiritual awakening.

4. The privilege of recovering from addiction is that we are constantly grateful for the goodness around us; we know all too well the hell of a life we left behind and how blessed we are to have found a way out of it. As for me, I could not have done it without a newly formed and more relaxed, affirming, and loving view of God. I believed He was in my corner and wanted my success. On one hand, my addiction still pains me when I think about the lives I hurt. On the other hand, I am eternally grateful for the inner knowledge I have of God's love, healing power, grace, mercy, and goodness.

Chapter 11

HOPE

It was a stunning spring morning at The Ranch. The trees were alive with new life: beautiful white and pink buds covered them like cotton candy. The weather was warming noticeably, and the birds chirped cheerily as I did my daily chores. In spite of this happy atmosphere, I was feeling nervous, like I did every morning. Each day in treatment felt like a week. It was a real struggle. For five weeks, I had followed every rule, completed every assignment, taken every suggestion, and even helped a few of the new people get settled in at The Ranch. I was doing the work, but nothing seemed to take away the nagging discomfort or emptiness I felt inside.

Since my decision to stay, there were moments when I still wanted to leave. I had committed to my sobriety, yes, but I had my doubts that I could change. *Getting sober* was doable. *Staying sober* forever seemed impossible. The emotional rollercoaster I'd been on didn't seem to have an end in sight. The Ranch Brothers kept saying, "This too shall pass." How I longed for that—that the pain would somehow pass. I repeated the words of Dave Pinegar in my head over and over, "The price of progress is the pain of change." On the bright side, I felt a small sense of pride that I hadn't been kicked out of or walked out of treatment yet.

I was on Outside Crew that week for morning chores. My assignment was to spray off the walks, sweep the porch, and take care of the animals. I especially enjoyed feeding the horse, Mikayla. She and I had developed a special bond since she watched me arrive that first day in the white van. I walked out to the barn and forked over Mikayla's breakfast of dried alfalfa and garnished it with a sprinkling of oats.

"Good morning, girl. Here's your breakfast in bed. Welcome to the Ritz," I whispered with half a smile.

Mikayla enthusiastically crunched on her breakfast while I ran the brush across her left side. Those mornings gave me a chance to contemplate and prepare for the insurmountable day ahead. The hard work outside helped me forget my own problems—at least for a minute. Maybe that's why they said that chores had therapeutic value.

Maybe they were right.

Suddenly I heard one of the Ranch Brothers yell out to me from the front door, "Hey Coombsy, HR wants to see you in his office!"

My heart skipped a beat and started to race.

HR Brown was the boss. He owned The Ranch. Why did he want to talk to me? Was I in trouble? I felt like I was being called to the principal's office. I made my way to the main house and walked slowly up the steps onto the porch, as if I were mounting gallows. I leaned against the weathered column, loosened my laces, and kicked my muddy boots onto the porch. Then I straightened them up nicely against the frame of the house.

I entered through the lobby and approached HR's office door to the left. I paused, took a deep breath, and lightly knocked. Maybe he wouldn't hear me, and I could go back to my chores? Avoidance was my usual tactic when faced with pressure, but I couldn't shirk it this time. Not at The Ranch. *Nothing slips by these people.*

"Come in."

I slightly cracked open the door and saw him sitting at his desk. HR was a strong, friendly Greek fisherman in his fifties, with loving, deep-brown eyes. He smiled at me from beneath his bushy eyebrows and waved me into his office.

"Hey, Jason. Come in," he warmly directed. I sat. Trepidation turned to curiosity. I was surprised that he knew my name. As I sat down across from his desk, I noticed a row of framed pictures of his family, bird hunting, and his dogs: three of his passions.

"How are you doing, Brother?"

Brother? He considers me a brother?

Carefully choosing my words, I told him what I thought he wanted to hear.

"I am doing amazing. I love it here. Thanks for askin'."

He listened intently to my cheerful line. The truth was that I was *doing* fine, like breathing and eating, but I wasn't *feeling* fine. I still felt hopeless, like my efforts were futile. Often, I seriously considered dropping out because I couldn't picture myself happy, healthy, and free. After failing countless times, why would it be any different? Ultimately, I lacked self-efficacy—the internal confidence in my ability to stay sober permanently.

I couldn't tell HR the truth. I had to appear like I was doing great, or he might think badly of me. I still cared more about what people thought of me than I cared about being rigorously honest.

Even so, HR could tell I was struggling. He reached into his pocket and pulled out something. He extended his arm and opened his fingers. In the palm of his hand was a large, bronze coin. I squinted my eyes to read the inscription. In the center of the triangle was the number twelve, written in Roman Numerals. Along each line that made up the triangle, it read: Unity, Service, and Recovery. Arching above the triangle across the top of the coin read the words, "To Thine Own Self Be True." I looked up at HR, curious as to what he was about to say. He folded his hands together and smiled.

"Jason, this year marks my twelve years of being sober. Twelve years ago, I had a gun in my mouth because I didn't think it was possible for me to stay sober—to change."

I felt the hair on the back of my neck stand up because it was like he read my mind.

Suddenly, he did something that blew me away.

"Here," he said, extending the coin for me to take. "I want you to have this, and I want you to make me a promise. Promise me that we will meet up again in twelve years. On that day, I will give you my twenty-four-year coin, and you will give your twelve-year coin to a newcomer. Deal?"

I stared at the coin, then back at him in complete disbelief.

HR saw my reaction and continued, "Recovery *is* possible, Jason. You are a leader. It is your spiritual gift. The Ranch Brothers here will follow your example, for good or bad. Serve others. Be honest. And trust God in all you do. If you do these things, I promise you that your life will get better." Then he said something that took me by complete surprise. "I believe in you." There was truth in his eyes. I could see it because I had finally started being able to look people in the eye again, but I had to look away after a moment.

I sat there in my chair, feeling unworthy to accept this incredibly meaningful gift, but also felt something new rising within. HR didn't even know me, but he believed in me. His words breathed new life into me. Maybe I could stay sober. Maybe I could do it right this time if I simply followed their proven suggestions. Maybe recovery was possible, even for a disappointment like me.

I felt a rush that rivaled a hit of crack cocaine, which also surprised me. My heart flooded with hope.

That was it. The new feeling was *hope*.

Maybe, just maybe, I could stay sober. Not just a couple weeks—with supervision—but twelve years on my own volition without the threat of a judges' gavel, or cops or court or getting tossed out of rehab. Maybe I could help other guys do the same. Was this possible? Maybe it truly was possible. My self-efficacy grew in that moment like a budding rose basking in the spring sunlight.

For the first time since my dance with the devil began, I could believe that long-term sobriety might be possible for me. I believed it—almost. I wanted it—for sure. I desired it even more than I craved relief from ongoing emotional withdrawals.

Yes, without a doubt, that moment with HR, holding his coin in my hand, visualizing my own twelve-year coin—and thinking that maybe, just maybe, I could earn mine, too—feeling that exalting rush of hope . . . that was when the game changed.

HR made the difference. He saw me as his brother, not a drug addict, not a criminal, not a bum, and not a loser. He saw me as a friend and an equal. Even a leader. He embodied the principles of honoring my individuality vs authority, drawing out my ideas vs. opposing his on me, demonstrating empathy, and supporting self-efficacy.

WOW.

A long moment passed in complete silence. Tears filled my eyes and rolled down my cheeks. He then stood up from his chair, walked around his desk, and embraced me with the love a father had for a son.

There is power in that kind of love.

That was a pivotal moment. Hope. Not guarantees, just hope, and a new confidence planted like a seed, ready to grow.

SIX KEYS TO GET UNHOOKED

While I advanced through the stages of change, my parents and family learned how to maintain their own balance and happiness in good times and bad. Though parents and spouses can encourage their addicted loved ones, the hard work is up to them. And as you can see, the outside influence of other men and women contributed a great deal to my progress. They ultimately understood my issues and believed in me. Think of it like this: a parent—even if he is a surgeon—can't operate on his own child. You need another expert physician to do this. Your job is to lovingly apply these tools found in this book, and patiently wait while the transformation takes place. Moreover, your job is to become as healthy as possible for the time when your addicted loved one will rely on your strength. There will be times after they get sober when you will feel the same fears and old behaviors flare up. Be ready so that you don't contribute to an unnecessary wrestling match with your addicted loved one and possibly contribute to a relapse.

Similarly, when your loved one is in recovery or rehab you can support him with words of encouragement as they are allowed, but the best thing you can do is work on your own recovery and become a new you! I know that sounds crazy, but I have never met a loving parent or spouse who didn't get lost for a time in hyper-concern and focus over a teen, adult, child, or partner caught in addiction's grip. Addiction does a number on everyone in the family. Al-anon and its principles will allow you to stay centered and peaceful, come what may, as your loved one does the work of recovery. (Or not.)

Below is some additional help that will keep you feeling at peace.

1—Bibliotherapy

Bibliotherapy is an expressive therapy through the use of books, and often it is coupled with writing. As my parents began their healing, they were given a list of books that would help them to get on the offense. They began reading books like *Codependent No More* by Melody Beattie, *On the Family*, and *Healing the Shame that Binds You* by John Bradshaw. In the quiet of their own home, they were able to become educated, empowered, and inspired.

Research shows that reading is a productive activity that can promote good mental health, increase empathy, sharpen the mind, and impact behavior. Reading also increases participation in therapy, reduces recovery time, and provides more opportunity for insight and behavior change. Studies on the efficacy of bibliotherapy show it to be helpful in treating depression, anxiety, and substance dependency. I personally know that reading breaks through limiting beliefs, narrowmindedness, and mediocrity. A helpful book is like having a friend who is there for you twenty-four hours a day. All you have to do when the anxious thoughts and worries come is open a book. Similarly, audio books and many talks by experts in addiction and recovery can be your companion on road trips or walks as you listen to them.

For a list of recommended books, visit www.brickhouserecovery.com/unhooked.

2—Counseling and Therapy

I am a big believer in professional help in order to get to the top of the learning curve faster. My parents became unhooked from my addiction because they not only engaged in bibliotherapy, but they sought the help from professional counselors and combined this with group therapy.

In a short amount of time, my parents achieved deep healing with professional help. Plain and simple. There are many layers of pain, fear, and emotional trauma that need attention in our effort to make a complete recovery. A good professional knows how to effectively guide you through the healing process so that you can feel better faster.

If you can afford it, please seek help from a professional. My advice is that you find one through word of mouth and referral. When you find the right one, it is worth its weight in gold. If you cannot afford a professional counselor, you may be able to find a mentor or sponsor who is just as helpful.

3—Find a Tribe

Why is finding your tribe vital in becoming unhooked? Here are a few benefits of support groups. First of all, when we are entrenched in a heavy life mess like addiction, we feel alone, isolated, and often afraid to be judged by others. Support groups smash through these feelings while offering us replacement emotions, such as feeling understood, knowing we're not alone, and a sense of empowerment, direction, and support.

These groups are attended by others who have walked our path and learned what coping skills to use in any given situation. The venue allows us to listen to others share openly and honestly about their struggles, and ultimately, how they worked through them. This creates an environment of answers and empathy that will help you reduce distress, depression, anxiety, and fatigue. If you need a safe place to express what is happening in your family, a support group will invite you to share openly and honestly, without fear of your story being shared elsewhere beyond the confines of a trusted group. The healing is incredible as you break out of isolation and open up to others. But if you want to just go and listen, that is welcomed, too.

Probably the most powerful reason support groups work is that they provide us a venue to be of service. You can help other people with your story and insights you've learned. It is in *giving* that we receive. It is a win-win. We all need to be needed.

Since not all support groups are created equal, you may want to attend at least three to six different meetings before finding the "one" that fits. During your hunt for a support group that fits, you will meet a variety of people from all walks of life who approach addictions differently. Try to stay open minded and focus on the positives by taking what is helpful from your meeting and leave the rest. There is no perfect group, just as there are no perfect people. But if you shop around, you will find one that "fits" and feels like home to you. Another option is to call your local Al-anon office and ask them for their recommended meetings in your area. There are also online meetings as well. You can find information at www.brickhouserecovering.com/unhooked.

When the time is right and when you are ready, a "sponsor", or an Al-anon guide, can be a powerful coach to help you progress and grow by working through the healing process of the Twelve Steps of Al-anon. Al-anon provides understanding and support for the family members of alcoholics and drug addicted people. What we can't do alone, we can do together. A sponsor also does not charge money and has the advantage of being free and available more often than a professional counselor or therapist.

Many people find lasting recovery through them because they are a practical and simple path to healing and emotional sobriety. The American Society of Addiction Medicine affirms the benefits of 12-step facilitation therapy, which might I add, applies to the family members as well.

Since the day I became sober, I attribute each and every mental, physical, emotional, and spiritual breakthrough to working the Twelve Steps. If taken seriously, these steps will help you in each life domain, problem area, and relationship you have. If you choose to engage in this process, via Al-anon or something similar, you will begin to take the focus off of your addicted loved one and become laser focused on the life domains and areas of opportunity for you to become who you want to be—a new and improved version of yourself. If you get hung up on any of the aspects of the Twelve Steps that don't resonate with you, simply put on your emotional raincoat and keep experimenting with this work. This is a powerful healing process that will absolutely drive results. Trust me!

If you would prefer taking another approach, there are also wonderful resources out there to help. Again, visit www.brick houserecovery.com/unhooked.

4—Keep a Gratitude Journal

My parents broke free from the mental obsession and fear for me and started their own recovery journey by consistently writing in a journal. They specifically took inventory of their days and their reactions, and recognized areas where they could seek to improve the next day. This has made a massive impact on their ability to spot their behaviors, identify if the behavior is contributing to the problem or solution, and rapidly launch into healthier behavior at once. For me, this tool to gain personal awareness by taking daily inventory has sustained my long-term emotional sobriety and deserves credit for much of my happiness and fulfillment today. An example of a daily inventory might look something like this:

Overall, today I felt more connected and optimistic than I did yesterday. I'm so grateful for the progress I'm seeing in myself, even though my son doesn't seem to be changing at this time. I'm grateful for the new understanding that I don't have to ride this rollercoaster anymore. I am grateful to know I can put on my emotional raincoat and get off the beach while he experiences his own journey towards change. Lately, I've been really trying to be more honest with myself by looking deep inside at why I feel anxious and begin to worry more. I'm trying to surrender these feelings, but I still have some work to do. I guess I'm still attached to the outcome and need to work on letting go and trusting the process. After my conversation with my son this afternoon, I recognized some impatience and judgment toward him flare up. Some of my comments to him made me feel bad, like the way I used to feel when I'd react to his behaviors. I'm going to put my focus and attention on the steps to surrender and being more patient and non-judgmental tomorrow.

The outline I use every day is:

1. Express gratitude. What we focus on expands.
2. Identify areas of progress.
3. Identify areas you want to work on.

Keep it simple.

I have found this practice essential in connecting my mind, body, and spirit. Research shows that keeping a gratitude journal increases determination, attention, enthusiasm, and energy. In fact, research shows that higher levels of gratitude are associated with better sleep, lower anxiety, and depression. The feeling of gratitude directly activates the brain regions associated with the neurotransmitter dopamine. Dopamine feels good, plain and simple. People who keep a gratitude journal show greater improvements in optimism, and it influences improvements in behavior, such as exercise patterns. It can also be attributed to reduction in physical aches and pains. On a side note: I want to emphasize the value of good sleep, nutrition, and exercise. When we get good sleep, fuel our bodies with the proper nutrition, and exert ourselves each day, the dopamine flows, causing us to feel better. When we feel better, we cope better. (And isn't feeling better the whole idea here?)

Okay, back to gratitude: when we appreciate the positive aspects of our situation, and we find gratitude in the little things, we will deal with life's challenges better.

One of the best parts of recovery is waking up to small pleasures again. If it's not easy for you to think of what you're grateful for, start with the little things, such as running water, electricity, and transportation. Even a good cup of hot chocolate! The laughter of kids. The sun peeking through trees. Use all of your senses to recall the things that bring pleasure. When we live in extreme anxiety and depression, we can grow numb to simple pleasures. For many, the simple pleasures no longer give them joy because their lives have become altered by constant fear. It takes time for a fear-soaked individual to heal and enjoy normal, small joys again.

Sometimes we take simple things for granted and we can stop to imagine how our lives would be without them. No matter how bad our situation feels, it could always be worse. As we learn to focus on the good in life, life will be good. If we focus on the problem, the problem increases, but if we focus on the solution, the solution increases. Bottom line: what we focus on expands.

For a helpful PDF I use to write my personal inventory, visit www.brickhouserecovery.com/unhooked.

5—Tracking Outcomes

The best way to gain great awareness on your progress is to consistently track your outcomes. Through an ecosystem of specialized digital health tools, we help parents, spouses, clients, professionals, employers, community groups, and government agencies effectively track outcomes, while providing training, telehealth, and support to those seeking healing and long-lasting freedom. As I write this book, we currently have four powerful tools with more on the way. They are available on desktop and mobile devices to help address the following struggles:

1. **LIFT** is an evidence-based recovery tool designed to help individuals facing *depression and anxiety* find deeper levels of recovery and healing. This is a powerful tool for family members struggling with an addicted loved one.

2. **TURN** is an evidence-based recovery tool designed to help individuals overcome *substance abuse* and maintain long-term recovery. Every single one of my clients is required to use this tool . . . and it works.

3. **FORTIFY** is an evidence-based recovery tool designed to help individuals overcome *sexual compulsivity* and find greater happiness and lasting love.

4. **Recovery Suite** is a separate tool created specifically for mental and behavioral health professionals, Employee Assistance Programs, Human Resource Departments, and government-based programs. This is the tool I use at Brick

House Recovery to gather aggregated outcomes to see how we as an organization are moving the needle.

Don't worry, this isn't a hidden sales pitch. The basic program for these apps is free, but I highly recommend you check out the premium upgrade for a minimal cost. Because I honor your commitment to change, I will give you a special "unhooked" discount. Find these tools and get your promo code at www.brickhouse recovery.com/unhooked.

6—Pour into Others

Everybody has a story, but only the brave ones are willing to share it with the intent to bless the lives of others. As we break out of our isolation, anxiety, and depression, we will find much needed purpose, strength, and hope as we share our experiences with those that may be struggling, too. This gives added meaning to your life, and quite simply, feeling that your life has bigger meaning is what makes it worth living!

As you share your story in a safe place, you release yourself from secret pain. You will evolve and grow beyond the struggle. You'll actually rise above it and eventually become grateful for your experiences. In a safe and accepting group context, you can gain insightful wisdom of what happened, what went wrong, and practical ideas of what you can do to alter your attitude or your course. Awareness is the key to your brighter future. We humans tell our stories to learn from them, broaden our perspective, and transcend our struggles. Furthermore, as you share your true, authentic self with others, not only will you create real connections, but you will be giving others permission to be their true, authentic selves in return.

As you get comfortable sharing your journey—its ups and its downs and wisdom gained from all of it—in a group setting, you will become more comfortable sharing. Others will glean wisdom from hearing what you've been through and what you are learning.

As you well know, parents and spouses can feel so isolated and alone when they are on the hamster wheel of addiction, and you now have hopeful solutions to share with them. As you meet others who are struggling with their addicted loved one, please share this book with them. Share it on social media. Share it in your network of friends. Share it anywhere you feel it might help another person. Sing from the rooftops about the progress you are making and the insights you received. As you bless the lives of others, your quality of life will increase. Let's combine our efforts and make a difference together. Welcome to the recovery movement!

Chapter 12

TRANSCENDENCE

IT WAS MY FIRST DAY at my brand-new job—cooking and selling hot dogs. I had been out of The Ranch for almost two weeks and sober for more than seventy straight days. I did as my counselors had suggested. I took a simple, low-pressure job right out of treatment. They talked about the importance of rest, relaxation, and settling into life correctly to avoid relapse.

Before leaving treatment, one of the therapists, Steve Brown (HR's brother), had said, "Jason, *convalescence* is as critical for someone leaving rehab as it is for the cancer patient leaving the Intensive Care Unit." Because I had never heard that word before, I had to ask him what *convalescence* meant. "Time spent recovering from an illness or medical treatment; recuperation."

This was hard for my race horse Type-A mentality. Man, I felt the need to play catch up—to hightail it back into a fast-paced job, earn great commissions, and enjoy all of the perks and prestige that I'd lost years before. However, I'd learned to take suggestions, even though I was humbled by this simple job.

The leap to become employed again was a big one. I spent the last two weeks just out of treatment by playing ping pong at the sober-living house, staying up late watching movies, sleeping in until 11:00 a.m., and attending multiple recovery meetings a day to try and enjoy my new sober life. It had worked. So far. I was still sober and having fun. I didn't think sober fun was possible!

Then it was time to work.

So, there I was, diligently working my new job at a hot dog stand out in front of a hardware store on the east bench of Salt Lake City. Since I had a college degree and experience at high paying, fast paced sales jobs, I must admit I felt I was working way below my pay grade at a hot dog stand. But Steve's words echoed in my ear, "If you want to stay sober, practice convalescence and find a low stress, flexible job that will support your daily recovery commitments." I trusted his hard-earned wisdom.

Aftercare, which is the last phase of drug and alcohol treatment, was held on Tuesday, Wednesday, and Thursday evenings at The Ranch. Here we learned what professionals called "best practices"—the tried and true ideas and ways to maintain emotional sobriety in the real world as we transitioned from inpatient rehab to out-patient. It serves as a transitional phase of treatment to help adjust to the pressures of bills, life, and the stress of the real world, minimizing the risks of relapse.

Sure, the hot dog job was flexible enough to support my Aftercare. However, dressed in my uniform, apron and all, I was pitifully embarrassed. The hot dog stand happened to be strategically positioned on the sidewalk next to the front doors of the hardware chain.

The smell of grilled onions and slightly charred sausages drew everyone's attention to stop by on their way inside. *What if someone I know decides to buy some power tools or light fixtures and stops to eat first? Where can I hide?*

Around lunchtime I wiped down the condiments on my prime piece of real estate. Sure enough, my feared worst-case scenario was about to play out. My humiliation and anxiety peaked as my ex-wife's brother approached the store. He caught a whiff of grilled onions, looked toward the stand, and spotted me there. Ashamed, I looked away, pretending I didn't see him. I was pretty sure, however, that he saw me. *How can he not?*

There I stood resplendent in my white t-shirt with an artistically placed mustard stain on the sleeve. Out of the corner of my eye, I watched him discreetly shift directions and walk past me into the store. Not a word was said. I felt like the most inadequate human being on the planet. How much lower can someone get in the prime of their life? There I was, a once-successful husband with a promising future, a college graduate with a once-lucrative career. Now I was making a lousy six bucks an hour, cooking stupid hot dogs for complete strangers. The shame burned. I felt pathetic. Right then the negative self-talk started up, as usual.

"I should never have taken this job! You're such a loser, Jason! You will never amount to anything!" my addict voice yelled. I felt like the brunt of a cruel joke. I was a joke. My self-hate, which had been suitably subdued through the last two and a half months, flared back up with a vengeance.

A sigh rolled up from deep within me.

I lit up a cigarette and took a deep inhale. Then I remembered that this feeling I had now had always preceded a downward spiral in the past leading me to a relapse. Each downward spiral looked something like this:

1. Something would *trigger* me, creating anxiety or depression.

2. Then my *shame* would kick in and the addict voice would reinforce my inadequacies and insecurities while robbing me of my emotional sobriety.

3. My ego would step in to cover my pain, hijack my commitment to sobriety, encourage isolation, and shut down my gratitude for achieving sobriety in the first place.

4. Self-hate and resentments toward others then would effectively cut me off from the Sunlight of the Spirit.

5. The insanity would return, and I would take a drink or use a drug.

6. Once the physical allergy was ignited, all bets were off and my life would circle the drain.

This had been my pattern, time and again. Insanity. Insanity...

Not this time! I'm going to work my relapse prevention plan. They say it works when you work it.

I quickly recited a familiar portion of the Serenity Prayer in my head, something every recovering person should memorize:

God grant me the serenity
To accept the things I cannot change;
Courage to change the things I can;
And wisdom to know the difference.

What could I change right now? And then I knew: I knew I needed to change my negative attitude. If I didn't, slipping back to the self-seeking escape found in drugs and alcohol was a guarantee.

This was a life or death moment, and I had to treat it that seriously.

I was reminded of a simple little game I used to play in treatment to get me through the tough days. How many people could I get to smile in fifteen minutes? Each smile counted as one point. If I could make them laugh, it was a triple-point bonus. It was a silly, childish game, yet I knew it might be just enough to get me through this humiliating experience.

If I was going to get people to smile, however, then I needed to stop hiding behind the grill and start interacting with customers. Right then, a man wearing jeans and a plaid flannel shirt walked up to the menu board. *Okay. Game on.*

"Good morning, sir. Can I grill you up a tasty hot dog?" I asked with a warm smile.

"I'll take a bratwurst, please," he said, not coldly, but not really paying much attention.

"Comin' right up!" I replied brightly. "How is your day treating you?"

"Fine," he answered politely. "How's yours?"

"Today is a good day," I said sincerely. "I am seventy-three days sober, which is a miracle for a guy like me."

That got his attention, and an awkward smile.

"Yeah. I just got out of rehab," I shared. "Would you like grilled onions on your bratwurst?"

The customer's demeanor changed almost instantly. One thing I discovered about recovering people in early sobriety is that we tend to share more than is welcomed or wanted. It is the famous "addict over-share." This time, however, it seemed to work. "Today is a good day because I'm sober" was certainly an interesting variation of the normal, polite, and incessantly boring social clichés and repartee. Suddenly the gentleman began to share, confiding in me.

"I have a son. He's . . . addicted to drugs." His face became twisted in heartfelt remorse and frustration. "My wife and I have tried everything, but we honestly don't know what else to do." I looked—really looked—into his eyes. He felt lost, confused, and angry just like my father had been.

"As his parents," he almost begged, "what do you suggest we try?"

I had to stop and think for a minute. My mood and attitude completely shifted from being self-absorbed to genuinely wanting to help this father. It was as if time stopped and I could see my own father desperately seeking answers about how to help me. My heart swelled with empathy and compassion for this disturbed father. As tears welled in my eyes, I said, "All I can say is to love him," I responded without hesitation. "Love him through it all." I paused, seeing my father's face in my mind.

This man and I proceeded to engage in a conversation that lasted over twenty minutes. I shared my story. I shared what my parents tried, what worked, and what didn't work. I was honest and even shared the painful parts. Suddenly he looked at his watch and thanked me as he wiped the tears from his face with his napkin. Before I knew it, he hurried into the store as if he was late for an appointment.

Something rose out of that experiment that I had not counted on. As I processed that interaction for the rest of the day, I began to suddenly feel profound purpose in the lessons I learned from my suffering because now they had become helpful to others. I felt something I hadn't felt for a long time. I felt needed. I felt useful, almost like I had a purpose in life.

That morning, I had thought of myself as a loser who worked at a lousy hot dog stand, but something had radically shifted. I was meant to be in that place, at that time, to make a difference in this man's life. That father shared some private feelings that he could not share with his friends, but he could with me. My truth was creating truth. My openness was opening others.

The days went by and I shared my story with every customer I could. I was overwhelmed by the number of people affected by addiction.

From time to time, the addict negative voice would creep in. "Who are you to think that you can help? You probably won't even stay sober!" Negative thoughts about the harm I caused others, especially my parents and family, loomed overhead. "You will never be able to fix all the wreckage of your past!" the addict voice constantly reminded.

Just keep helping people, I told myself.

It was obvious that people craved insight, understanding, and answers about addiction and how to help, just like Mom did when she found out about my problem. They really wanted to tell someone about their struggles, someone who would listen, understand, and ease their broken hearts.

My difficult road to sobriety positioned me to offer them hope and guidance. Even though my sobriety was new, my own fresh and recent experiences had priceless value to these customers.

I realized that I do, indeed, have something to offer. Gradually, but very powerfully, my focus turned outward to helping others. By helping others, I found incredible strength far beyond my own.

I found myself as I forgot myself.

Suddenly, my mentor Steve Carlston's words popped into my mind from many years ago in his downtown Los Angeles office: "Jason, when I was a young professional just out of college, a guy helped me get started along my path. Now it is my privilege to help you. And someday, it will be your turn to help someone, too. And that is how 'becoming successful' works."

Those profound words were now coming true. My dormant purpose awakened inside of myself, and it felt strong and powerful. From that moment on, I would dedicate my life to helping people with addictions.

There was no turning back now. It was my turn to carry the message of recovery to the world.

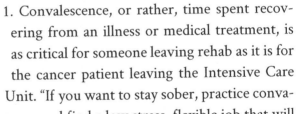

1. Convalescence, or rather, time spent recovering from an illness or medical treatment, is as critical for someone leaving rehab as it is for the cancer patient leaving the Intensive Care Unit. "If you want to stay sober, practice convalescence and find a low stress, flexible job that will support your early sobriety."

2. When our loved ones are in treatment, or recently completed treatment, allow them the gift of having fun—sober bowling, ping pong, late night movies with recovery friends, and frequent meeting attendance. Although the signs of early sobriety indicate lack of family balance and responsibility, be patient. Learning how to have fun, live life, and be sober is imperative for long-term recovery. They really need to remember that fun is possible without alcohol or drugs attached. Play is a form of therapy, and a vital one. Responsibility and balance will come in time.

3. Often times, people in early sobriety will rely on nicotine, caffeine, sugar, and various other compulsive behaviors to cope with their new life of abstinence. Although it is not ideal, remember that we are encouraging "progress, not perfection." Recovery is not an event. This is a life-long journey that will unfold over time. If they are staying away from drugs and alcohol, don't harp on other behaviors. A healthier lifestyle will take time, one step at a time.

4. We will feel a profound sense of purpose in the lessons we've learned from our suffering as we share them with others. When times get tough, just keep helping people. By helping others, we will find incredible strength far beyond our own. We will find ourselves as we forget ourselves in the service of others.

Chapter 13

FINALLY, FREE

FROM THAT MOMENT ON, I meant business.

There is no finish line in the world of addiction recovery, however; we will hit ceilings that require breakthrough after breakthrough in order to keep growing. In order to keep from falling back into the dark, seeping waters of relapse, I had to clean the slate. Not just any slate. My slate, the slates lathered with the scum of broken promises, heart breaks, and outright wrongs done to others. In order to achieve a full measure of emotional sobriety, I had to clean up my past, right my wrongs, and live in harmony with my fellowman—as best I could do.

Starting with the less foreboding ones, I began working down the list of names and institutions to which I needed to make amends.

One by one, I followed a simple outline, genuinely making sure it was more than just a simple apology. Unlike the hundreds of times I said "sorry" to people, I knew that true amends must be sincere. First, I had to own my wrongs. Second, I had to ask the person how I could make things right with them. Third, I let them set terms and willingly accepted them, as long as they were reasonable.

Each time I chipped away at the list, I saw one name I felt ashamed to call: Steve Carlston. Fear rushed through my body over and over. Just the thought of how many times I had dragged his reputation through the mud made me cringe with stabbing regret. Yet I knew in my core that if I was to stay sober and alive, I needed to make *all* of my amends.

I sent him a text.

"Steve, long time no see. I hope this is still your number. I have something extremely important to talk to you about, and I would like five minutes of your time. Can I schedule some time with you?"

In true Steve Carlston form, his response was warm and friendly. Unexpectedly, he offered to buy me lunch and I jumped at the chance to have an hour face to face with him. We scheduled a time a few days later at a little deli downtown, near a television network he managed.

On that cold March afternoon, I noticed the dirty ice in the gutter near the beautiful city high-rises. The contrast triggered a memory of my once lucrative "high rise" sales career, my former wife and marriage, and my eventual fall–to the gutter–of home-lessness and despair. I remembered to force a gratitude prayer every time haunting memories flooded my mind, threatening an attack of anxiety. I truly was grateful for the fact that I wasn't chained to my addiction on the streets any longer.

Steve and I arrived at the restaurant at the same time and we embraced. His tall, athletic build engulfed me with loving empathy and a palpable genuineness. Steve always had a way of making me feel comfortable, even though I was positive he could tell I was uncomfortable that day. I felt even more uncomfortable than the first time I had met him—back when I was a young, unsure intern in the office of a powerful man.

My face was hot and flushed at another memory of one of the last times I had seen Steve. It had been a solemn occasion at my Uncle Bob Coombs' funeral. I was deep in the throes of addiction then, unable to face Steve or the pain of losing my uncle. I had bolted to avoid Steve, hiding myself away in the bathroom to do a few lines of cocaine to gain composure. I stayed there until I was sure he was gone, no longer in the company of my family. My heart was now heavy with the memory of such cowardice.

Steve had heard about my years of struggle through the grapevine, and yet he was willing to meet me. He was still in my corner. Even as we sat down at the linen-covered table, it was hard to grasp such genuine generosity.

"Wow, Jason," he said, with a warm smile and shining eyes. "It is so great to see you healthy and happy." His remark gave me some courage. It was time to make restitution.

"Steve," I said, clearing my throat. "The reason I contacted you after all these years is because I need to make things right with you. In fact, my life depends on it."

"Absolutely, Jason. What is it?" Steve inquired with a look of concern.

Sheepishly, I dropped my eyes and stared at the table cloth. "Well, you know how you stuck your neck out for me all those times I needed a job? It was because of you and your influence that I was able get those wonderful positions in the first place, and I squandered each of those opportunities in my addiction. Worse, I dragged your reputation through the mud."

I took a deep breath. I clasped my hands together to stop the shaking and continued, "I feel horrible about it and I want to apologize. What can I do to make things right with you?"

Slowly raising my eyes to make contact, I couldn't hold his gaze. I quickly stared back down at the table, embarrassed.

Steve's reaction caught me by surprise. He waited for me to raise my head again, and looked at me, man-to-man. With a huge smile, he seized the opportunity to mentor me, like he did in his office in Los Angeles many years before.

"Jason, I don't regret helping you find employment. We all need people in our lives who will lend a hand in times of need. In fact,

I believe that what you have been through makes you an expert in addiction. You can take your life's lessons, your experiences, and your insights in order to help others avoid addictions, and recover from them."

I stared at him in astonishment. Instead of berating me, or accepting me and quickly changing the subject, he was treating me like an equal.

"You see," he continued, "you and I were meant to meet fifteen years ago. I was able to help you. Now you have the opportunity to give back to others and help them along their path."

It was then that Steve reached into his bag and pulled out a book. Its royal blue cover with bold, white writing caught my attention. The title said, *Aspire! Discovering Your Purpose through the Power of Words* by Kevin Hall.

"Jason, here is one of my favorite books that has helped me discover my purpose. The author Kevin Hall is a dear friend of mine. I want to give you a signed copy of his book if you promise me you will read it."

Feeling inspired, I took the book in my hand and agreed to read it since these were Steve's terms.

After lunch, we went our separate ways. Once again, I felt incredibly high on life. A little arrogantly, I tossed the book in the back seat of my car, cranked up my music, and drove home.

The book sat untouched in my car for two weeks. One night during a graveyard shift at my new job at an adolescent treatment center, I decided to grab the book and read the first chapter. I did, in fact, make a promise to him and I intended to keep it.

For the first time in my life, I was absolutely captivated by a book. I stayed up the entire night without a wink of sleep in order to finish it. Amazed and surprised, I realized that the entire book aligned with everything I had learned in recovery. It expanded on principles that had saved my life: humility, honoring my God-given gifts, honoring the Divine within others, relying on my

Higher Power, serving others, and being willing to share my suffering to help others avoid it.

Something powerful shifted within me that night as I nearly read the entire book cover-to-cover. With an unstoppable passion to fulfill my purpose of helping others with addictions, my life took on a deeper, more personal meaning. I began setting specific and lofty goals for myself, and decided I would not let my fears hold me back from reaching my potential.

Within days I applied to graduate school, and in a matter of weeks I was accepted in the Master of Professional Communications program at Westminster College in Salt Lake City. I dove in with commitment and a hunger to learn as I had never done before. As fate would have it, I met the most amazing woman in class. Brin was not only stunningly beautiful, she was kind, compassionate, and absolutely brilliant. She accepted me for who I was, recovering from addiction and all. No one on the planet was happier than I was when she said yes to my question, and we were married six months later.

During that same time frame, and with Steve Carlston's support, I was hired by Dr. Kevin McCauley and the co-founders of the Institute for Addiction Study. In my new role, I became acquainted with the very best experts in addiction treatment and began my career in the industry.

That experience prepared me to manage a residential treatment program while finishing graduate school. In that setting, I worked hard to enhance my abilities and skills to effectively support, influence, and motivate my clients and their family members into recovery.

After completing graduate school, I ventured out into the finance industry, where I learned the art of business in southern California. Money was no longer an issue, and I was climbing the ladder of success in many people's eyes.

However, after a profound spiritual experience while sitting in the sand on Huntington Beach, I felt inspired to return back to the addiction treatment industry with force. My supportive wife and I took the leap to Boise, Idaho to start our own addiction treatment center, Brick House Recovery, and we haven't looked back.

Our family goal is to connect you and our clients with the best principles and resources in order for your family to recover. For us, there is no greater joy than to have a front row seat to this ever-unfolding miracle show.

A few years after opening Brick House Recovery, a miracle happened that topped all previous miracles. In the middle of the night on March 18, 2016, Brin gave birth to our set of twins—a tiny baby girl, Indie May, and my mini-me, Radin James.

The night they were born, I could not help but relive the day my son Nathan was born years ago. I vividly recalled the shame of once being that unfit and broken birthfather. I reminisced the tears of joy when I held him for the first time. I also vividly remembered the gut-wrenching pain of placing Nathan into the arms of his new adoptive family. I recalled the intensity of my feelings as I wrote him the letter while sobbing in my car. I made him the promise that I would become the kind of man and birthfather he could be proud of.

Today, as I strive to be a loving father to Indie and Radin, deep down I know that I am living up to my promise to Nathan—to be a good example to him. I can't think of a better feeling than this.

Last but not least, my relationships with my parents and siblings have never been better. I have worked extremely hard over the years to earn their trust back with each and every interaction. Trust is fully restored in our family.

The principles of recovery have given me and my family a new life. Today my recovery is injected with hope, clarity, and motivation. No longer am I a slave to my struggles, fears, anger, and addictions. No longer do my shame, inadequacies, and limiting beliefs control me. Through the help of my parents, ex-wife, family members, professionals, and my recovery family, I have been gifted a full recovery.

Over the years my family and I have opened up our lives and shared our story with thousands of people because we know it is vital that we share our message of hope with the world. We discovered that our vulnerability breaks down walls of separation and opens doors to connection. You see, genuine connection is the opposite of addiction.

As a family, we have come full circle. In fact, my mother came up with an idea for a family Christmas service project: we would serve those who lived on the same streets I lived on while homeless. As a family, we purchased a shopping cart full of clean new socks and after driving in a blizzard on Christmas Eve, we walked those streets handing them out to any woman, child, and gentleman we could find. Memories of the cold winter I roamed those streets flooded my mind. I looked into those windows and saw my reflection, now happy and healed and whole. I was filled with gratitude as I contemplated my two babies, my wife, my warm home, and my recovery. I realize that all of us have our own unique struggles, and the battle is real. However, it is so worth the fight.

Today, my mother tells me that those painful experiences have allowed her to more fully enjoy this tender part of her life. It has given her life a richer meaning and purpose. Because I crawled out of my hole, and most importantly, she crawled out of hers, we are now helping people find hope. The truth is, from our lowest moments, we often discover our highest purpose, our path, and our reason for living.

When you feel discouraged, find comfort in the words of Holocaust survivor, Viktor Frankl: *"What is to give Light must endure burning."*

Part Two:
THE FAMILY'S PERSPECTIVE

THOUGH YOU MAY FEEL like your family is alone, and that you are the only family going through such craziness and chronic drama and pain, I hope that by reading this book you will know you have plenty of company. Because addiction sends ripples out into the family structure, and healing from addiction is most effective when the whole family heals, I asked my mom and my dad and my sister to share their own emotional journeys as I fell into addiction, and the rollercoasting years of trying to recover and failing, and finally—solid recovery and a new and wonderful life. I believe their stories will help you feel less alone and will offer honest encouragement and help.

My Mother's Story

My son has an addiction. Gratefully, today Jason is in recovery. Alcohol and drugs had never been a part of my life or my world. I didn't know that someone so close to me, my own child, could have a secret life; one that I knew nothing about.

I was blindsided.

Jason had been a beautiful, healthy, active little boy. The third of our four children, they were all very close in age. My husband and I welcomed, loved, and enjoyed our busy little family. Everything seemed fairly normal with our children as they grew. We supported them through school as well as all of their sports and church activities. I thought we were raising happy and well-adjusted children. Certainly, we were doing the best we knew how.

After high school, Jason spent two years in Brazil doing missionary work for our church. Once he came home, enrolled in college, and attended a study-abroad in Israel, he met and married a lovely girl. When he graduated from the university and found a wonderful job with great opportunity to grow, his future seemed full of promise. I felt he was accomplishing all the important things that would insure him a happy, successful, and rich life.

Then the other shoe dropped.

The bomb fell. Or whatever phrase one would use to describe the moment one's life turns upside down and inside out.

I can still see the shame in Jason's eyes that late summer night when he confessed to his father and me, "I am addicted to drugs."

No, you're not addicted to drugs! A voice quickly yelled back in my head. *No! You can't be addicted to drugs. You are my son and you know better.* Taking a few pain pills for a neck injury isn't the same thing as being addicted! *Don't even talk like that!* Oh, how my mind insisted this was not true.

Jason began to tell us a very sanitized version of what was going on in his private life. This was the beginning of sharing secrets that could no longer be hidden. From that night forward, the lies and secrets slowly unraveled—the pieces starting to fit together, and my life was never the same. I didn't have a clue or any knowledge that my son was experimenting with drugs, let alone that he had progressed to the point of total dependency and criminal behavior. His life was full of secrets and facades.

Admitting my son was addicted to drugs was more than I could wrap my head around, let alone accept and believe. Maybe this is why the professionals call "denial" the first stage of grief and loss. It isn't something you want to believe. Maybe I was not yet ready to believe or to feel that kind of pain. But, as time went on and I was slapped and punched with reality again and again, I slowly allowed my protection, my defenses, and my denial to come down.

I have been asked, "When did you first realize that your son was struggling with drugs?" I would have to say I knew when I couldn't deny, justify, or rationalize any longer . . . when secrets couldn't be hidden, and when my spiritualizing, managing, and controlling everything didn't work. Once the secret was out, everything began to change. Our family began to feel the pain and sorrow of this disease—and Jason became sicker and sicker.

From the beginning, I believed I could help Jason and that my husband and I together could fix this. Jason was an amazing kid, and if he would just follow the steps we would lay out for him (and if we infused some money into the situation) we could get this behind us and forgotten—legal issues and all.

We could help him salvage his life. *Why wouldn't we want to help our son?*

Jason seemed so willing and grateful for someone to rescue him. We hired an attorney. We took over his finances, so bills were paid on time. We found an old used car for him to drive when his car was totaled in an accident while driving intoxicated. I even went so far as to make him his own "to do" list.

We had a lot to learn. I had a lot to learn. We were in a "full court press" on Jason and his life. But Jason was not ready to change, no matter how desperate we were for him to change. I was definitely uninformed about this disease, and especially about knowing what we could do that would really be helpful. I know I added to his shame and self-hatred. I know now that our way of "helping" kept him from experiencing the negative effects his behavior was having on his life. This approach kept him from becoming ready to move through that stage to another on a journey to change.

My world as I had known it was unraveling at the seams. Many of my attitudes, thoughts, and ideals crumbled. I had tried to do everything in our home that would keep this kind of ugly thing away from us.

What went wrong? What did I do wrong?

Jason had always been and continued to be loving, kind, and tender with us as parents. He tried hard to protect and keep from us much of the pain and consequences of his usage. But eventually it always found us. I can't imagine the pain, guilt, and self-hatred *he* must have experienced during this time, but all I could see and feel was my own pain and sadness.

Why doesn't he just stop? Why is he choosing this life?

"Just try harder!" I said to him multiple times. "You can do this."

There was also:

"What? You're out of money again? Where has it gone?"

"Why don't you start going back to church and find some new friends?"

"Why don't you spend some more time with your family instead of those poisonous people?"

"If you quit, we will take you on a trip, or buy you something nice."

Bargaining, guilt, expectations, and especially . . . shame, shame, shame. I didn't know it, but these weren't really helping him. We cleaned him up and put on a few bandages here and there, but nothing-long term. We had no idea what stage he was in his addiction, so we forced our will upon him. Jason pretended to comply—first with us, and then with the courts and jail systems.

Jason promised that he would do better and that he was sick and tired of it all. He promised he had given up that life and he had changed. Over and over again we heard these words. I wanted to believe the promises, resolutions, and repentant spirit. But nothing seemed to change. The words appeared empty.

What I didn't know then was that he was not capable of keeping his promises. Looking back now, I believe that a part of him wanted to change. But the negatives of his behavior were not yet outweighing the positives of him using. I didn't know or understand that lying was a symptom of the disease. Through his drug use, he had caused the part of his brain that performs those abilities— judgment, morality, and values—to not function. They were numb, dead. He could not access or implement much of what he had been taught or had once valued.

However, his survival instincts went into overdrive.

Drugs had become his oxygen. He needed to breathe. He could not survive without them. Drugs were his obsession every minute of every day. He fought for his "oxygen" at all costs. My son was so sick.

I heard it said that addiction is a family disease. This was not something that I understood. I thought that my son was sick but the rest of my family was fine. His addiction was the problem.

Boy, did I have a big learning curve.

As hard as I tried, I couldn't fix his addiction. As much as I hated to admit it, I was powerless over this disease and him. No matter how great my advice was, no matter how much money we spent, no matter the number of lectures, tears, scolding, bribes, or bargains, we could not stop his addiction.

We couldn't even slow down the spiral. Jason's life was spinning out of control. It was excruciatingly painful, and it felt as hopeless as it sounds. As each day, month, and year passed, Jason got more and more sick, and so did we.

When Jason attended a court-ordered treatment facility, a counselor in a family class gave us some powerful advice. "You and your husband have worked hard," the counselor said, with great compassion. "You created a good life together. You deserve to continue to have a life and not let his addiction take it away from you."

My husband Doug and I looked at each other uncomfortably. *Isn't that what parents are supposed to do? Take care of their son . . . at all costs?*

The counselor continued, "I want you to imagine that your addict is sitting in the middle of a lake and he is dropping boulders in the water. He doesn't feel a thing—not one thing. But the ripples from those boulders are causing waves that are creating a tsunami for you. If you don't get off the beach, you will be killed."

So we tried to get off the beach. Doug and I began to use some boundaries. We learned that boundaries not only protected us but allowed Jason to feel the consequences in his life. It wasn't our job to buffer him from the pain of his behavior. That pain was the force that would motivate him to change. At times we were encouraged; other times we were devastated.

Then one night, after texting us for days telling us that he needed to talk to us (never a good sign), Jason came to visit us. It had been only six months since our son had graduated from drug court, but he was in trouble again. Weeping, he asked if we would help him— one more time. The negative experiences of continual substance abuse were overwhelming him. He was at a new level of scared.

My husband asked, "How can we help you, Jason?" From the look in Jason's eyes, we didn't really think our son had any idea what could help him.

We made him a last chance offer to enter a drug treatment facility we had heard about. We weren't willing to sit on the beach anymore, getting pummeled by his waves. Jason could tell for the first time that we really meant it.

He turned down our offer that night, saying he did not need to go to a residential facility. He felt he could do this with some out-patient help. Jason thought he wanted his freedom, but after eight weeks of slips and painful relapses, our son admitted he needed more help. Jason finally took our offer and entered a sixty-day residential treatment program followed by a ninety-day outpatient program.

This treatment center—as I now believe all good treatment centers must have—offered a program for the family, parents, or wives of the residents. In order to attend this class, we were asked to commit to a twenty-week program.

As part of Jason's treatment plan, Doug and I were required to attend a three-hour family-group class every Wednesday night at the facility, attend two Al Anon meetings each week, each get our own sponsor, work our own Twelve Steps, write a nightly inventory, and read bibliotherapy books about co-dependency, addiction, and healthy emotional family systems.

My first reaction was, *Wait a minute! I'm not the one who needs help.*

I didn't feel I needed this or had the time to give to this intensive program. However, Jason wasn't the only one who had reached a new level of scared. I was desperate! If my son didn't buy into this program, I knew that he would eventually die. That fear was destroying my life and my family.

I was desperate for my son to commit to doing whatever these professionals were asking him to do. I wanted him to buy in to this opportunity— to believe he could live a different life. If I was unwilling to attend and participate in family group, it would send the wrong message to my son.

Also, I was anxious to learn what I was doing that had not been helpful. I needed some new tools to communicate without venomous comments and toxic behavior. I needed to learn how to give encouragement and show patience— in the right way. For years I had felt baffled, sad, and sickened by all that had happened. I wanted some answers and information. *What had gone wrong? What could I have done differently? Why us? Is there any hope?*

Very reluctantly I agreed to the intensive family program. I was not at all prepared for what I would learn during those twenty weeks . . . or what I have continued to learn.

That night our instructor lovingly looked into my eyes. "The most powerful and effective thing you can do to help your son get well is to get busy with your own recovery." So I jumped in with both feet.

I was nervous and afraid as I walked through the doors of Al Anon meetings and the treatment facility. *What am I afraid of? Everything!* Instead of being able to control and hide, my fears and pains were going to be out in the open for everyone to see and hear.

I discovered quickly that those rooms were the few places I could go where I felt understood, valued, and accepted. Classes and support groups gave me strength. They permitted hope and gave direction. It was always a beautiful experience as we shared and learned from each other. They became sacred rooms to me.

I was relieved to find out that I didn't cause this disease, I couldn't control it, and I couldn't cure it. But I also learned that I could contribute to it. By looking honestly at myself, my attitudes, judgments, expectations, fears, and feelings, I began to slowly understand what I was doing to contribute to Jason's disease. Coming to this understanding and awareness has been the most difficult challenge of my life.

Addiction is definitely a family disease. We all contribute, and we all suffer. I also suffered from this disease. I didn't understand that addiction—chemical dependency or another form of addiction—is a symptom of deep-rooted shame. Hence, true healing must start from the inside. Without getting to the causes and conditions of the disease, we can never truly experience healing. I have gained a deeper understanding about feelings—that feelings are not good or bad, they just *are*. An uncomfortable or angry feeling is not *bad*. These feelings can be our teachers. Emotions can tell us when something is wrong. It is what we do with those feelings that is important. I am learning how to honor feelings— my own and others, and that the only way to heal them is to feel them. I have learned how to identify, manage, and heal painful feelings.

Also, I have learned that supporting my son didn't mean taking care of him, fixing his problems, paying his bills, or programming his life. To support him, it was imperative I got out of the way. It is about setting boundaries to protect me physically and emotionally while allowing the consequence of his behavior to motivate and teach him. I learned that pain is the motivator. I support him now by letting him learn for himself without me controlling the outcome.

Supporting someone correctly is not allowing ourselves to be consumed or obsessed with another person's life. I had to learn to look at my own life, relationships, resentments, character defects, and judgments. Where was my serenity? Did I know how to take care of myself emotionally? Did I know how to show self-love? Did I even know what that was?

I learned that not only was I powerless over this disease, but my son was powerless as well. There was a Higher Power that could restore my son and me to sanity. My challenge was to get out of the way and let Him. There was great peace and serenity in accepting God's will for our lives and the life of others.

Years ago, I read a book that said, "Recovery is not about finding blame; it is about taking responsibility." I would never minimize the pain and suffering that surrounds addiction. It seems endless and it grows like a snowball that turns into a deadly avalanche. It buries and smothers. But there is hope. No matter how this disease affects your loved one, I learned that you can get yourself to an emotionally healthy place. You can own your life, not theirs. You can enjoy the promise of serenity and acceptance whether they are ready for recovery and change or not. And you can stop contributing to their disease.

I understand that I do not have to be afraid anymore. I know that whatever the future holds there will always be some pain. But I have learned how to feel that pain and the actions I need to take to heal it. I know what it is like to be in a place of acceptance. I have experienced peace and serenity even in the midst of hard trials. How grateful and blessed I feel for what I have learned, what I have felt, and how I have healed. This journey would not have been one I would have signed up for, but it has been a most powerful, humbling, and sacred experience for me.

My advice to you, the reader:

1. **Don't be afraid of the disease of addiction.** It is frightening, but to deny it is more dangerous than the disease. Acknowledge it and it will help you to see the truth and reality in your own mind.

2. **Realize your addicted loved one thinks his drug is his oxygen.** Don't over-react by shaming him for breathing oxygen. It has become a need, not a want. It's life vs. death for him. Acknowledge that and move into the next step.

3. **Do not let your fear overrule your better judgment.** Your addicted loved one will come with tears, with anger, with abandonment, but remember that he has created these feelings through his addiction. **Do not rescue.** Let him struggle. He will progress through the stages of change quicker when you get out of the way.

4. **Walk the path with him while you do your own work.** You will develop a closeness that will amaze you, and you will develop some much-needed inner strength and learn to rely on a Higher Power that will give you what you need when you need it.

5. **Never give up.** Give up helping, but never give up on the love you have for your addicted loved one. Never forget the person that lies beneath the shackles of the disease and let it give you hope for the long-term. Miracles do happen.

As I see my son speaking to audiences, and expressing himself in his writings, I am humbled at how blessed we are to share our story of hope with families around the world.

My Father's Experience

One day I saw a young toddler sitting with his parents in front of me in church. The boy was being corrected by his father for his restless behavior. With a stern and uncompromising look on the father's face, he reprimanded his child. Then I watched, stunned, as the little boy took his father's lips into his tiny fingers and pressed them closed—as if his father's lips were the main problem in his life.

I wanted to laugh and to cry.

I knew that I was perhaps that pair of stern lips to my son, Jason. For years what came through my lips to my son was often negative and non-accepting. I had crushed his creativity, and when he wasn't doing what I thought he "should" be, I sought to crush his soul. Of course, I didn't *think* I was doing that. I thought I was doing what he needed—to be directed by me to do what was best for him.

When Jason was not behaving the way I wanted him to behave, he heard from me. Yes, I loved him, but I don't remember communicating that to him very often.

When Jason and his siblings were young, we would get compliments everywhere we went. Jason loved to be with us and he was the light in the room. Everyone just loved to be around him. When he got into junior high he changed. Suddenly he was not my boy—he was someone who cared all too much what his peers thought. He had to be the cool guy, and as he grew older, his need for an active social life superseded his time with family. I was harsh with him. I still ruled the roost. I detected that he didn't accept my rulership. He would act like he didn't care, and I shamed him until his spirit was crushed. It would break my heart when I would get the tough kid to cry. But I knew I had gotten through to him. Or at least, I thought I had.

I expressed my displeasure often in his choice of friends as he grew into a teenager. As a result, my son became more and more private and secretive about his friends and their activities. I found it less painful, I suppose, to be less and less involved in his life.

We knew that he had "dabbled a bit" with alcohol in his high-school years. He was arrested one night during spring break for shoplifting cough syrup to get high with some of his friends. The police officer was a friend of the family and let him go after placing a call to us. In my denial, I convinced myself that he was just a victim. I berated him for running with some ill-chosen friends. Of all our kids, he was the one who acted out. I was unable to see the good in him. Even when he went on his church mission to Brazil, all I could point out were his personality foibles and mistakes. When someone would write something good about him, I thought, *He's sure got them fooled.*

Years later, after he married and seemed to have life somewhat in order, one night he asked my wife Janna and me to come visit with him. When Jason announced he had a "prescription drug" problem and needed help, I suppose it came as no big surprise. At that time, I had no idea it was as serious as it was, and if anyone had told me, I wouldn't have believed it.

In my mind as a doctor I thought, *You've been in an accident. You got dependent on some pain pills. So what? We can fix this. We'll just get you off the prescription.* It was that simple: just change the prescription for something lighter and he could kick this. I wouldn't learn until years later that his addiction went way beyond prescription drugs.

Janna and I offered to help in any way we could, mostly by managing his finances while he "got a grip" and "changed his ways." I treated him just as I had when he was a teenager. I focused on what we needed to do to control and fix him. I focused on his financial problems (he and his wife were up to their ears in debt), hoping against hope that his drug problem would just go away if he would just shape up. I began paying off his debts, and with each dollar spent, I became more and more angry. He accumulated significant debt to instant check-cashing companies. Each time I went in to pay off another debt, I made it clear to the girl behind the window that if they ever loaned Jason another dollar, they would not see it back.

Still he kept going back, writing bad checks, and they would cash them—with smiles, I suppose. They probably knew I would bail him out; of course, I did—again and again—thinking I was helping.

At one point, Jason lost a good job because of misusing the company credit card. I remember writing a letter to his employer, hoping to make them see that he was a victim and not a perpetrator and begged them to give him another chance.

I made phone calls to another employer explaining, justifying, and running interference for Jason so he could retain his employment. To me it was vital he retain employment. I had no idea that what I was doing was harmful to Jason, not helpful.

During those difficult years, before Jason really wanted true help, he lived a secretive life, and because he didn't want to hurt his parents, I believe, he stayed away from us. His wife divorced him, he lost his small home, and was in and out of jail many times. I couldn't stand to see him living on the streets, so I provided an apartment and a car for him. He trashed the apartment and crashed the car a number of times.

At the time, I didn't know I was enabling him. I think it was more difficult for me than it was for him when I knew he had no place to sleep except out in the rain, the snow, and the frozen cold. I also had to watch his mother suffer when we didn't know he was safe, and that was perhaps even worse. However, the more we helped, the deeper into his addictive behaviors he progressed.

Quietly, in those years, unbeknownst to me, I was nursing my own addictive behaviors. It was so covert; I didn't really let anyone know about it. The secrecy should have tipped me off, but I didn't realize how much I was struggling, too. I was too sick in my secrets to see it.

The predominant emotion that I felt in those days was anger. I couldn't understand how Jason could "choose" this path when it caused him so much unhappiness. I was especially angry that he caused my wife and me so much pain. Although I have since learned that underneath most anger is fear, I couldn't see that at all at the time. I was a macho man. I had no fears. Deep down, however, I was afraid. I was terrified of financial disaster and afraid of the effects Jason's addiction continued to have on my life.

Most of all, I was afraid that I might have been the cause of Jason's addiction by the way I raised him. *My failures! My shame!* So I continued helping him out of difficult circumstances.

Finally, Janna and I made a pact: we decided we were not going to allow Jason to ruin our lives, particularly our long-term security and happiness. We also knew at a deeper level that if we needed to expend our financial resources to save him, we would—but that would not happen without a healthy dose of increasing resentment on my part.

We had heard many stories of families who expended their entire savings and future earnings on trying to save one of their kids, only to have relapse and death for their reward. There were times when I was so fearful and angry that I would have accepted his death as a blessing. I felt so much pain that I once looked very seriously at my wife.

"There are a lot of things worse than death," I said quietly. From the look in her eyes I knew that whether or not she agreed with me, she knew exactly how I was feeling.

It shames me to remember the thoughts that I had in those days. It was mostly selfish thinking on my part. I wanted relief from the daily pain. I truly felt that I was the victim and that my suffering was greater than Jason's. Indeed, I wondered if he suffered at all—that perhaps he just loved his drugs more than us (or anyone or anything else), and life was good for him as long as he could get what he needed.

Jason came to church with us on occasion, and one day when he went to the pulpit to speak, I was embarrassed. He didn't look good, and I thought he might be a little high. All I could think of were all the things he wasn't doing to fit in properly and embarrass me.

Why can't you be on time?

Why can't you sit without falling asleep?

Why are you reeking of tobacco?

Why do you totally disregard my wishes?

One of my most painful memories was a time when Jason and I met to purchase some cell phones together. I had assumed that Jason was recovering because he was getting drug tested by the court system regularly and he was out of jail. However, I noted an opened pack of cigarettes on the seat of his car and that Jason had tobacco on his breath.

At that time, smoking was a BIG deal to me. In my mind, almost no personal failing was as great as nicotine addiction. It represented to me such a huge departure from the way we raised Jason that I viewed smoking as open rebellion—a personal rejection of me and all my values.

Jason denied that he was smoking, but the evidence was clear, and I came completely unglued. I spewed anger and poison and shame and disgust—all my emotions about his addictions that had brewed inside me through the years. Only this boy could not push my lips closed to get me to stop. Nothing stopped the toxic scorn from spilling out and onto him. So much of my ignorant parenting was based on "My way or the highway—but before you go, let me shame you some more."

When Jason's pain became great enough, he came to my wife and me and asked again for help. This time, however, he meant it. To his great credit, he suffered and endured a painful road to sobriety and recovery through an inpatient program designed to treat victims of disease. Here they were not treated as criminals or "people who make bad choices." They were treated as sick people who needed to get well, yet were still held accountable.

Jason's counselor, Kris, called Jason a "rock star" and I found myself going back into old perceptions of him. Then she said something to me that made me open my eyes.

"When Jason walks down these halls, I imagine the chains clanking. He drags these chains around wherever he goes, but he's taking this disease on, trying to break those chains. He's struggling, and he's going to win. He's a great man."

Something miraculous began to happen inside of me as I surrendered. In fact, once I finally surrendered, I saw a light begin to come back on in my son's eyes. During that time, I attended a program for the families of the patients. A great personal, inner shift began occurring in me as I realized that I had many of the same behaviors and thinking as other addicted people. I realized that I had been harboring selfish, self-serving, spiritually destructive, and injurious attitudes and behaviors. I began seeking the kind of help that was working inside of my own son.

I began attending 12-Step meetings, eventually got a sponsor, and began working the Steps. I embarked on a spiritual quest and journey of my own. First, I began attending weekly meetings, where I admitted my powerlessness daily. Then I learned to meditate and pray frequently. This sparked a profound change within me.

I gradually became the person I believe God meant for me to be. I took daily inventory and tried to admit my wrongs to keep from repeating them. The reward became a keen peace of mind and a connection with God—even a new perception of a personal and loving God. Best of all, I began learning to accept myself and to be at peace with whatever God had in store for me each day.

I began learning to accept matters about me as "just about right," rather than stressing over what I had no control over. I also became so much more compassionate and aware of the pain of others.

I began learning how to love; even to love those who I thought might have hurt me. I guess that is how my Creator loves me—unconditionally. I wish I had learned this earlier in my life, but I'm appreciative to have learned it now.

I became intensely grateful for Jason, for his addiction and recovery, and for his path that led me to follow. I now look up to Jason with great respect and admiration.

I see now that his pain was far greater than mine ever was, and that he would have come to recovery a lot sooner if he could have. If recovery is difficult, regret is agony. I only regret that I didn't start this journey sooner. I now seek to be the example to that young father in church, not to crush the spirit of his little boy.

I love my son. There's a bridge that we've built now so that we can meet each other halfway. He and I now have a shared language, and instead of anger, we have a shared humility and compassion for each other and for ourselves, like best friends. We can talk about anything. That helps me to be open with him. We both got past our anger at each other and we stand on loving neutral ground; no judgement, just love. Having built that bridge has been priceless. I would never have chosen this path, but I wouldn't change it for anything in the world.

My advice to you:

1. **Acknowledge your loved one has a disease**. It may be hard at first. It may seem impossible at first, but it's not. Step out of anger and denial into surrender of the disease. It's only when the disease is acknowledged that progress can be made.

2. **Step out of judgment**. Don't let your old anger and worries about what others think matter. Make this about your relationship together and forget the outside world. They all have their own struggles.

3. **Don't rescue!** Let him feel the pain from natural consequences. Do not try to comfort him when he faces consequences. That will only keep him comfortable in his disease. Surrender to the fact he might have to sleep in the streets, or sleep in jail, or even die. Don't rescue.

4. **Try to love him.** Just love him and keep on loving him even though you may not feel like it. This involves a certain level of acceptance and surrender, too.

5. **Do your own work.** Start on your own 12-Steps or self-development program. Work on your own spirituality. A great master once said for each of us to focus on the beam in our own eye than the mote in another's eye. Love your addicted loved one and focus on your own personal work. This will lead to miracles.

To witness my son go from homeless to happy as he helps others recover from addiction, I couldn't be prouder of him. And today, I am actually proud of myself for all the hard work I have done to put me in a healthy place.

My Sister's Experience

"We begin to see that all people, including ourselves, are to some extent emotionally ill as well as frequently wrong, and then we approach true tolerance and see what real love for our fellows actually means. It will become more and more evident as we go forward that it is pointless to become angry, or to get hurt by people who, like us, are suffering from the pains of growing up."

– Bill W., Alcoholics Anonymous

The year 2006 was a pivotal year for me. This was the year my little family of two busy boys welcomed the birth of my sweet daughter. I was adjusting to the messy, hectic, sleepless life of a mother of three small children. It was a crazy, joyful, exciting time; it was also a time shrouded in heavy grief. I had just learned from my parents that my younger brother Jason was addicted to drugs.

During that year, my heart was filled with such polarizing emotions— overwhelming love and gratefulness for my little family, yet debilitating anxiety, guilt, worry, and fear for the life of my brother.

I wrestled with these feelings. It seemed that everything I knew was turned upside down. Everything I believed in was challenged. It was a year that I reevaluated what was important to me, the relationships that I had, as well as how I felt about God and who I believed He was. I changed a lot that year.

Jason and I had always had a great relationship, a unique bond between brother and sister. He is just two years younger than me. As we were growing up, we had almost nothing in common when it came to our interests and even our personalities. Regardless, I had always had a great respect for the things that came easy to Jason. He had a natural charm and charisma with people, and a comfortable way with others that I did not share. He excelled at sports, any physical activity that he participated in, and he was always up for an adventure.

People loved Jason. He didn't do much but be himself, and people were naturally drawn to him and wanted a piece of his time, his energy, and his attention. I was always proud that he was my brother. And I knew because of the sweet way he treated me that I had a special place in his busy, noisy life.

In my eyes, Jason had the potential, and the raw talent and ability, to do anything he wanted to do. He could be anybody he chose. I could sense, though, that he couldn't see this himself. I sensed that he didn't know his own strengths that were so apparent to me. I remember when Jason was a young teenager, a respected leader in our church told Jason that he was a natural leader and that there was nothing he could do to change that. He told him that people followed him, that people would always follow him, and that Jason needed to choose carefully where he would lead them.

Even at that young age, Jason seemed to have a flock of people who gravitated to him. I worried that these people took too much from him, and I was exasperated at times to see how he was pulled in so many directions. I once called them "Jason's leeches" to my mother. Maybe I was jealous of the leeches because they were getting too much of my brother; maybe I worried that they were just another distraction in his noisy life that would keep him from seeing who he could become. I never thought that I had any cause to worry that my baby brother might become addicted.

As I grew up, moved out of the house, got married, and began my own family, I still felt a closeness to Jason—even though I saw him less. My husband and I moved to Tucson, Arizona for my husband's residency program, but we traveled home several times a year to see our family.

I didn't sense any alarm about Jason. It always seemed like things were going well, but I did notice that he pulled away from us. He would leave family gatherings early, wouldn't follow through when he'd say he would be somewhere, and always there were people calling him, texting him, and occupying his time when he was with us.

Though my husband teased him about it, I knew this was just how it was. I accepted long ago that being with Jason meant sharing Jason.

I remember one day Jason was at our home when my husband Jamie and I were preparing to leave. As we got to our garage, Jason ran back inside to go use the bathroom. Jamie, realizing he'd forgotten something, ran back inside. When he returned, he had a troubling expression on his face.

"What's the matter?" I asked him.

"I found Jason looking in our medicine cabinet. He said he had a headache," my husband said. *Strange,* I thought. *Why didn't he just say something if he needed a Tylenol?* I thought it was puzzling, but Jamie was more upset. He had a friend in high school who had been caught rummaging around in his parent's medicine cupboard; it was later discovered that this boy was addicted to pain medication. To Jamie, this was a red flag. I tried to push that memory out of my head, and never thought about that incident again until years later.

It was Christmas 2005 when my parents came down to visit us in Tucson. I had missed the company of my parents so much that I was thrilled to have them in our home catching up on their lives and letting them get reacquainted with their ever-growing grandchildren. Quickly, I could sense that something wasn't right. There was a sadness in their eyes and they seemed to be holding back as I asked them how everyone was doing back home.

When I pinned them down with direct questions, they reluctantly shared with me what they knew about Jason. He was in trouble; he'd lost his job, and he'd just confessed to them that he was addicted to pain medication. I was speechless. I didn't know what to think. As I absorbed the information over the next few days, I asked many questions. What I didn't understand at the time was that my parents only had the version of the story that Jason had shared with them. He told them what he had to because he needed their help; but he couldn't tell them the whole truth. He was much too ashamed to confess everything, and a part of him still felt he could stop on his own without having to disclose too much.

It took many months for the secrets to unravel and for us to see how far my brother was into his addiction. I heard how his life was imploding; his job, his marriage, everything he owned as well as everything he'd valued seemed to be handed over to this insatiable monster, his addiction.

I couldn't understand it. I couldn't. My mother and I spent hours on the phone, sometimes several times a day talking for many months, crying and commiserating over Jason. I wanted to do something. I would have done anything! All I could do was suffer and worry and pray for my younger brother.

Would I ever have Jason back again?

Eventually Jamie felt we had to tell his parents. Our family had all met at their cabin in Bear Lake the summer prior, and Jason knew where the key was. I was crushed. I was ashamed to tell my in-laws they should be cautious, that my own brother could possibly do something wrong, like trespass on their property or steal from them.

I learned that when you have a severely addicted person in your family, you can easily become addicted to your addict. When they have a good day, you are elated. When they have a low day, you are miserable. My parents and I didn't recognize this. We were just consumed with worry, fear, and dread over each new development in the drama of Jason's life.

It was a painful time. It was difficult to know what to do with all that I was feeling. Unfortunately, some of the things I did were not helpful. I began to feel resentment towards other members of my family who were not reacting in the same way that I was.

Everybody was taking this crisis differently. Some retreated and stayed away from us and didn't communicate or "participate" in the family drama by staying busy with their own lives. I took this to mean that they were uncaring— that they were writing us off.

Others asked pointed questions, tried to find an easy blame, and seemed to feel animosity toward Jason for what he was doing to our family. This also made me angry because, for some reason, it hurt me for others to be angry at Jason. I still felt fiercely protective of Jason and hated for anyone to be judging him with a critical eye.

I was so sensitive and worried at that time that it seemed any innocuous comment would hurt me. I never acted out in that hurt and anger, but in silence I suffered and let the resentments fester.

In retrospect, I wish I would have known how to allow everyone to grieve the situation in their own way. I wish I could have given all of the members of my family that compassion and respect to come to terms with this difficult situation in their own way and on their own timeframe.

Surprisingly, I also felt a lot of shame with the situation. I carried that shame into all of my relationships and friendships. I didn't want my friends to find out that Jason was addicted. I didn't want them to judge the situation, my family, and him. I don't know why I felt that no one would be supportive and loving, but I learned that this level of isolation is common among those in this situation.

When Jason had been sent to jail for the first time, I knew that many of my friends from my hometown had probably heard. On a trip home, I was to meet some of my girlfriends for dinner. I dreaded going. I didn't want to talk to them about Jason and my family. I felt fiercely protective of my brother and I wasn't ready to talk about it. I remembered the times in the past I had gossiped about other people and their problems. I thought I had all the answers, and I didn't respect their privacy. Now, the story was *my* family.

Because of my shame and fear, I worried that my friends really didn't care about me, my brother, or my family. I assumed the worst— that once they got all the dirty details, they might deliver them to others, and revel in our shameful story. Because of this shame, Jason's secrets became my secrets.

Had I given my friends a chance, and had I opened up to them about all that I was suffering with hoping to find the compassion that I craved. If only I had been strong enough to be vulnerable in sharing my suffering, I may have been able to build the deep trust that I needed. In my embarrassment, I just couldn't do it. I defaulted to isolation and probably missed some great opportunities.

I realized that the friends I felt I could trust were priceless to me. Furthermore, I recognized how important it was for me to become that kind of friend. I wanted to become a person whom others felt safe with, a person who could honor someone else's pain and hold it sacred. It was important to be a friend who cared much more about the person than their "story." Looking back now, I am grateful for the struggle and the stretching. It actually gave me a clearer picture of who I wanted to become.

In my grief-stricken quest to understand Jason and why he couldn't stop using, I began searching out books and articles about addiction. In one week, I read the first two-thirds of the "Big Book" of Alcoholics Anonymous. My husband joked that I might be the only person to read this book who has never had a sip of alcohol in my life.

What I found in those pages fascinated me. I turned to them to learn about Jason, and found myself learning about life, my own life. The big book was full of practical advice of how to better one's life and relationships, how to right wrongs, and how to live in such a way to lift and help others—that we actually need to help others for our own well-being!

These were all things I had learned in church, but to see it spelled out in very clear steps inspired me wholeheartedly. While I read, I still thought about Jason, but I also reflected on myself and my own new journey in being a mother. I recognized things that I wanted to change in myself in regard to how I will raise my children, how I teach and discipline them, how I listen, and how I honor who they are.

Another important thing that I learned during this time was how much I needed God's help. As I went to a handful of Al-Anon and family group classes with my parents, I learned about the Twelve Steps that Jason and others were taught from Alcoholics Anonymous. I've had a firm belief in God since I was a child and practiced prayer regularly. Regardless, the Twelve Steps taught me an applicable way to access that power in my life.

The term "powerless" was new to me. I had never felt powerless before. When life was going along well, I always felt I was in control and I was capable of managing my own life. But when my world was turned upside down, and I was filled with grief and hopelessness, shame and despair, and I learned what it felt like to be powerless and surrender to it. I learned what sweet peace can come when I can access God's power, let go, and turn all of my angst over to Him.

In one family group class, the wise teacher taught me that God knew and understood Jason even better than I did, and He loved Jason even more than I did, and only He truly knew what Jason needed to learn and how he was going to learn it, and in what timeframe he was going to learn it.

Learning to trust God and allowing Him to watch over Jason was a different kind of faith. Learning to truly trust in Him and realizing that not only was He mindful of Jason, but that He was also mindful of me, brought me an indescribable feeling of peace.

I needed Him in my life. I was powerless.

I recall one instance in particular when I felt a deep powerlessness. My brother had just entered another addiction treatment center. This was not his first rehab experience, but I hoped it would be his last. I hoped that this would be the answer, that within those walls Jason could find whatever it was he needed.

Jason would not be receiving any phone calls or visitors for the first four weeks that he was there. Imagining how difficult this was for him and how lonely he felt, I knew I needed to write him a letter. I wanted to continue to reach out to him. The trouble was I had absolutely no idea what to say to him.

We had gone from being close siblings to a place where I couldn't even think of how to talk to him. Every sentence I constructed in my mind sounded so awkward, forced, and fake. I just couldn't send him a letter like that. I remember closing the door and getting down on my knees. I broke down as I told my

Heavenly Father in plain, simple words that I couldn't do this. On my own, everything I came up with to communicate to Jason was wrong. I simply asked Him to help me. I pleaded for the words to come to me; not words that would hurt or damage, but words that would help and heal. I cried some more, then dragged myself back to the computer to give it another go.

How strange it was that I didn't even hesitate. I began to type a letter to my brother. The message was very simple. I told him how much I loved him and how important he was to me and to our family. I told him I believed in him, and I told him that if he didn't mind, I would keep writing him to tell him these things.

The peace that I felt confirmed to me that this was all I could do. And it was all that was needed. It was how I had to handle my desire for Jason to get well at the residential program. I had to realize it was not in my hands.

Overtime, Jason began to heal and get better. All I could do was pray and hope that it would continue. I did worry after Jason returned home how our relationship itself would heal. Would it always be awkward between us? Would it ever feel natural with him again?

One night, many members of our family gathered in Idaho at my oldest brother's home. After the kids had all gone to bed, Jason took the opportunity to open up to us about his own worries, and the awkward feelings that he experienced when he was around our family. Apparently, these inadequacies had haunted him for years. Humbly, he apologized and said that these were some of the things that he was struggling to overcome. He let us ask him questions, and in answering was open, honest—transparent, even. He wasn't afraid to let us see the "real" Jason, even the side of him that was insecure, scared, and vulnerable. Not many people that I have known are willing to be that vulnerable, and I appreciated it. I could relate to how he felt, and I loved him for it. That night was the beginning of me trusting him again.

Since then, Jason has continued to be transparent with us. I haven't peppered him with questions or hammered him with interrogations. I respect his privacy. But the times that I have spent with him he has opened up to me, and this has helped our relationship become better than I thought possible.

It sounds strange to say, and probably impossible to believe, but I'm very grateful for that time in my life. I'm grateful to my brother for allowing me to be a part of his recovery, which brought me to some recovery of my own. My family has learned some incredible lessons that we wouldn't have learned if it hadn't been for Jason. Today, we are a better family because of it. We are not perfect, but that's the best part. I don't feel that we need to be perfect. Accepting this is very freeing and allows me to feel more love and acceptance of myself, my children, and the people in my life.

Several times I have had the opportunity to witness Jason speak to large and small audiences. Each time I have been in awe at how willing he is to put his ego aside and share with others about his own struggles and fears, and his own experiences with overcoming his demons and rebuilding his life. It inspires me. His willingness to share and be vulnerable helps other people, and it has directly benefited our family by building trust.

A Spouse's Experience in Her Own Words

To All the Little Baby Birds

The Spouses

A dear friend Michelle offers hope to wives and husbands:

Three years ago, a counselor handed me a copy of *Courage to Change*. He asked how I felt about assisting Dan (my husband) in his recovery from addiction. I was of course willing to do anything, and told him I would read any book and study whatever he told me. I really thought I was going to learn some magical knowledge or skill that would support Dan in his sobriety. I was, I just could never have anticipated the package it would come in.

Several years and several recovery programs later, Dan and I are truly different people. Our family and marriage have endured the same storms you are facing now: feelings of anger, betrayal, pride, judgement, resentment, and tons of chaos. So, the big question everyone wants the answer to is, *how can I help the addict in my life?* The answer is not what you want to hear, but it is what your soul is starving for. Gently and powerfully focus on your own healing and recovery. That is the answer. Do your own work and let go of the need to control another's path. Let them have their experience and concentrate your energy on *your* path, *your* mission, *your* healing, *your* weaknesses, and let those weaknesses become *your* strengths. You want the magic pill? It is love, forgiveness, and surrender.

I have looked over my journals of these difficult years and cannot hold back the tears as I see so easily now what a gift this has been for my personal development. I would not wish this pain on my greatest enemy (P.S. I don't have any because I'm in recovery now). However, there is no other way for me to have changed so much in such a short amount of time. I was literally brought to my knees. On June 8, 2015 I wrote:

> *I feel like a little baby bird, helpless and fragile, being held in the strong and gentle hands of God. I am not being placed safely back in my old nest, but rather lovingly carried up the mountain to the highest peak. While we walk, I've been given short reviews of lessons learned to prepare me for the summit. I begin to realize that the answers to my questions are getting easier, quicker, and becoming part of my nature. I almost don't even need to ask the questions anymore because my soul intrinsically knows the answer. We are getting closer to the summit; I can see it now. I can feel the wind and the bright sunlight beating down on my face. I know it is time. This fragile, broken little bird has been prepared with careful thought and precision. I know that God will now set me free to soar as he knows I will. He knows how weak and flawed I am, but he*

also knows my heart. He knows that this little baby bird will fly when I am let go at the top of the mountain, and so do I.

I am sure that as you read this you think that there's no way I could possibly understand how addiction has ravaged your life. When addiction became an unmanageable force in our lives, I was pregnant with our fourth baby. Our fifth (surprisingly) followed one year later. We lost our very successful business. My children had to transfer out of their private school and away from friends they loved. I had to go to work. We've dealt with the law, and all the other treats that accompany drug addiction. Dan has spent nine months away from our home in treatment and sober living in the past two years. I have felt like a single mother. I know first-hand the pain of addiction. I also know how quickly and easily beauty can be restored if you choose it. Above all I know that the more I let go, the more I remembered how wonderful Dan really is. Prior to these years, I would have described him as a great man, a great father, and a great provider. I could see more easily that *this addiction* was not *him*; it was his pain manifesting itself. If you can see this truth in your loved one, you will be able to help them, yourself, and your children more powerfully. It really is all about compassion and forgiveness.

Pain and fear can ruin you or rebuild you. The choice is always yours. There is guaranteed continuation of pain if you choose to blame and resent the addict in your life. There is simultaneously guaranteed peace and grace that follow the decision to forgive and the courage to mend your own character defects. The courage to focus inward will change your environment, your relationships with everyone, and above all your heart. Indeed, it will change your very nature. So, to the little baby birds of the world I bring a gentle message. *You're already suffering from addiction . . . you may as well get the gift that it bares!* Commit to your own transformation and lay claim on the greatest gift life will ever give you: wholeness.

Jason's Final Words

I realize that there are many pathways. The experiences shared in this manuscript are sacred to those of us who have poured out our hearts and lives. We do it not for recognition or self-aggrandizement. We do it to help the one family member or addicted loved one who is seeking escape from these chains. May you find comfort in this journey as you apply the principles imbedded in these pages.

I would love to hear about your journey, so let's stay connected. God bless you along your journey to healing and freedom.

Warmest regards,

Jason

ACKNOWLEDGMENTS

A SPECIAL APPRECIATION for my birth son Nathan. He gave me *the* one reason to rise up and try again. Also, thanks to my wife Brin for her endless sacrifice as I strive to magnify my life's purpose and divine calling. My twins, Indie May and Radin James, for the light and purpose they evoke in my soul. My mother for her prayers, love, and resilience through the years of deep sorrow and tribulation. My father for his humility and example of redemption. My siblings for rallying around me when I needed them most.

Thank you to Kevin Hall for writing the book *Aspire,* and for the bountiful connections that set me on my path. Truthfully, this book would not exist without his profound influence in my life.

Dave Blanchard for adopting me as a student and coaching me through Intentional Creation. He expanded my vision and changed the course of my life. Dr. Kevin McCauley for taking me under his wing early in my recovery and inspiring me to write this book. Thomas Cantrell for the time as my creative editor and the sacred experience at the homeless shelter where I finally made peace with my past. Bridget Cook-Burch for the years of early-morning consulting and co-creating the storyline of this project. Greg Johnson for taking a chance on me and encouraging me in the midst of countless rejections and dark discouragement. Becky Johnson for her depth, personal touch, and validation through the final editing process. Deidre Paulsen, Colleen Whitley, Mother Barbara Wilson for their insightful edits. Francine Platt for her inside graphic design. William Vogel, LCSW for his clinical insights over sushi and years of mentorship as the Clinical Director at Brick House Recovery. And finally, Bishop Brent Daines for leaving the ninety-nine to retrieve me from the chains of hell.

JASON D. COOMBS, MPC

www.BrickHouseRecovery.com

JASON COOMBS is the CEO and Founder of Brick House Recovery and the author of the book *UNHOOKED: How to Help an Addicted Loved One Recover.* Brick House Recovery is a nationally accredited, faith-based substance abuse treatment program in Boise, Idaho.

Jason earned his bachelor's degree at the University of Utah and went on to achieve his Master's in Professional Communications. He currently sits on the Clinical Advisory Board for Impact Collective and is the co-creator of RecoverySuite.com.

Jason continues to expand his reach as the addiction epidemic is taking over the nation. This rise in addiction costs our country $700B annually in health care, crime, and loss of productivity, and Jason found a niche to serve where there is a desperate need: he consults various organizations and corporations, with a passion to help corporate Human Resource teams about how to safeguard the successful recovery of addicted employees. This fresh approach saves corporations thousands of dollars in loss of productivity, treatment costs, and termination/hiring costs.

Jason has the heart for helping people. You would never know it now to meet him on the street—that Jason Coombs was once in the throes of a horrendous addiction that left him homeless, penniless, incarcerated, and near death. He found his purpose by way of his long, inner struggle and transcendence from the ashes.

Jason and his wife, Brin now live in the beautiful and serene hills of Star, Idaho where they enjoy open space, star gazing, and fresh air. They have a new set of twins (boy and a girl). Jason enjoys playing the guitar, triathlons, hiking, snow skiing, fly-fishing, and meditation in the great outdoors. He has a deep passion for traveling and adventure.

CONTACT INFORMATION

For discounts on upcoming products and events visit:
www.brickhouserecovery.com/unhooked

To find out more about Brick House Recovery call or visit:
208-286-4274, www.brickhouserecovery.com

To book Jason to speak or for consulting, contact him directly
at: info@brickhouserecovery.com